GETTING PUBLISHED

Getting Published

A Companion for the Humanities and Social Sciences

Gerald Jackson and Marie Lenstrup

First published in 2009
by NIAS Press
NIAS – Nordic Institute of Asian Studies
Leifsgade 33, DK-2300 Copenhagen S, Denmark
tel (+45) 3532 9501 • fax (+45) 3532 9549
email: books@nias.ku.dk • website: www.niaspress.dk

British Library Cataloguing in Publication Data

Jackson, Gerald
Getting published : a companion for the humanities and social sciences
1. Academic writing 2. Scholarly publishing
I. Title II. Lenstrup, Marie
808'.066

ISBN: 978-87-91114-76-2 (hardback)
ISBN: 978-87-91114-77-9 (paperback)

Typeset by NIAS Press
Produced by SRM Production Services Sdn Bhd
and printed in Malaysia

Contents

Preface

And he dreamed the dream of all those who publish books, which was to have so much gold in your pockets that you would have to employ two people just to hold your trousers up.

– Terry Pratchett in *Maskerade*, 1995

FEW GET RICH IN ACADEMIC PUBLISHING. A handful of scholars have earned respectable royalties from books they have written for a broader (more general) readership; Jared Diamond and Steven Pinker are examples. Likewise, some academic publishers make a profit, but rarely do they achieve more than the 10% return on investment considered a minimum in other industries.

Academic publishing may be a high-status industry, but there is more money and greater profit in selling soppy romance novels and scented tissue paper. That said, *success* is a different matter, something that is quite reasonable to strive for and which should not be measured in monetary terms alone. In this book we aim to maximize your chances of success as an academic author, but let us be realistic: it is highly unlikely that you will end up with pockets sagging with readers' gold. There is a much better chance that you will find the whole experience rather daunting: writing is hard work, a publication contract is no certainty, and good reviews followed by really satisfying sales can be elusive.

You ask, perhaps, why publish at all if it is such a thankless occupation? That is a fair question for most authors, but not for academics. Publication is far and away the most important avenue for academic, scholarly and scientific communication. The quality and quantity of publication are the main measure of the relative excellence of both academic institutions and the individuals working there. A range of good publications will help an academic gain recognition among colleagues and students, may well be the decisive factor in promotions or new appointments, will increase the chance of grant awards – and should also be, quite simply, a source of personal satisfaction at having brought new and exciting work to the attention of the global academic community.

However, we have seen time and again how the authors we work with ask the same questions, raise the same concerns, fall prey to the same misunderstandings, and cause the same practical hiccups for publishers. There is clearly a general gap in the knowledge and understanding that authors have of the publishing process and how best the process can be exploited for their own purposes – a gap that cries out to be filled with clear, practical, reasoned advice.

What this book will do for you

It may be a cliché, but it is still true: knowledge is power. In this comprehensive but concise companion we aim to give you

Knowledge of how the book industry works, how and why publishers decide to accept or reject a manuscript, what constraints and motivations shape academic publishing, and how new developments in printing technology and in electronic publishing and marketing are making waves and causing changes.

Knowledge of the differences between successful and unsuccessful manuscripts, how to take these differences into account at the very earliest stages of your work, how to determine and satisfy the aim and readership of your work, and how to present your manuscript for the maximum chance of acceptance.

Knowledge of how you as an author can affect the success of your book after acceptance, how to work efficiently towards publication with all the various specialists in the publishing house, and how to help ensure that your work reaches the largest possible readership.

We even offer you ***knowledge of how to self-publish*** without the backing of a traditional publisher – although we see that as a last resort.

This book is unique in its international outlook and should be equally useful whether you hope to publish your work with a press from Singapore, Germany or Canada. It is also unusual in its focus on the humanities and social sciences, which allows us to concentrate on the particular concerns of these areas of academic endeavour. And lastly, it is the first book of its kind to pay proper attention to the effect of, and opportunities arising from, new developments in IT, print technology and new media.

New academic authors will obviously get the most benefit from this book (not least the chapter on turning a PhD thesis into a book). However, more experienced authors looking to improve their understanding of the publication process and increase the success of their books should also find much of interest in these pages, especially in our overview of how writing and publishing is changing with the (electronic) times.

The book opens with an introduction to the people and functions in the book industry, and some background about the current state of play. There follow three chapters that are aimed at overlapping groups:

- Chapter 2 on planning a book, for those starting a book from scratch,
- Chapter 3 on turning a PhD thesis into a book, for newly minted PhDs, and
- Chapter 4 on writing shorter texts, for those aiming to produce an article or a chapter in an edited book.

For the rest, we have structured the subjects in the chronological order in which they will become relevant to most authors on the journey towards publication.

We cannot take all the pain and effort out of the process, but knowing what you are in for and up against can bring a measure of control and help avoid a lot of grief. We provide down-to-earth, practically applicable advice that will be of direct use in the conception, writing, presentation and promotion of your next book. After reading these pages, we hope you will feel much less mystified about the inner workings and logic of the academic book industry, but even more so we hope that you will feel far better equipped to plan and write an attractive manuscript, select the right publisher to pitch it to, present an informative book proposal to that publisher, negotiate the terms of a publication contract, work efficiently at all stages of the production process, and enhance the marketing and promotion of the resulting

What's in a name?

There are several terms used seemingly indiscriminately by the publishing industry, but with nuances of meaning.

A *book* is the physical object that is produced, while a *title* is a way of referring to a unique *text* which may, for instance, have been published both in *hardback* and *paperback*, i.e. as two different kinds of *book*. The *work* is the entity that the author has produced, both in *manuscript* (more correctly: *typescript*[1]) form before it is published and after publication (possibly in several volumes). *Monograph* is often used synonymously with *title* and *work* when only a single author has been involved – although we have recently seen oxymoronic references to 'multi-author monographs', so perhaps *monograph* is also coming to include collaborative works.

In practice, you need not worry about which term you use. The nuances are fine and professional usage sloppy. You will not go wrong if you talk about your *book* – as we do in this ... erm ... *text*.

1 Since *manus* means 'hand' in Latin, the term 'manuscript' should, strictly speaking, only be used to refer to a handwritten text. In practice, though, most people both inside and outside the publishing industry use the term to mean a text of a certain length produced by any means, whether manual or technical.

book. Not least we hope that we will leave you with the knowledge and tools that will empower you as an author and help make your encounter with the publishing world a positive and rewarding one.

A clear focus means clear advice

Our scope is focused, which allows us to give specific advice to a clearly defined group of authors.

Our focus is on ***academic works.*** Academic publishers differ from other industry sections in the high number of new titles produced, the low number of copies sold, the imperative for global reach, and in their operation of the peer review process. Academic authors differ from other authors in the reasons they have for writing, in the frequency of their output, and in their reluctance to remain with one publisher throughout their careers.

Our focus is on ***the humanities and social sciences,*** although much of what we say may also be applicable to other fields. What we think

Have you got what it takes?

Book publishing offers you, the author, professional recognition, advancement in your career, the recognition of your colleagues and students, and the opportunity to influence the way people think about your subject. Is that enough motivation for what will be a long, difficult and potentially abortive exercise?

Your readers want to find new material presented in an attractive and accessible form, without having to sift through mountains of data to find a few specks of diamond dust. Is that what you are offering?

Commercial realities demand that every publication must pay its way, so ***your publisher*** wants an author who understands the book's readership, brings something new and creative to modern scholarship, and boosts the success of the book by being an efficient partner to work with. Is that what they can expect?

of as the human sciences differ from the natural sciences in the level of funding available for research and publication, in the relative reliance on books over journals as the preferred medium of communication, and in a more relaxed attitude to the speed of dissemination.

Our focus is on ***monographs***, although we have also included a chapter on journal articles and chapters in edited volumes. The investments of time for the author and of money for the publisher are far higher in the case of monographs, and the risk of failure therefore much more significant. Consequently, planning and market awareness are of paramount importance for monographs, and post-publication involvement on the author's part is more likely and more desirable. In most other respects, though, our advice will be equally applicable to shorter publications.

However, our focus is ***not confined to printed books***. We also consider works published electronically, an increasingly important growth area for both authors and publishers.

About the authors

Why should you take any account of our advice? Apart from the basic qualification of having between us some 30+ years of experience in academic publishing, we bring to this book a few qualities that we hope will set us apart from the authors of other books on publishing. Gerald Jackson has guided hundreds of authors through to publication as editor in chief of NIAS Press, where he engages daily with editorial and production matters, as well as the wider issues of running a small publishing house. Marie Lenstrup has worked in academic publishing for many years and now runs ASBS, a marketing agency and consultancy for academic publishers. Between us, we cover all the bases. Our experience comes from small organisations, so we have been directly involved in many different tasks within a publishing house (and the publishing world beyond) and understand how the needs of various functions can interact – and sometimes counteract. We have both regularly acted as consultants for other presses, thus our insights are not limited to the view from our own two backyards.

Beyond the book

The problem with books is that their contents are like bugs preserved in amber: while they may be very beautiful bugs, they are rather dead bugs nonetheless. To avoid this situation, we are augmenting the contents of this book with updates and useful extras. We are also involved in various forums on publishing and as much as possible we aim to go out and talk directly to academics on these issues. To learn more about such resources and activities, simply go to the NIAS Press website (www.niaspress.dk) and search on the title 'Getting Published'.

Acknowledgements

We are very grateful for the comments and advice we have been given by friends and colleagues, which has been extremely helpful in the process of turning the sow's ear that was our draft manuscript into what we hope is a potential silk purse. In particular, our heartfelt thanks go to Robert Cribb, Patricia Crosby, Leena Höskuldsson, Kimberley Hundborg, Colins Kawai, Paul Kratoska, Keith Leber, Henrik Lenstrup, Henrik Kloppenborg Møller, Sofia Palli, Samantha Pedersen and Jonathan Price. Last, but by no means least, we recognize and appreciate the great tolerance and support of our respective spouses, Lene and Jon.

CHAPTER 1

Behind the scenes

As repressed s[illegible] butchers, so th[illegible] publishers.

IN THIS BOOK WE FO[illegible] hopes, needs and ef[illegible] players in the book in[illegible] stages of the process o[illegible] through to a book in a [illegible] start on this, it would be useful first to have a look at who these industry players are, what it is they each do, and what the environment in which they do it is like.[1]

The people inside the publishing house

The three main functional groups of staff within an academic publishing house are the editorial department, the sales and marketing department, and the production department. Depending on the size of the business, there may also be layers of management and all the supporting departments that one finds in a business of any size, such as human resources, accounting and office management. But there

1 Like all branches of human endeavour, publishing has its own 'dialect'. For those unfamiliar with some of the terms and concepts found in this chapter or elsewhere in this volume, we have included a compendium of publishing terms as Appendix 3.

is nothing special, and thus nothing particularly interesting, about what these auxillary sections do in a publishing house, so let us leave them to one side.

Editorial, production and marketing staff are the people with whom an author is likely to come into contact in the normal course of events, and they will also be in regular contact with each other throughout the publication process, consulting on matters small and large, and making sure that the process runs as smoothly as possible.

Editorial department

The main task of a ***commissioning*** or ***acquisitions editor*** is, unsurprisingly, to commission or acquire texts. Commissioning implies an active role in defining a book project and finding authors to take it on, whereas acquisition implies the more passive role of simply acquiring material that already exists as authors' ideas or actual manuscripts. In practice, though, editors from academic presses tend to take on both roles, and the different titles are likely to reflect nothing more than the domicile of the publishing house. European editors are often called commissioning editors, while their American counterparts are normally called acquisitions editors.

Contrary to popular belief, academic editors do not often spend their days in soft chairs surrounded by big piles of manuscripts, nor their evenings in cosy restaurants chatting up prospective authors. They rarely read entire manuscripts submitted for publication, mainly because even where the publishing house is large and its editors are therefore specialized, they cannot know all subjects well enough to judge the academic merits of a manuscript. For this, they rely instead on advice from peer reviewers. And they only occasionally woo authors with fancy meals, mainly because the good presses receive so many unsolicited manuscript submissions and proposals that editors are free to spend (most of) their evenings with their families.

So what *do* academic editors spend their time on? Well, they do engage in a certain amount of cold-calling on academics they hope might become authors. Thus, they travel around to academic conferences, and at times from university to university, and meet those academics who they believe could make good authors. It is the commissioning editor to whom authors offer material, and it is he or she alone who assesses both solicited and unsolicited book proposals and manuscripts to decide whether to take a book project further through the formal review process to potential acceptance for publication. When a proposal is accepted, the editor negotiates a contract with the author, may provide advice during the writing process, discusses any changes that are necessary either as a result of the peer reviewers' recommendations or for financial reasons, and

With their offices ceiling-high in books and paper, their relaxed style of dress and demeanour, and their interest in wide-ranging and esoteric subjects, academic editors are well camouflaged in their hunt for academic authors.

ensures that the final text when submitted lives up to the standard that has been agreed. After final submission, the editor often remains active as the author's go-between in relation to all the other staff at the publishing house.

In orbit around the editorial department, but not directly part of it, may be one or more ***series editors***. These are usually academics who are highly regarded in their respective fields and who have agreed to lend their expertise and professional networks to the publisher. Some series editors engage in active commissioning, while others are able to take a more reactive approach and simply wait for proposals to be submitted to them, either directly from authors or via the publisher. If a series editor recommends that a work be accepted for publication in a book series, it is unlikely to be turned down as the series editor is also *de facto* a peer reviewer.

The commissioning or acquisitions editor is supported by a ***desk editor*** or ***editorial assistant***. The title of desk editor implies that this is a class of editor who is more sedentary, and that is indeed the case. The desk editor does not actively go out to find new works and new authors, but will instead take on a great deal of the practical work involved in the peer review, in communications with the author, and in liaising with other departments within the publishing house. Desk editors may also get directly involved with copy-editing the final text and making or suggesting concrete changes.

More commonly, though, text corrections are the province of ***copy-editors***. When a manuscript has been written by a non-native speaker, the copy-editor may have quite a time-consuming and involved job to do. It is no small thing to ask an academic not only to undertake a difficult piece of writing, but also to undertake this in a foreign language, and it is only to be expected that inelegant phrases and language errors will occur. However, unless an author is very well established indeed, the publisher will require the author to deliver, perhaps through outside help, a manuscript whose language is in a reasonably good state of correctness. That means that copy-editors should be able to concentrate on ensuring that the manuscript has internal consistency of style both of writing and of layout (and perhaps also that it is consistent with a house style), that all references are present and correct, and that both the language and the arguments flow without obstruction from point to point.

If a book has a good-sized publication budget (which is rare for academic books in the human sciences) or if the author has a helpful grant (which is fortunately much less rare), the editor and author may decide to seek help from a ***picture researcher*** to illustrate the book. Obviously, the more a work leans towards discussions of fine arts or the like, the more essential it becomes to have an illustration expert involved, but for most academic books picture research would be an unnecessary luxury. So most presses do without a picture researcher on staff, but will be able to draw on a freelancer if and when the need arises. As a rule, academic authors must provide their own illustrations.

The editorial department may include one more specialist: a ***rights editor or rights manager*** who is charged with selling on rights to the work to other publishers. That may involve selling the rights to certain markets, e.g. selling US market rights, or selling translation rights to certain languages, such as the French-language rights, or lastly it could be a question of selling rights to certain editions, for instance paperback rights. These rights are sold to a rights manager or an acquisitions editor from another press, bringing us right back to the beginning again.

Production department

The ***production manager*** (or ***production editor***) is in charge of arranging all the physical, practical jobs that are involved in getting from a finished, edited, polished text file to a printed book on the warehouse shelf. While no publishing house can survive without editors and few would imagine surviving without sales and marketing staff, it is a curious fact that quite a few small and even some medium-sized publishers have no in-house production department. They find it is enough to have a production manager (and at times even that role is filled by someone who is already working in another function), and to have him or her arrange all the necessary design and typesetting work through a group of freelancers. Today, these people will often be found half-way around the globe – indeed, publishing in academia is very much a global activity. The production manager is normally also in charge of arranging printing and delivery through outside firms.

The most important tool of the production manager is the diary. A manuscript must pass through a large number of production stages and a large number of hands before it becomes a book, and it is the production manager's task to ensure that it does so smoothly, speedily and efficiently. This is no small task. Just as every public building project one has ever heard about is running late and over budget because of 'unforeseen circumstances', so book production can be plagued by glitches and delays. If the work at one stage takes a little longer than expected, then the person due to handle the next stage may be busy on another deadlined project, and the freelancer after that may have gone on holiday, so that when it comes time for the author to approve something he or she has just gone off for three months' fieldwork in the back of beyond. Thus do production schedules spiral out of control, and production managers' ulcers blossom and grow. In reality, the production manager's day is taken up with liaising and planning and fixing and rearranging to try and keep everybody happy and productive.

The production staff or freelancers will always include ***typesetters*** – a wonderfully antiquated title harking back to the days when book production involved setting moveable type, just like good old Gutenberg, the spiritual father of all printed media. These days, typesetters are men and women with seriously large computer monitors, incomprehensible jargon involving kerning and leading, and strong opinions about typefaces. They use various specialized software to turn authors' word-processed text into highly polished pages where every aspect of the text appearance can be controlled and modified.

Cover designers also use highly specialized software to produce their designs, and work with an intimate knowledge of picture manipulation, colour and fonts to produce covers that are attractive to look at and ideally also a bit intriguing to encourage potential buyers to pick up the book. At the same time, cover designers must satisfy a number of practical concerns such as ensuring that their designs leave enough room for the text to be fitted on the cover, that they will work both if the cover is seen front-on and spine-out only as in libraries, and that their covers can be produced to a high standard without breaking the bank.

In addition, most presses have freelancers they can draw on for proof-reading and indexing. Generally, the author is asked to undertake these tasks, but if there is sufficient room in the budget, or if time is of the essence, or if for some reason the author is unable to find the time, then there are people out there making a living as ***proof-readers*** and ***indexers***. Some (rich) publishing houses can afford the luxury of having proofs read by both author and proof-reader, with a third person collating the two sets of proofs.

Only the very largest publishing houses have specialized ***print buyers*** who shop around with the various printers to find the best deal as regards price, quality and business terms. In most cases, the logistics of buying the services of printers and bookbinders and of arranging shipping and delivery to the publisher's warehouse are part of the production manager's work.

Sales and marketing department

Sales and marketing are very often lumped together into one department, and those outside it may think of these two functions as almost one unit. However, the functions are rather different, and tend to attract different types of people. Put very briefly, marketing is about market positioning and about producing, structuring and organizing product and brand information and ensuring that it reaches the right customers or partners, at the right time and in the right format. To achieve this, marketing staff typically employ various forms of one-way communication, from direct mail to e-mail alerts to print advertisements. Sales, on the other hand, is a two-way affair where sales staff are in dialogue with customers to negotiate terms, take orders and close deals.

Marketing staff tend to be assigned to produce all of the material related to particular book projects, rather than specializing in particular types of material and producing that for all book projects. This is probably because so much of the work involves writing, cutting, pasting and massaging the same basic material: the book description and bibliographic details. Once a marketing executive has produced a book description for a catalogue, it makes no sense to ask another staff member to start from scratch and produce more detailed material for a website, or to extract bullet points to quickly grab the wandering attention of busy booksellers. So while marketing staff are to an extent jacks of all trades, they can get quite intimately involved with specific books.

They may be helped by specialist ***reviews managers*** who make it their business to know exactly who is who among the editors of relevant journals and newsletters, and to know precisely the profile of each journal so that they can ensure that all the appropriate publications receive review copies, and that copies are not wasted on publications that are either unlikely to produce reviews or unlikely to be read by the target customers for a particular book. Reviews managers are helped in this task by review editors at the journals as they will often go through publishers' catalogues to indicate which books they find particularly interesting. And reviews managers also hope for help from authors who may have contacts that can improve the likelihood of a review being carried by a journal or who may know of new or local or highly specialized publications that are new to the reviews manager.

At larger publishers, there may be a specialized section of ***promotions and public relations (PR) staff***, although in many cases these will simply be general marketing staff wearing a slightly different hat. The work here centres on organizing and running events such as book launches, providing support for lecture tours, arranging book displays at academic conferences (sometimes handled by a specialist ***confer-***

ence manager) and planning and managing stands at trade fairs. PR staff are also responsible for communications with mainstream media – but realistically, this is rarely relevant for academic books.

Sales staff can be assigned particular fields in one of two ways: either they are ***product managers*** handling certain subsections of the publisher's list such as journals or textbooks or religious studies, or they are ***account managers*** handling sales of the entire catalogue to specific customers based either on location or type of customer, such as chain bookshops or library suppliers. Their job is to oversee the processing of orders, keeping their customers informed of progress and delays (such as when an estimated publication date slips, or when items ordered are temporarily out of stock). They also negotiate with new customers the terms under which books are supplied, i.e. agree on discount levels, the length of the credit period, how and when buyers are allowed to return unsold stock, etc.

The office-based sales staff are mirrored in the field by ***sales representatives*** who travel around visiting bookshops and trade intermediaries, meeting with their buyers to present the crop of new books, discuss what stock levels would be right for each individual shop, and review how well last season's books sold with a view to determining whether any should be restocked. Sales reps are invariably organized along geographical lines in the same way as account managers, to limit the amount of time they need to spend on transport and maximize their time with buyers. They can provide extremely valuable input back to the office-based staff because they are the first to hear reactions from the book trade as to which types of book sell, which do not, how the market is going generally, and what appears to be the trend for the future. Any complaints and grumbles they hear from booksellers about pricing and service and the physical appeal of books can also be highly informative.

The last group of people under the sales and marketing umbrella are ***order processing*** and ***warehouse staff***. The office staff key in orders, send out invoices, and chase outstanding payments. In addition to these practical jobs they maintain accurate records of all books and their sales histories which editors and marketing staff can draw on in making decisions on whether to issue a contract for a new book, determining formats and prices of new books, and planning select marketing campaigns. The warehouse staff work in huge, hangar-like buildings with row after row of towering shelf units holding boxes and pallets of books. They pick and weave their way between forklift trucks delivering new stock and rattling book-wrapping machinery to pick and pack books for dispatch, receive and unpack new stock, and handle returned stock from customers. Sometimes they are also responsible for the practical work involved in printing on demand, one of the new technologies transforming publishing.

Few publishers have an in-house global distribution network. As such, it is common for publishers to appoint regional distributors who (on payment of a commission) undertake these sales and marketing functions in a specific territory.

The people outside the publishing house

Whether or not the staff at a publishing house work with specialized colleagues or with freelancers and commission agents to produce their books, they will certainly work with a number of outside agencies and companies to bring these books to their ultimate readers. In this section, we look at who is who at the trade end of publishing, that is to say whom publishers interact with to print, ship, market and sell their books.

The orderly progression of a manuscript and book is from AUTHOR (via agent) to PUBLISHER via printer to MARKET to READER.

In academic publishing in the humanities and social sciences, few authors have ***literary agents*** (and those who do will not need to read this book), so in most cases the contact between author and publisher is free of intermediaries.[2] Agents earn their money by com-

2 On the other hand, established authors aiming at the cross-over market (i.e. books by but not necessarily for academics) do sometimes engage the assistance of a literary agent.

mission (i.e. a percentage of an author's royalties), hence naturally they will only be interested in taking on authors they expect will earn enough royalties to provide good commission income. That, sadly, excludes some 99.9% of academic authors. At the market end, however, is a world teeming with different specialists all hoping to do their bit towards (and earn their bit from) shifting as many copies of each book as possible.

Producing the physical books

Printers are the most obvious partners for publishers. It is rare for an academic publisher to have an in-house printing operation – that is something more common for very short-lived publications such as newspapers or magazines. One major reason for this is that different books need different printer set-ups, so there is a clear incentive for publishers to shop around for each individual project to find the printer most suitable in terms of technical ability and price.

Some printers are set up for printing large quantities, producing books in their thousands or even tens of thousands, although that is admittedly a rare occurrence for an academic book in the human sciences (but not at all unreasonable for, say, a medical textbook). Other printers have set themselves up to be able to offer competitive prices on the smallest of printing jobs, down to just a few hundred copies, or even single copies in the case of digital printing. Yet others have invested in machinery that enables them to provide really high-quality image reproductions for books on art and design, or to handle extra-large sizes, or to print on unusual papers. Trade fairs are full of printers from all over the world touting for business, and it can be pretty difficult for a small publishing house to review the burgeoning selection of printers to pick the ideal one for a particular book. So ***print-buying agents*** or ***print brokers*** are also able to make a living, helping publishers make the choice, and helping them negotiate good prices and terms.

After the book pages have been printed by one specialist printer, and the cover perhaps been printed by another specialist printer, everything is assembled by a ***book binder***. Now the only practical job that remains is getting the stock delivered to the publisher's warehouse.

Although there are numerous printers in Western Europe and North America, a large number of publishers choose instead to have their books printed either in Eastern Europe or in Asia because they find that the prices charged by printers in developing economies are low enough to more than outweigh the extra cost of getting books shipped great international distances to their various warehouses. And that is where ***shippers*** come in. There are perhaps a good half dozen specialized book shippers who are set up to handle the transport of these heavy, fairly bulky, but happily non-perishable products. Book shippers help keep costs down by allowing publishers to consolidate their shipments, i.e. the shipper handles the practical work involved in receiving goods for transport from several sources (such as different printers and co-publishers), bundling every-

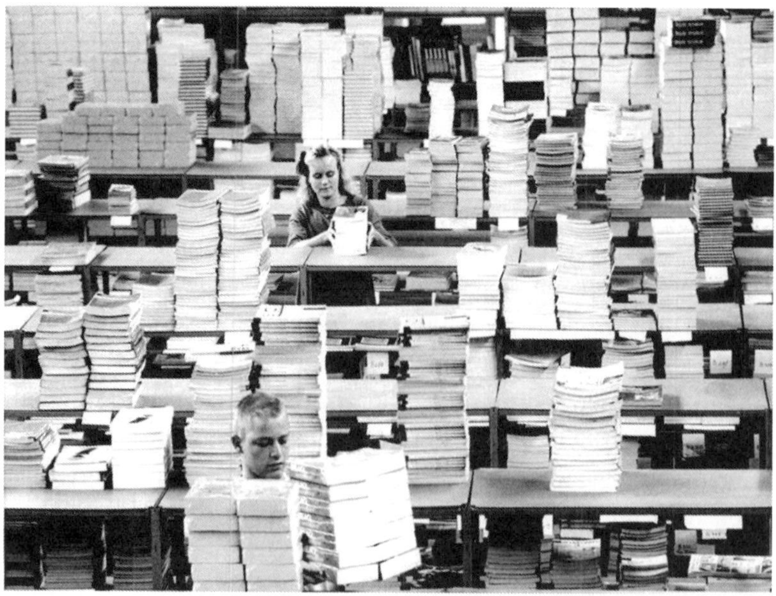

Behind the scenes at the warehouse, where the lofty ambitions of academe meet the gritty (even sweaty) realities of distribution.

thing together, and sending it as one shipment, attracting one set of customs and document charges. And book shippers will bundle together shipments from several publishers in one container so that each publisher only pays for the space they actually use.

Bringing the books to customers

At last, the academic text is now fully groomed, dressed up and delivered to the ballroom door, all ready to meet its fate. Luckily, a number of suitors and match-makers are standing ready to help it make a successful debut.

Bibliographic database services provide an absolutely central and indispensable service to the book industry and are rewarded for their efforts by payments from both ends of the distribution chain, i.e. from publishers and from booksellers alike. Bibliographic services receive information about new books from publishers and warehouses, structure and organize this information to fit with their vast databases of already published books, and add their own classification information to book records in order to enhance searchability. This results in a very comprehensive dataset covering, as near as practically possible, all books available for order in a particular region. The bibliographic service sells this dataset to libraries and to booksellers. When you walk into a bookshop to order a book not on the shelves, chances are that when the bookseller looks up the book you are after on their computer, they are using a dataset from a bibliographic service.

Sourcing books is made easier for booksellers by ***wholesalers*** who act as intermediaries bringing together the most sellable books from many publishers and offering a one-stop shop for booksellers who have neither the time nor the inclination to deal with each individual publisher but who prefer instead to place one order and receive one invoice from a good wholesaler. Indeed, some bookshops will only carry titles that are stocked by their chosen wholesaler, in effect using the wholesaler as a sort of gatekeeper and first filter between the bookshop and the ocean of new titles produced each year.

Everyone knows ***bookshops***. Chain shops and independent shops, generalist and specialist shops, physical and Internet shops, all are clamouring for our attention and our book buying budgets. But perhaps not everyone knows how bookshops make their money. In many industries, the producer will set a wholesale price which is the price charged to the retailer, and the retailer is then free to set the retail price completely independently of the producer (but obviously with an eye on the competition). Books are somewhat different. The publisher sets a recommended retail price and then offers different levels of discount to different customers: so the larger the bookshop, and the larger and more regular its orders, the higher the discount it can demand. Since most countries have by now abandoned fixed-price agreements on books (mainly because these were frowned upon by lawmakers as possible distortions of competition), book retailers are also free to set retail prices independently. In practice, they usually present any deviation from the publisher's recommended retail price as a discount to customers – thus the half-price sales and the three-for-the-price-of-two offers which may refer to full prices that only ever existed in the publisher's catalogue. But the sale of academic books, since they are specialized items, is unlikely to be much affected by small variations in price and more likely to be affected by the efficiency of customer communications, hence specialist bookshops (like Internet bookshops) aim to get to know their customers so they can communicate directly about new books that might be of interest. Good specialist and academic booksellers aim to build communities of loyal, regular customers, and such booksellers are highly valued by publishers.

The last major group of players important to academic books are the ***library suppliers***. These specialists work for libraries by helping them pick the books on which to spend their dwindling budgets. The library supplier has detailed information about the profile and wishes of each library they work with on the one hand, and on the other hand they gather together information about new books from a great many publishers. These two sets of information are compared, and the library supplier provides the library with a recommendation as to which books should be acquired. Libraries get this service for free, and often even get a small discount from the library supplier, who survives on the difference between this small discount and the much larger one they can command from the publisher.

The state of the book industry

Publishers and booksellers are like farmers (perhaps every profession on the planet is like farming): conditions are never right, there's always some threat or problem standing between them and the success they feel they so richly deserve.

Oh no, woe betide us!
The fixed-price agreement is outlawed.
Library budgets are cut and cut and cut again.
The dollar exchange rate has collapsed.
Internet shops and discount sales are squeezing us dry.
Everyone will be wanting e-books now.
How will we ever survive?

Like the boy who cried wolf, the book industry has repeatedly announced the imminent death of the printed book. Admittedly, all these laments are based on actual issues and challenges experienced over the last decade or so, challenges publishers and booksellers have had to meet by adapting and developing and changing their way of doing business. The main issues affecting academic publishing right now are many.

Competition from the Internet. Our brave new world has brought about countless new ways to inform and to sell information in the widest possible sense. IT developments has been a major factor behind the decline in sales to libraries since ever larger chunks of libraries' budgets go toward the hardware, software and human expertise (wetware) needed to stay plugged in. But just as the Internet and other technological advances can present a threat, they also present a potential opportunity for publishers to expand their activities so that they are the providers of, rather than competitors to, electronically produced and delivered content.

Declining library sales. In The Good Old Days, library sales alone were enough to ensure that almost any new academic book would sell upwards of 1,000 copies worldwide so that it would at least break even financially. But successive reductions in the book-buying budgets of most libraries have changed that happy state of affairs to one of increasing gloom. Academic publishers can now expect to sell no more than 150–200 copies to libraries worldwide, and for some specialized books that figure can fall as low as just 50 copies. It does not take a financial genius to see that this level of sales is unprofitable and that it is therefore imperative for publishers to find new sources of sales revenue.

More books than buyers. Sales to individual scholars have also fallen, in part because of the great proliferation of material that makes it nearly impossible for scholars to maintain comprehensive, personal libraries, and perhaps also because in some fields scholars appear not be buying the kinds of books they are writing. In recent years we have seen a great increase in the number of PhD theses being turned into book manuscripts by post-docs who need publications under their belt in search of an academic career, but at this precarious stage in their lives, few among these authors have the funds to be strong book buyers.

Lower sales mean higher unit prices mean lower sales... There is a classic vicious circle of falling print numbers and rising costs. In traditional offset printing, it takes a lot of effort, and thus a lot of money, to set up the presses for a printing job, but once you press the start button the running costs are low. That means that small printing jobs of just a few hundred copies result in high per-copy costs, while large jobs of thousands of copies can bring the production cost down very significantly. So, the lower the projected sales volume of a book, the lower the quantity ordered, and the higher the per-copy cost. Increased cost must of course be matched by increased price, which can make customers reluctant to buy, resulting in even lower sales volumes and even higher costs.

Print on Demand (POD). A promising solution to the problem of the high cost of small offset printing jobs is the new digital POD systems. Here, publishers do not print books for their warehouse shelves, but only print as and when orders are received. Printing digitally means that there are few set-up costs, so the unit cost is the same whether you print one book or 1,000. Many book warehouses now have the systems to provide POD services, and machines are being trialled in a few large bookshops. The trouble is, though, that while the unit cost of printing small quantities or even single copies is much lower than for offset printing, it is still too high to leave room for any realistic profit for most publishers. In practice, POD is therefore mainly used as a service to authors, keeping their books in print indefinitely. But the hope is that in the near future unit prices can come down to a level where POD-only publication becomes a real option.

Commercialization (or closure) of university presses. Just a decade or two ago, even those books that were too specialized for most libraries to buy, and therefore not commercially viable for privately owned publishers, could find willing publishers among university presses that had juicy grants to help them publish what was worthy rather than what was commercial. But cuts in university funding throughout Europe and North America has forced parent institutions to take a much more mercenary approach to their presses, and the vast majority of university presses today must cover their own costs through book sales (although many still get rooms and services provided free by the universities, and some also get a contribution towards salaries). Presses have responded in various ways. Some have chased commercial success by publishing outside academe. Others have asked for or required publication subsidies from their authors. And some, sadly, have sold up or closed down.

The electronic revolution. Weirdly, during the same period that book sales have fallen off dramatically, overall student numbers have been rising strongly worldwide. But while this has certainly had a positive effect for textbook publishers, it has not had the positive effect on academic publishers generally that one might have hoped for. It may be too soon to say anything definite, but it seems from conversations with academics and publishers that there is a tendency for students today – or perhaps just under-graduate students today – to prefer Wikipedia and Googling, cutting and pasting Internet content instead of buying, reading and transcribing quotes from a book. This is bad for academic publishers, but could be worse for academe itself if 'Internet scholarship' favours the quick fix over the long, coherent argument.

The book industry and you, the author

The net result of these various developments for authors has been largely negative. The most noticeable difference is that academic publishers have had to take a more hard-nosed, commercial approach to the books they publish. In concrete terms, the key effects have been:

- Increased commercial behaviour.
- The rising power of publishers' marketing departments and the decline in the power of editorial staff to decide what is published.
- Greater aversion to financial risk, hence to taking on a book project that looks commercially unpromising or expensive to produce.
- A big increase in the number of 'crossover' titles (of interest beyond an academic readership) and interdisciplinary titles.
- Greater willingness to publish purely commercial titles with little or no scholarly value for the general public.
- Reluctance to publish highly specialized studies.
- Reluctance to publish edited or multi-author volumes, these being (sometimes unfairly) seen as inferior to monographs.
- More 'fad' and 'me-too' publishing as publishers seek to emulate the successes of their competitors.

It is harder to get a book proposal or manuscript accepted, and it is harder to make an academic and commercial success of those that are accepted. Each new book project must stand or fall on its own merits, and publishers must take the bottom line into consideration when signing up an author – because, quite simply, any publishing house that loses money today will be closed down tomorrow.

But there are also positive aspects for authors. The electronic revolution opens up the real possibility of self-publishing for those with the energy and technical ability, and opportunities for self-promotion have become much more varied even for the technologically challenged. Print-on-demand technology means that books need never go out of print, and that surely is a wonderful thing both for the author and for future readers. Some may wonder if the information age will eventually be crushed under the weight of its own success, but for now the Internet offers choice, range and speed to scholars everywhere.

Everyone in the academic book industry – this whole extensive machinery – is there for the express purpose of making the most of your manuscript. It may not always feel that way. There may be times when you feel that getting a clear answer out of your publisher is like trying to nail jelly to the wall, and likewise there are times when publishers feel that getting authors to meet their deadlines is as hopeless as herding cats. In the last analysis, though, you must trust that we are in fact all dedicated to the same aim of making your book (and every other book accepted for publication) a success. Bluntly, we would soon be out of a job otherwise. And less bluntly, academic publishing is no goldmine, so those working in the industry are likely to be there *both* to pay the mortgage *and* because we find it a worthwhile, intellectually engaging and just plain enjoyable line of work.

CHAPTER 2

Planning your book

The last thing one discovers in composing a work is what to put first.

– Blaise Pascal

THE INCREASINGLY TOUGH ECONOMIC CIRCUMSTANCES of academic presses, as described in the previous chapter, have implications for how you and other authors conceive and write an academic work. Bluntly put, if you simply sit down and write the text that you feel like writing, you should not expect any publishers to get excited enough about the resulting work to invest in publishing it. And if your work does not get published, then what was the point of writing it in the first place? There are vastly more manuscripts written than books published, so ensuring that you have the best chance of success as an academic author is the main purpose of this book.

On the other hand academic presses must now work harder to make each of their books a commercial success. For instance, publishers are no longer content to let a book sell 'on its own merits'; they actively promote all their titles. Nor are they content only to sell in their home market but are busy building global sales networks. The chances of your book making an impact on the global scholarly community in your field, then, were never better.

But if success is to be achieved, you must *plan* for it. Planning is neither simple nor quick; it requires much more than sketching out a rough table of contents that you later flesh out into a book. It requires you to think seriously and deeply about not just *what* you wish to publish, but about *how* and *why* you want to do so. In turn, you must also analyse your intended readership, the market and the commercial viability to ensure that what you plan as a manuscript stands a realistic chance of becoming a book. Without such an analysis, you are at great risk of failing to write what your readers want, and therefore what your publisher is prepared to invest in.

Understanding needs and desires

While there are many aspects to planning your book, it is useful to start by considering your needs and desires, and those of your readers and your publisher.

What does your publisher want?

Participants at a recent seminar on getting published were asked to suggest answers to the question, 'Why do publishers publish?' Two key assumptions emerged, each supported by a large section of the audience. These were:

- The desire to bring scholarship to the light of day is the main motivation for publishers.
- Publishers mainly publish to make money, but also quite like bringing scholarship to the world.

It is interesting that only half the participants expected profit to be publishers' primary motivation – even though today, that is in fact the case for most publishers.

This audience was pretty representative of opinions generally. A common reaction is to agree that *commercial* publishers are profit-oriented but to contend that university presses and their like have a higher purpose. It is true that university presses (as well as the publishing departments of research institutes, learned societies and so on) traditionally worked to select, communicate and promote scholarly excellence. But they were also expected to earn some kind of income to cover at least part of their costs. Today, almost everywhere around the world, there is less money available to fund altruistic publishing, and the need for publication programmes to 'pay their way' has become universal. So while scholarly considerations may still be a major motivation for many presses and indeed may remain their *raison d'être,* modern commercial realities demand that every publication must pay its way.

How does this affect you as an author? And precisely how should it guide your actions when planning your book? Essentially, your publisher must aim to make a profit on your book; it needs to earn more than it costs to select, edit, produce and disseminate. This means there are two things you must think about: income and expenditure.

Success is not one thing

Many people think that a high sales volume is the only measure of a book's success. You may think differently, and under the right circumstances your publisher might agree. The important points to be clear about are (1) what you want to achieve, (2) what you have to do to achieve it, and (3) whether you are prepared to put in the necessary effort. The point is illustrated by the following two books on seemingly similar subjects which were conceived and packaged very differently. Both were successes in the eyes of their authors and publishers.

A Jewish Archive from Old Cairo

This book tells the story of how a 1,000-year-old collection of Jewish written materials (including shopping lists, personal reminders and other artefacts of everyday life) was found, restored and interpreted. The author believed the subject would be of interest beyond the scholarly community and convinced his publisher to release a paperback edition with colour illustrations. He then embarked on an extensive lecture tour of both academic and Jewish communities across Europe, where his enthusiasm

- ***Income.*** Sales are not the only income for a book but they are important. When conceptualizing your book, you need to envisage a readership (market) sufficiently profitable to your publisher. Otherwise, subventions can help uncommercial works get published, and some publishers ask for them when they believe it can make the difference between acceptance and rejection.
- ***Expenditure.*** Avoiding unnecessary costs is equally important. Bear this in mind when both planning and writing your book. Does the manuscript need to be this length? Are these colour illustrations necessary? Will the language need a lot of editing? And will this be a fiddly, time-consuming book to typeset?

Obviously, if what you are contemplating is a demanding, unprofitable book, you will have difficulty finding a publisher willing

for his subject and his skills as a speaker sold books by the dozen at each event. The author was, presumably, happy to have his work reach as large a readership as possible, and the publisher achieved sales figures well above average and profits to match.

Catalogue of Arabic Manuscripts

This is a comprehensive catalogue of Islamic material covering 1,000 years, now held by the Royal Library in Copenhagen. The Library and author saw this as a resource for scholars and were concerned more with accuracy and detail than with breadth of appeal. They raised a grant that made it viable to produce a large-format hardback book with many colour illustrations and with text samples reproduced in the original Arabic (very expensive to typeset) that was bought by the key libraries in this field. The Library and author were happy to have exactly the type of book they believed was needed for future research, and the publisher was pleased to have produced a prestigious work without being out of pocket.

to take the work on. If you want your work to be published, it must be clearly targeted at a readership that is large enough that a sufficient number of copies can be sold. Your publisher will also hope to find an author who can boost the success and profitability of the book by being an efficient partner to work with both during and after publication – fast, committed, not afraid of networking. Is that what they can expect from you?

What do your readers want?

Your readers are unlikely to care whether your publisher makes money or not. (Indeed, they may not even notice who the publisher is.) Rather, they want to be presented with new material in an attractive and accessible form. They do not want a rehash of known literature, but they do want a text that is situated in current debates, and preferably one that moves the debate forward. They do not want to wade across acres of common knowledge to find a few golden nuggets of useful new material, but they do want to be presented with enough background material to enable them to judge the value of a book's arguments. Moreover, while (some) readers may be happy to be intellectually challenged by a difficult subject, very few are prepared to put up with badly conceived topics or sloppily structured arguments, clumsily written.

If you dream of writing a crossover or interdisciplinary title, you will have to think about readerships in the plural. Ask yourself if there is anything in your specialist topic that can be of more general interest to neighbouring subjects, to other academic areas, or even to non-academics. For instance, can you make a history of dentistry in Indonesia be relevant also to broader themes in Indonesian history? To the history of dentistry in general? Or perhaps even to the history of ideas about health and beauty in Asia and the rest of the world? And can you thus widen the readership without losing sight of the original target group for your work?

The interests of publishers and readers coincide at the point of sale. Publishers need readers to buy (or get libraries to buy) their books. Readers buy books that meet their needs and desires. Is that what you are offering? Will you be able to convince a publisher of this?

What do you want?

Understanding your own needs and desires is equally important. We have already discussed motivating factors such as professional recognition, advancement in your career, the admiration of your colleagues and students, and the desire for fame and fortune. If these reasons provide the motivation for what will be a long and difficult exercise, a crucial task for you will be to ensure that what you produce matches the interests of your publisher and readers so that in turn they can fulfil your wishes by publishing, reading, and valuing your work.

Success in life is never guaranteed. But certainly you, the author, will have a better chance of coping with (and even thriving in) the publishing environment if you go for a viable (i.e. sufficiently large) readership, know your readers and give them what they want. In short, when you plan your book, you need to think market, think reader.

Questions to ask yourself

Before you start planning the book in detail, you must conceptualize for yourself exactly what type of work you aim to produce. The questions we suggest you should ask yourself cover issues that publishers will want answers to when they decide whether to take on your manuscript, and that marketing staff will ask you when the time comes to tell the rest of the world about your book.

Type of book. What kind of book are you writing? You need to be very clear whether you are writing academic non-fiction or trade non-fiction (see box overleaf) because this will determine what you write (and how) as well as which publisher would consider your manuscript.

Which market?

Non-fiction publishing is divided into several fields. Once quite distinct worlds, now the divisions between them are becoming blurred.

Academic non-fiction

Academic non-fiction is published by university presses and other scholarly publishers, many of them commercial. This generally takes the form of a scholarly monograph or edited volume, but some will make the transition to reference works or textbooks (see below). Numbers of copies printed and sold are usually in the hundreds, book prices are high, and generally this is a reasonably safe if sometimes unprofitable business. Scholars generally have a good chance of getting published here, but they will not get rich.

Crossover and interdisciplinary titles

These are academic works targeting a wider readership by crossing boundaries. It is extremely rare to see works bridging the chasm between academic and popular non-fiction, but a well-written scholarly work can attract a wider readership with a specialist interest. For instance, local histories and social histories with a regional focus will be of interest to family historians researching in that area. Works aiming to span several academic fields are increasingly common as presses are wary of narrow, specialist works. The great danger with this approach is that, due to the necessary compromises required to please multiple readerships, the book fails to please anyone.

Educational texts/textbooks

Some academic works are adopted as required or recommended reading for higher education but they are rarely textbooks *per se*. University-level textbooks in their true form tend to be commissioned by specialist textbook publishers after exhaustive market research. Often they are written by teams of specialists working within carefully specified parameters. Educational material for schools has a similar origin (though a school curriculum may also play an important part) but may have an even stronger instructional nature. As true textbooks bear little resemblance to the scholarly works primarily focused on in this book, their authorship falls outside our scope.

Reference works

Dictionaries, encyclopaedias and other reference works may occasionally originate from a work offered to a publisher by an author. In general, however, like textbooks these tend to be commissioned works written by teams of specialists. Again, such authorship falls outside the scope of this book.

General non-fiction

Published by 'trade' presses (publishers catering for the general public), general non-fiction comes in a myriad of genres ranging from celebrity memoirs and do-it-yourself manuals to serious studies of contemporary interest. At the 'higher' end (which includes books more likely to be written by a scholar), the ideal book should wear its scholarship lightly and the text should be clear and comprehensible to the general reader. In this high-volume, high-risk world, a book can sell in the hundreds of thousands or fail dismally with only a few hundred copies sold. Prices are often aimed to attract the impulse buyer. Scholars have only a small chance of getting published here, but the rewards for the lucky few can be highly tempting. Bear in mind, though, that general non-fiction aims to disseminate rather than create knowledge, and such a book may be of little value for your academic career.

Purpose. Why this book at this time? Is the intended use only as a research monograph to inform a specific field or might it double up as a supplementary text or professional reference work?

Readership. What are the subject area(s) and readership level you wish to address? Can you quantify the size of this readership? Where is it to be found? What are its characteristics? (For instance, does it roughly equate to the readership of a key journal or association membership in your field?) Is there is a wider academic readership that you might not have considered, such as colleagues in related fields or other disciplines? Could you perhaps even adjust the manuscript to appeal to an even wider readership including non-academics, such as niches among the professions or particular interest groups? If your study aims to serve the interests of several readerships, how can these be quantified?

Discourse. Can you locate your study in an existing academic discourse? If not, any publisher will want to know why. The danger will be that you are considered 'off planet' and/or offering a book of only marginal interest. But even if your work is part of an active scholarly debate, there is a risk that interest in this topic will have become exhausted by the time your book is published. Ideally, you should be writing at the start of such a debate, not at its peak. Is there an existing book series into which your book might logically fit?

Format. What type of study is being published by others (and what not published)? That is, what type of study would be most appropriate to write? Does this match what you have in mind? What is the proposed length of your book? A closely argued, 1,000-page definitive work would hardly be appropriate in a field dominated by short and snappy introductory texts. Would there be a lot of tables and illustrations, and would any of these need to be in colour? Their added cost could cause a publisher to reject such a book.

Competition. What published works would compete with your book? You need to know not only the academic discourse but also the published literature (in book form – journal articles will not usually affect sales of a book). What are their relative strengths and weaknesses? What makes them a serious competitor to your book? When were they published? Established giants are not invulnerable if regarded as a bit 'long in the tooth'.

Value. In comparison, what would be the strengths of your book? What features and benefits would it offer the reader? How would it compare with direct competitors and related works dealing with this issue? How and why would it be superior? More appropriate to the reader? More up to date? If breaking new ground, how? If offering a new approach to the subject, how would this be beneficial? And what would be the weaknesses of your study? How might these be addressed or transformed into benefits?

Special features. Are there specific localities where a wider interest in your book might be likely? Is there any upcoming event (such as an anniversary or a related TV series) that could be tied in with your book? Have you a unique selling point that transforms your book out of the ordinary into a 'must buy' item?

Author. Who are you? What qualifies you to write on this subject? Have you any qualities or background that make your book special? Have you connections that will help sell the book? For instance, do you belong to any associations, networks, mailing lists, etc., whose members might be interested in your book? Have you any experience (such as in dealing with the media) that might help you promote your book?

The answers to all these questions should help you define for whom you are writing and why they should be interested in what you are writing. If you have more than a few 'don't know's, then you do not yet have a sufficiently clear idea of your purpose and direction in writing. In that case, you might find the exercise overleaf useful.

Clarifying your focus

To cut out the waffle and help you focus on the essence and uniqueness of your study, you can try to describe your book to a potential reader (ideally someone unfamiliar with your previous work and current field):

- Write out a description that is no more than a page long.
- Get reactions from your reader.
- Review and condense your description down to half its original length.
- Repeat until you are down to a crystal-clear description of just one sentence.

Mapping the book

Only now, after you have conceptualized your book, should you proceed to plan it in detail. Essentially, you need to build a structure for your book, one that not only considers how best to present your argument but also ensures that it is of a suitable length, that it includes what needs to be included (and excludes the rest), and that it has the narrative pace and coherence that will draw the reader through your text – in short, that it is a satisfying (even uplifting) experience for the reader.

Precisely how much detail you go into depends very much on your personality and approach to writing. Some authors write intuitively, sketching only a bare outline of what they wish to say beforehand; somehow they are able to assemble a complex argument from within and present this fully formed on the page. Others might be called Lego or jigsaw writers, meticulously assembling building blocks of headings and snatches of text; the final text is added piece by piece to this solid structure. Each approach has its virtues. Intuitively written text often has a greater vibrancy and inner consistency whereas the text of Lego writers is less likely to omit areas of fact and argumentation. The best authors are able to draw on the strengths of both approaches – but only a few can be the best, so do not despair if you find it hard to encompass both approaches in your own work.

The draft table of contents

Now at last the time has come for you to get concrete and draft your table of contents. The various elements that a book can be made up of generally come in this order:

Title page
Table of contents
Lists of figures and tables
Preface
Acknowledgements (if not part of preface)
Author's notes, lists of abbreviations, chronology, etc.
Introduction
Body chapters
Conclusion
Appendices
Glossary[1]
References/Bibliography
Index

Not all books contain all elements, but before you start it is useful to have thought through if, say, your book should include a list of abbreviations or a glossary, as these are much easier to write as you go along rather than after the main text is finished.

But the main area you should concentrate on now is the introduction, body chapters and conclusion. In planning out the order and content of these, you must keep considerations of structure, length and focus in mind.

---

1 This is the standard position of a glossary. In Europe, short glossaries may also appear before the introduction.

Structure

Even the most intuitive writers have some structure in mind before they start. Key requirements in your draft table of contents are:

Organic unity and pace. Your book must 'hang together', i.e. have both internal consistency and coherence. It needs a red thread running through it. And it needs a sense of pace, tempo and momentum – a narrative drive. Bear this in mind even if drive is hard to visualize in your structure.

Direction. Unity and pace are best achieved if there is a clear sense of direction in your book. For historical material, this is often achieved by a chronological presentation. Space is another good unifier, an orderly journey from point to point providing both thread and drive. Not all works (or disciplines) are suited to such treatment, however. You may need to find another device to give a logical and lively progression to your text. Different fields have their own way of handling narrative; check out what works well in your own.

Signposting. An important way of (often subconsciously) indicating direction is by the names you give your chapters and sectional headings (and the same is true of your book's title and subtitle). Arguably, these signposts should give an instant glimpse of the entire book. For instance, the two sets of chapter names in the imaginary biography below are targeted at very different readerships, one aiming to give

Two different approaches to a biography of Bill Clinton

Academic headings	Trade book headings
An Arkansas childhood	'Billy Boy'
Youthful dreams	An encounter with JFK
University years	A Rhodes Scholar at Oxford
Early political career	Back home and into politics
The race for the presidency	Into the ring
42nd president of the United States	Victory

a sober sense of chronological direction, the other hoping to entice the reader by vaguer and more intriguing chapter names. We shall revisit the issue of smart versus sober naming in the section below on selecting a title for your book. Either way, as you revise your study, remember to reassess the titles of your chapters and sectional headings.

Length

A book's extent depends on the type of work, and you should investigate what length is appropriate for your book. If, for example, you see your study in a certain book series, then check other volumes in the series to get an idea as to what length looks to be standard. You will notice that many academic books are between 272 and 320 pages in length. The golden extent for many publishers is 288 pages.[2] This is equivalent to a text of about 90–100,000 words without tables or figures. (To find the number of words in a book, count the number of text pages, count the number of lines per full page, find the number of words per line [count 4 or 5 lines and take the average], then multiply the three figures.)

Books falling outside the standard range of 272–320 pages can be problematic. Under-length books are often regarded with suspicion by scholars: perhaps they have not covered their subject properly. (It is of course entirely appropriate that some types of book are short: simple guides, for instance, or material of an informative/instructional nature like this book.) On the other hand, over-length books are more likely to be tolerated by scholars but are the bane of publishers' lives. They cost more to produce in almost every area (editing, typesetting, proofing, indexing, printing and binding) but rarely can

2 Why is 288 pages a golden extent? Because this length is sufficient for the author to develop their argument fully. It is also perceived as a full-sized book hence it is quite acceptable for the publisher to charge the full normal price. For the publisher, it is an economic size – 18 printed sheets (books tend to be printed on 16-page sheets) give a nice balance between the costs of cover and inside pages.

the price be commensurately higher without losing sales. Because of their greater weight, they also cost more to send (in shipping costs for the publisher and later in delivery charges for the customer).

Length obviously depends on how much you have to say. The question to keep in mind is, are you trying to say too much (or too little) for the type of book you are writing, for the readership you are targeting? Setting yourself a target length when planning your book and each chapter within it is, then, vital. If nothing else, it will force you to decide what material to include and exclude. Ideally, it will also force you to write clearly and concisely, in turn strengthening your voice and the force of your communication.

Focus, beginnings and endings

It is not unknown for an author to offer a work that starts with a broad description of almost everything and ends with microscopic analysis of a single, tiny thing. This does not work: its focus is dysfunctional. A well-rounded study needs to start by setting its subject in context, move on to bring in specific issues over much of the book, and finally bring everything together with a new perspective on the subject.

Especially important are the introduction and conclusion. The former should draw the reader into the book, the latter leave the reader with a feeling of completion. In a way, your book should be like a feast that tempts the restaurant patron with look and smell and afterwards leaves her pleasantly sated, but not feeling over-stuffed. When planning your book, you need to think through how you can achieve this.

However, interminable overviews of the literature, exhaustive itemization of methods used in the research, myriad citations and endless footnotes – these are the trappings of theses, not books. Do not even *think* of including a lengthy literature review or a methodology section in your planned book (and keep citations and footnotes to a sensible level).

Choosing a great title

More than likely, people will get their first impression of your book from its title. A great title will not lift a book with inferior contents, but an inferior title could sink a book with great contents. Moreover, the title defines your subject area, the level at which you are writing, and often indicates the relationship of your book to others in the field. It should be crisp, descriptive, informative, explicit, and it should broaden the appeal of your work as much as possible.

Clear, not clever

Clever book titles are common in North America. Clever thesis titles are common everywhere. Often aimed at readers outside the narrow special area dealt with in the book, they are usually followed by a more explanatory subtitle (the 'real' title, aimed at subject insiders). Typically, clever titles are puns or sayings, and they rely on some knowledge of the subject. An example might be *Riveting Ideas: Ship Design in the Modern World* by Jane Smith. It is our firm opinion, though, that since a book's title may be the only indication of content to booksellers and librarians it should clearly point to this content. Remember that you are not writing a work of fiction with intriguing and artistic title to match. Your book will be read or not read on the merit of the subject matter, and it is highly unlikely that a fun title alone will turn it from an academic treatise into a seasonal stocking-filling impulse purchase.

Key words

It is impossible to overstate the importance of key words. Consider how you yourself find the books you buy or borrow. You cannot rely only on searching by subject because books may not be ordered this way, or they may not be clearly classified. Hence, unless you know of a book already (from a review or bibliography, for instance), you will have only the words in the title and subtitle to go by. Sometimes you have to enter key words in specific fields for searches, and in our example above that means a search for 'ship design' would not include 'Smith: Riveting Ideas' in its results. Do your book a favour and give it a title that ensures it the best possible chance of being found in searches.

Short, simple and concise

Books should be findable, but beware of over-long constructions. It really is not necessary for your title and subtitle to present a complete synopsis of the book. Aim instead for a title that tells the reader just exactly enough that they will know whether this book is for them (and that does not fill the front cover with text but leaves a little space for a good cover design). You could even try to do without a subtitle altogether.

Consider that on a library bookshelf it is only the spine that will be seen, and here there is rarely room for a long title, and hardly ever for a subtitle. If the spine title does not tell a potential reader what to expect, the book may remain unread.

What makes a good title?

When thinking about your book title, bear in mind the following points:

- Your title should be meaningful.

As you can see from this slice from the cover image of our book, there is not much cover surface visible for most books on library and bookshop shelves.

- It should describe what your book is about in a clear and concise manner.
- It should maximize the possibility of your book coming up in a database query or web search on your subject.
- For all the above reasons, use the most important key words in your title.
- Avoid the use of quotation marks, colons, semicolons and question marks as these can cause problems when referencing a title.
- Check that the title has not been used elsewhere already, and especially not recently nor at any time in your own field.
- Definitely do not recycle a title you have used for your thesis (as this would imply that your book is a warmed-over thesis).

In line with these points, arguably a good title for Smith's book would be *Modern Ship Design* with no subtitle. Admittedly this is a fairly pedestrian title – a truly great title needs that extra pinch of inspiration and flair. Take for example the title *Love, Sex and the*

In celebration of odd titles

Clearly, not all authors and publishers share our attitude to devising great titles. Their interest seems to be more in odd titles. Famous in the publishing world is the Diagram Prize for Oddest Book Title of the Year. Recent short-list titles include

- *The Stray Shopping Carts of Eastern North America: A Guide to Field Identification*
- *Tattooed Mountain Women and Spoon Boxes of Daghestan*
- *How Green Were the Nazis?*
- *D. Di Mascio's Delicious Ice Cream: An Ice Cream Company of Repute, with an Interesting and Varied Fleet of Ice Cream Vans*
- *Proceedings of the Eighteenth Seaweed Symposium*
- *Better Never to Have Been: The Harm of Coming into Existence*

Filipino Communist. Consider by comparison *Love, Sex and Filipino Communism*, which has nowhere near the same effect. The mental image of one terribly excited Communist does wonders for the title.

Work on your title. At this stage, it is just a way of referring to your study, it is by no means written in stone. As you finalize your book plan – and later as you write the book – come back to the title, walk around it and take a hard look. There may be something better inside the text.

Annotating and evaluating the table of contents

As you finalize your book plan, it is very useful if you annotate each element in your table of contents – in essence, write a short abstract for each chapter. Not only does this provide a well-signposted 'road map' when you begin writing your book, keeping you on track and allowing you to refer and defer to material you have not yet written; it is also an invaluably clear and concise description of your manuscript to include in your book proposal when approaching a publisher.

Of course, your road map is only useful if the terrain it maps is attractive to visitors. Take a stroll through its imagined lanes. Do you get a sense of direction and purpose? Is your journey interesting, even intriguing? Does its promise make you want to complete your journey? Or is the pathway convoluted, does it climb unnecessary mountains and is it punctuated by crossroads leading to blind alleys?

Try to ask yourself these questions calmly and dispassionately. If there are blemishes in your plan, work to correct them. Do not allow your final detailed plan to become a straight-jacket; there are always things you will need to change as your writing progresses. But getting your plan as good as possible will save you time and grief in the later stages.

When you are happy with your polished plan, then is the time to start writing.

CHAPTER 3

From thesis to book

The average Ph.D. thesis is nothing but a transference of bones from one graveyard to another.

– J. Frank Dobie

IF YOU ARE LOOKING TO REWORK A THESIS into a book (or, say, are the supervisor of someone in that position) then this chapter has information specific to theses that is not found elsewhere. All other readers should feel free to skip this chapter.

The pressures of junior scholarship

This volume is about getting your book published; we do not believe that a thesis in its pure form is publishable, and as a consequence we are not going to discuss the highs and lows of writing a thesis here – for that, you have your supervisor. However, theses (which by definition are required to be original contributions to scholarship) have been the basis of many great monographs, and that makes them highly relevant to this companion.

Most junior scholars will have been living off a doctoral grant that suddenly expires, so finding a new source of income is imperative. For those looking to make a career in the academic world, this is the crunch time. The available options may be a junior teaching position or a post-doctoral grant for a limited period of time, neither of which is a sinecure, and neither of which is particularly well paid – but both of which could well involve a stressful and time-consuming move to a different part of the country, or even a move abroad.

Invariably there is also the firm expectation from peers and superiors that a series of publications will be delivered, not least a monograph. Indeed, building a good list of publications is an absolute must if you are to progress in your climb towards the pinnacle of the ivory tower. The pressure is on from Day One.

So, you find yourself with very little time on your hands, with a massive pressure to publish, and with a major piece of writing recently completed. Is the solution blindingly obvious? Sadly not.

Why is a thesis not a book?

Some of the pointers in Chapter 5 on preparing the manuscript may be useful to you when writing your thesis. What we do *not* suggest, however, is that you set out to write a monograph and submit this as your thesis. At first glance, this might look like a neat way of avoiding the laborious task of reworking the thesis after its completion. The reality, however, is that such a monographic thesis would most likely be unacceptable to your supervisors and external examiners because it would lack several elements normally deemed vital in a thesis that tend to be pared down or absent in a book. In other words, do not even think of it.

Whether a thesis is submitted as photocopied and ring-bound A4 pages or as a properly printed and bound book-shaped object, its contents are fundamentally different to what we expect to find in a scholarly book. The main differences are shown opposite. Note that the thesis and monograph are both equally valid forms of scholarly communication; they simply have different forms and purposes that require quite different treatments by their authors.

Common in some countries is the requirement that PhD candidates deliver many copies of their doctoral thesis as part of their defence – handing over up to 300 copies is not unusual. In other countries, theses are 'published' by their authors' university departments or faculties in book form. Of course, only a few copies are needed to conduct the defence; often the majority are used to fund the host university's library exchange programme.

Main differences between a thesis and a book

	A typical thesis	A good scholarly book
Form	Often book-like	Book
Length	Often a lower limit, but not always an upper limit	Limited by market forces
Author	Student	Writer (with obligations to readers)
– purpose	To prove competence and academic credentials	To communicate ideas
Readership	Panel of examiners	Colleagues and anyone else interested in the subject
– purpose	To examine student	Learning
Focus on	Author	Reader
Scholarship	Exposition required	Absorbed and built on
– role	To demonstrate knowledge	To frame discourse
Approach	Defensive exposition	Open disclosure
Treatment of subject	Often highly technical and very detailed	Avoids unnecessary technical detail
Language	Often obscure, abstract and heavy on jargon	Clear with judicious use of technical terms where needed
Structure	Often progressive recitation	Organic unity, narrative thread
Narrative flow	Orderly exposition but argument not built; often excessive signposting	Builds argument, linking chapters with subtlety; has pace and momentum
Ending	Often ends quite abruptly	Wrapped by conclusions
Methodology	Detailed description required	Description only if and when relevant
Quotations	Necessary, often extensive	Limited use
Referencing	Often far more than strictly necessary	Only what is necessary
Evaluation – before	Feedback from supervisor; final assessment by panel of examiners	Publisher's commercial assessment, peer-review process and editorial input
– after	Formal defence	Peer reactions in journals and other external forums

Traditionally, these theses were photocopied, with great wads of A4 paper thus received by somewhat unenthusiastic exchange libraries. Increasingly, however, we see them produced in book form, often striking in appearance. University libraries are still exchanging these with other libraries, but the excess copies these days are often passed on to a book distributor to see if through sales they can wring a little profit out of the 'book'. Aesthetically it may be pleasing to have such a thesis on one's bookshelf, and it may be flattering to see it listed in a publisher's catalogue.

However, we would argue that in fact this 'book' could harm your future academic career, often quite severely. Why? As we have said, a thesis is not a book, and nor is it perceived as such by scholars, who – like libraries – have limited budgets. Rarely do you see them actually buying a copy of a thesis, should this be commercially available. Fair or not, theses do not have a high perceived value. Thus, perhaps 50 or 100 copies of your thesis are exchanged, a handful sold, and a dozen given away in connection with your defence. The depressing fact is that this could be enough to deter a publisher from taking on your study and working with you to produce a monograph that would have a perceived value and might earn you a reputation – and a job offer.

As a PhD student you may well have no say in this matter at all, but we believe this is a practice that should at least be questioned by students and their supervisors, and discussed with those within the university who do have a say. It is entirely possible that the technical ability to produce attractive 'books' cheaply has overtaken academic and collegiate concerns without an active decision ever being made, and that the powers-that-be prove willing to consider whether the small advantage to libraries is worth the potential great disadvantage to PhD graduates.

What to do with your thesis

So, given that no reputable publisher will allow you simply to slap a cover on your thesis and call it a monograph, what do you do with it? You need to consider two points in conjunction:

- What kind of book do you wish to write? Consult Chapter 2, particularly the sections discussing markets and all the hard thinking required in planning a successful book.
- What needs to be done to produce that book? Assess your material to see what is useful and what needs to be added or rewritten, and assess your schedule to determine whether you will be able to do the work within a reasonable time.

So, what options do you have, then?

Delay making a decision. This is often the result of thesis fatigue and the need to do something else for a while. Delay can be positive; not least, it allows you to stand back from your study and gain some perspective. The risk, however, is that you lose momentum and never properly return to the thesis topic. If you delay, you should set yourself a deadline to ensure that you do eventually make an active decision.

Do nothing. This is a time-honoured and very common default decision that allows you to spend your time on other projects. The trouble is that, if you did a good piece of research for your thesis and actually came up with something new and interesting, then you could be wasting a treasure-trove. Moreover, much of the research work has been done; to start a new research project and see this through to a published work could take far longer than it would take you to rework your thesis, or even to write a completely new manuscript on the basis of the thesis research.

'Mine' your thesis for articles. Certainly, it is quicker and easier to write an article than a book, and faster publication means that you can assert your 'ownership' of new ideas and research material before others have a chance to steal your glory. That said, there are many benefits that articles do *not* deliver, such as the opportunity to develop a lengthy argument, to avoid sharing the limelight with other authors, and to prove your academic mettle. Remember, however, that the book vs. article choice need not be an either–or situation; many authors shape the bulk of their thesis material into a full-length book, but also spin off articles from material either not used in the book or sufficiently changed so that a publisher will agree that this is essentially different (and unpublished) material. In theory, it is possible to take an editorial chainsaw to your thesis, chopping it up into many article-sized logs. The reality, however, is more likely to be that only two or three of your chapters are suitable for reworking into articles; if you discount the book option, the rest of your thesis will be wasted.

Make minimal changes (or in other words, produce a 'warmed-over' thesis). Thesis fatigue, the pressures of new projects, or sheer laziness – there are many reasons for looking to take a short cut. If one really must publish a monograph, why not simply slap a new title on it and run a quick find/replace on the text, swapping all occurrences of 'thesis' or 'dissertation' with 'study' or 'book'? You can (and people do). Just don't expect to get the work published. Why? Because a thesis is not a book.

Do a partial makeover. This is the most common strategy, essentially to extract and build on one or more elements of the thesis, with any leftover material being reworked into articles or used to form the basis of subsequent research. The virtue of this approach is that you build on a strong base of coherent material; the downside is that reworked text is unlikely to be as good as text written from scratch for its particular purpose.

Rewrite from scratch. The most radical solution – to completely rewrite your material from the ground up – normally gives vastly superior results, but many junior scholars lack the time and mental energy to carry such a huge task through to its conclusion.

Assessing your material

It is clear that you cannot get published without at least some work, but how much work is enough? As always, that depends – not least on what you are aiming to achieve and what shape your thesis is in. For this reason, even before you start putting in all the work that is necessary, you need to think ahead. Here, if you haven't already done so, you should (re)visit Chapter 2, especially the sections on determining what you want for yourself and your book, and what potential readers of your book will be wanting.

Apart from the considerations involved in planning any kind of book, for the specialist task of converting a thesis into a book you need to ask yourself these additional questions:

- What material do I have that is new and interesting to other scholars?
- Is there enough good material in my thesis to work into a book?
- If more material is needed, what is this? What will be involved in obtaining it?
- How can my final material be presented in a coherent and interesting way?
- How long will the revision work take?
- Will this (old) work fit in with the (new) work that I am currently engaged in?

There are some who would argue that a thesis should never be reworked into a monograph since the radically different nature of a monograph requires that it be written from scratch. Arguably, this is true of some theses, but there are also many cases where a thesis already carries within it the germ of a monograph (usually hidden somewhere in the middle chapters) that can be brought out and expanded. Be aware, though, that if you are going to make a good job of it, the process of rearranging material, polishing it and writing new links and conclusions can become almost as time-consuming as writing new text from scratch.[1]

---

1 It is not without reason that a nameless wit has revised the Pareto Principle, observing that the first 90 per cent of an activity takes up 90 per cent of the time, while the last 10 per cent of the activity demands the other 90 per cent of the time.

It takes stamina to get from the rather daunting event of the PhD defence to the very much jollier occasion of the book launch.

Certainly, there are dangers in reusing material, particularly when patching together disparate pieces of text; this can jeopardize consistency and fail to create a coherent voice and storyline within the work. Nonetheless, there is a very understandable temptation to reuse old text that on rereading you find really rather good. If you are very careful and critical when you read through your draft text to ensure that it really does flow and link seamlessly, there is no reason why you should not be able to produce an excellent book manuscript from reworked thesis material.

Getting started

Once you have satisfied yourself with real answers to the above questions and decided to go ahead with a book, you must plan it out in detail. Many of the points you need to consider are discussed in Chapter 2, but there are a few extra issues pertinent to theses arising from the different processes involved in revising a thesis and writing a book from scratch.

Deciding when to start. There is no one right time to begin. Start too soon and you will lack the distance and detachment from your thesis that is needed if you are to write a monograph that is fresh, lively and free of 'thesis baggage'. Delay too long and you may lose momentum and your ready grasp of the subject in all its complexity; worse, your material may begin to show its age. In any case, soon enough your hand will probably be forced by the need to make important life and career choices.

Planning by preparing a comparative table of contents. If what you are proposing is a monograph derived from a thesis, then especially useful (not just for planning but later also for making an approach to a publisher) is to map the similarities and differences between the two works. An example is overleaf. On the basis of such an analysis, you will be able to draw up an annotated table of contents that both describes the content and indicates where the material comes from. It is this annotated table of contents – *not* the comparative map – that you will use to 'sell' your book proposal to a publisher (as it is the proposed book, not the original thesis, that is of interest).

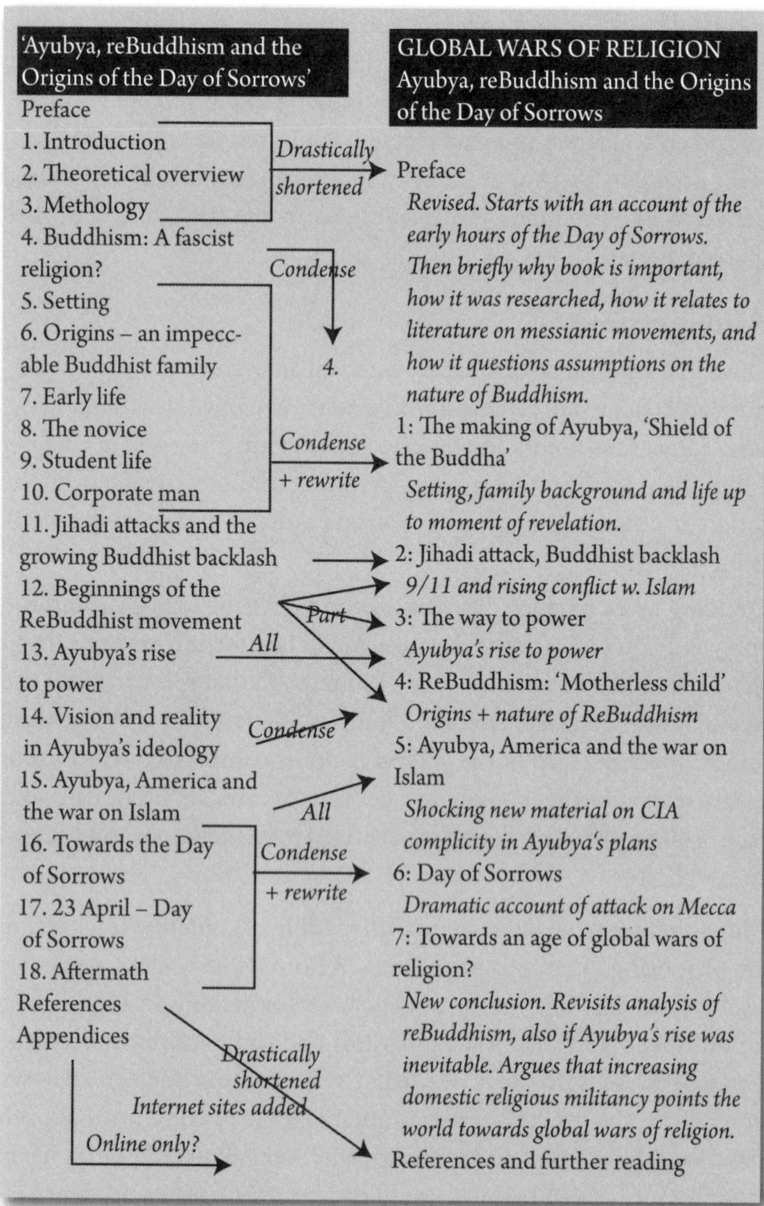

A visual plan of attack for turning an imaginery thesis, 'Ayubya, reBuddhism and the Origins of the Day of Sorrows', into the book, Global Wars of Religion.

Things you will need to cut

As is clear in the thesis–book comparison above, there are many elements in a thesis that do not belong in a book. These need to be reworked, trimmed to their bare essentials or even chopped away completely. Do not look at such editing as just a butcher's job. Your work is in fact a rough diamond that by careful cutting and polishing can be revealed in its full glory.

Literature review. Your study belongs to a specific scholarly discourse and will be framed by this. As your intended readers are already familiar with this discourse, it is sufficient that you lightly refer to this and indicate how your work adds to the debate. Certainly, it is unlikely that a 100-page review of the theoretical literature to date will be of interest.

Methodology. Likewise, readers will want to know enough about your research to help them assess the validity of your argument but no one will be interested in the minutiae of your methodology.

Quotations. Supporting an argument with the words of an authority in the field is reasonable, but do this judiciously and elegantly: paraphrasing rather than direct quotation is easier to read. If you have a lot of direct quotations in your thesis, look to eliminate most of these in your book.

Tables. Remember that every table is a distraction; it draws the reader away from the text. For each table, ask yourself: Is this one necessary? Could it be summarized and reworked into the text instead? Would it be more effective as a figure? Can it be reproduced legibly on a book-sized page?

Footnotes/endnotes. These are another distraction. The situation is worse when the note reference system is used because, with comments and citations mixed together, pertinent comments can be buried in a torrent of citations. For each note, ask yourself: Is this one necessary? Can citations be clustered or even (for multiple references to the same book) collapsed into a single citation? Can you indeed reduce the number of works cited?

References. How many people actually read bibliographies – apart from to check if their own work is listed? Cutting your reference list to only those works truly relevant to your new book will not only save time and effort for everyone; you will also save a few trees. However, academic value is (also) measured by the number of citations a work enjoys, so leave in those references that you feel have earned their place.

Appendices. Arguably, an appendix is where indigestible material is left to rot, somewhat out of sight. If you were unable to integrate such material into your thesis you need to look hard at its usefulness in your book. Consider placing such material online instead.

Excess material. Some of your thesis text may be very good but too long or too far off topic to be included in your lean, focused monograph; this excess text must be condensed, rewritten or completely discarded. The result need not be a complete loss; these 'offcuts' may form the basis of several good articles (see the next chapter).

Problematic material. There may be all sorts of reasons why material that was used in your thesis is problematic in your monograph (straight copies of maps from another author's book, for instance). It might be simpler or more appropriate to have such material reworked or cut than seek permission to reproduce them unchanged. Another example is text that is potentially libellous; this may scare away every publisher you approach. Whatever the reason, have your eyes open for such material and deal with the situation before it causes problems in the publication of your monograph.

Stylistic issues. More difficult to remove from your text is not so much what you have written but the style in which you have written it. Examples are language that is obscure, abstract and heavy on jargon, explanations that are highly technical and overly detailed, and text plagued by excessive signposting. These and other stylistic issues are dealt with in Chapter 5 and in Appendix 1.

Things you will need to add

If, as is often the case, the significant contribution that your thesis makes to scholarship in your field is found in its middle chapters, then it is unlikely to be enough that you pare away everything else; something needs to be added.

Coherence. Your book will need to have organic unity, held together by a clear narrative thread. There is double value in doing this. By tracing the trajectory of your argument, you will quickly see what other material you are missing (and what more needs to be cut).

Background material. Theses often have too much background material but sometimes – because the examiners are experts in that field – assumptions are made about what readers will know. What is needed is sufficient background material to orientate readers and prepare them for the 'meat' of your study.

New material. Again, the usual problem with theses is too much (not too little) material. But if you have at all refocused your study from what appeared in the thesis then gaps will have appeared that must be filled. Likewise, your subject is unlikely to be static; it will need to be updated to take recent events, publications, etc. into account.

Introduction. Most thesis introductions are rather pedestrian, whereas a book can greatly benefit from a short but lively introduction that whets the reader's appetite for the text that is to follow.

Conclusion. Many theses simply end; they fail to draw the threads of their argument together into a coherent and satisfying whole. Whether or not your thesis is like this, you will almost certainly need to rewrite your conclusions to bring them up to date and to reflect the changed character and focus of your study.

Index. An index is not required until your book is in production, but even at this early stage it is smart to start thinking about its contents. Such thinking has an added value; because all that your index will be is an alphabetical 'mind map' of your study, once you begin jotting down the various entries and subentries to be included, you can quickly discover things that might be missing in your text.

Whole books have been written on transforming a thesis into a monograph but we believe that in this chapter we have covered the essentials and refer you to Chapter 2 for fuller advice on planning a monograph. If you now feel all planned out and ready to write, then it is time to turn to Chapter 5 with its advice on writing a book. If, however, you also have leftover material from your thesis that was impossible to include in your book, then you will find it worthwhile taking a look at Chapter 4.

CHAPTER 4

Producing a shorter (or collected) work

An essay should be like a miniskirt: long enough to cover the subject, short enough to be interesting.

– Wilma Roby

AT FIRST GLANCE, this chapter may not be for you. If your interest is in writing a book, why concern yourself with writing a journal article or contributing a chapter to an edited volume, let alone *editing* such a volume? However, here we deal with two points that may nevertheless be of interest to you:

- Shaping leftover material from a thesis, book or research project into articles or book chapters.
- Taking material actually used in your book and reworking it into an article.

Why write articles?

What you are reading now is a book. It is, moreover, a book that largely focuses on getting an academic book published. That said, we are not blind to the fact that most scholars also contribute articles in journals and chapters in edited volumes; indeed, there are many scholars who *only* write such shorter scholarly works. It is not surprising, then, that strong arguments are put forward in support of the book while denigrating shorter works, and that equally strong voices disagree:

> 'The book is dead; the future lies in concise scholarship, published quickly and electronically.'
>
> 'No one takes bite-sized "salami publishing" seriously; it has little more weight than a contribution to Wikipedia.'
>
> 'In terms of the points awarded in research assessments, there is more "'bang for your buck" in writing several articles than one book.'
>
> 'You won't get tenure with a string of articles; the list of books published is what counts.'
>
> 'It is quicker and easier to write an article than a book.'
>
> 'Only in books can authors properly develop their argument.'
>
> 'You can assert your "ownership" of new ideas and research material far quicker in a journal, long before others have a chance to steal your thunder.'
>
> 'Some journals are very slow to publish, and in a journal you're one of a crowd; in a book you keep the limelight all to yourself.'
>
> ... and so on and so forth ...

While compelling arguments are made on both sides, we would suggest that in fact books and articles are two sides of the same scholarly coin. Indeed, we suggest that you have it both ways – write a book *and* a handful of articles. The trick is how to do this so that you enhance your reputation without repeating yourself *ad nauseam.*

Reworking (or recycling) material

Some journal articles are written from scratch; many more are derived from conference papers, lectures, working papers and the like. There is, however, another important source of material for articles: theses, book projects and ongoing research. In culinary terms, articles arising out of this type of material are the academic equivalents of off-cuts and refries.

But is this what you really want?

Of course, while there are excellent reasons for writing articles, *this may not be what you wish to do*. For instance, you may have limited time to finish your book and can do without the distraction of writing an article. Even if article authorship is not for you, you do have alternatives to getting short texts into the public domain. For example, you could post a working paper on your institute's website, present a paper at a conference, or contribute an essay to a relevant professional magazine or newsletter (often these have vastly higher circulations than any academic journal in the same field). In other words, do not trap yourself into an either-or mindset.

In the previous chapter, we discussed mining a thesis for articles. But in fact any research project may generate material that is unsuitable for inclusion in a book but would make an interesting contribution to a journal or edited volume. There may indeed be similar excess material in the book that you are writing right now. For instance, as you revise your manuscript, you realize that your analysis of place in the early work of James Joyce does not really belong in your new biography of the great novelist but would make an excellent article in a certain journal, if properly developed. Such 'off-cuts' are unlikely to be viable articles in their own right but, with foresight and a little work, they can provide the basis for a splendid 'meal' nonetheless.

Likewise, some book chapters can be reworked into journal articles. These need to be viable and interesting in their own right, as well as capable of being presented in a quite different form. In theory, you could spin off articles from all of the key chapters in your book. However, you risk ending up with a dead book, one with nothing new to say and which no one wants to publish. Many publishers will ask if the book manuscript you present to them is original and unpublished; if your answer is in the negative, you will have to explain why. It is not at all uncommon for books to contain material already presented (in different costume) as articles elsewhere, but each publisher has a level above which they start to worry that there is not enough unique material to make a book marketable – often this pain threshold lies somewhere in the 25–40% range.

How much reworking is necessary? As much as it takes to ensure that your article bears little resemblance to the original chapter. To do less risks seriously annoying both book publisher and journal editor. Thorough reworking is also smart because many journals demand that contributors sign over copyright in their article to the journal. With cosmetic differences only, you would need to obtain – and maybe even pay for – permission to use your own text in your book. In any case, the structure, style and content of a journal article are quite different from those of a book chapter. Most likely, their target readerships are also subtly different. For all of these reasons there are no excuses for ducking a thorough rewrite.

The convention for reworked material is that this is first published in journals – hardly surprising given that journal issues are usually faster to produce than books. On the other hand, it may be in your better interests (or your publisher may demand) that you delay submitting your article until production of your book is well under way. That said, a good journal article can be an excellent advertisement for a subsequent monograph, and publishers who produce both books and journals are often happy to see material from one help promote interest in the other.

In fairness and as a courtesy, if your article reworks material from your book, then you should always inform readers that it is based on material appearing in so-in-so chapter of your book. (Your book should make a similar reverse attribution to your article.) Such attributions have the added benefits of advertising your book/article.

Planning and writing your article

If you have not already read Chapter 2, it would help to do so now; there is much on the planning and conception of articles that is common to books. Likewise, you would benefit from reading the chapters on book writing that follow before starting to write your article. Bearing that in mind, the following points are necessarily brief.

Chicken or egg? The next section deals with finding the 'right' journal. This step almost needs to be taken first since the choice of journal will have an unmistakable effect on how your article is written. On the other hand, you cannot consider your publishing options without thoroughly defining the scope and nature of your article, the discourse to which it belongs and its intended readership. The only solution to this dilemma is to take both steps in tandem – and proceed with care.

Read before you write. The best writers read a lot; they are immersed in the literature of their field (*and* of other fields) as well as in the minutiae of their own research. This gives more than knowledge; it also offers perspective and a subconscious understanding of what is expected, what works, and what is appropriate.

Understand your needs. This will have a crucial effect on what you write and where you aim to publish it. An article that is 'assessment fodder' (its sole purpose being to boost your department's research evaluation results) can be handled quite differently from an article announcing a major breakthrough in your field.

Map your subject. No article (nor any book) stands alone. It may well be breaking new ground but nonetheless it has a starting point in an existing discourse, debate, field and discipline. Orienting yourself right from the beginning makes it far easier to write your article: there is then direction, coherence and relevance to its contents.

Think readership. Defining a target readership and understanding the needs and interests of your intended readers is a crucial part of that orientation; it will help you write a far more successful article.

Know your journals. Several journals may serve the subject and readership you are reaching out to. But each journal will have its own 'personality' and preferences. It is also likely that it will work to fairly strict rules on page length for each issue, balance of sections, number and type of articles, treatment of subject, etc. There is no point offering a 50-page annotated bibliography to a journal that only publishes short empirical pieces, for instance. Immerse yourself in what your preferred journal has published before (check out not just the most recent issue but at least a year's output to detect any variations over time) and above all else read its Notes for Authors. It is your job – not the journal's – to understand what is required. Good journals are offered more relevant articles than they have room to print and thus have little incentive to take on work that fails to observe the requirements listed in the Notes.

Structure your text. Often, articles are prefaced by an abstract then introduced by an exposition of the issue, the theoretical and empirical background, and a description of the methodology. Invariably, the text is supplemented with notes and concluded with a list of references. That said, conventions on the organization and content of articles vary across fields and between journals. Understand what is expected of your article (as above by reading the Notes for Authors and checking other published articles in that journal).

Do not reinvent the wheel. Most articles have a similar structure of 'meat' wrapped in a sandwich of introductory and concluding material. If you plan to write several articles based on much the same research material (be this 'off-cuts' or 'refries'), then you will save yourself a lot of time by doing a thorough job at the beginning (with your first article) on such common elements as background, methodology, discourse, references, etc. Even so, do not stretch your material too far or use the same positioning text for different articles. Because each article has its own needs and internal dynamics, some reformulation and rewriting will be necessary.

Consider length. Again, know your target journal(s). Usually, they will not consider articles falling outside the normal length.

Watch your style. One of the worst, most boring things to change in a text is the formatting of the citations and references. Get this right by consulting your target journal's Notes for Authors *before* you start writing. Do the same for all of those other stylistic issues including spelling and grammar. Most journals do not have the resources to correct your shortcomings in this area (and they may indeed reject your article because of its failure to adhere to their standards). Therefore, the time invested getting your text into shape before submitting it will be repaid several times over at a later stage.

Finding the right journal

There is no single 'right' publisher for any book, nor one single make-or-break journal for your article. If you are thoroughly versed in the field at which your article is aimed, then you should know the key journals there. Augment this list with searches for articles in your field published in journals you have overlooked or perhaps never heard of (using general search engines like Google as well as more specialist ones like JSTOR and Google Scholar). After browsing through their contents online (if a journal is not online in some form, it is probably not worth your while), you should come up with a short list and a gut feeling of which is your top pick.

Sometimes a journal editor is prepared to consider replying to an enquiry about their likely interest in your article but many only wish to consider a 'bird in the hand' (articles actually submitted); they have no time for 'birds in the bush'. Unfortunately, they also tend to take a very dim view of authors submitting the same article to multiple journals. Doing so might seem time-effective to you, but the journal will have to invest time and effort in getting your article peer reviewed so editors will want to be sure this work is not wasted. If you are tempted to chance it, remember that there are only so many good external reviewers in a given field and that the same reviewers may well be approached by several journals. The net result could see you being blacklisted. It is of course a different matter if you decide to split your reworked articles, offering each to a different journal. This may be the best way to broaden their impact, especially if they cross-reference each other.

The orthodox position is that only peer-reviewed journals have any academic credibility. This can become an issue if you are seeking research funding or a job; all those articles listed on your CV that are published by non-refereed journals may be discounted or even treated as negatives. Even so, by no means all non-refereed journals are bad/inferior. Some undertake a meticulous in-house review process rather than outsourcing to external peer reviewers who (let us be frank) are not always equally thorough or consistent in their evaluations. Probably the crucial distinction should be between journals that have a review process and those that do not – but do not expect all academic bureaucrats to share this judgement.

There is no reason why you should not be ambitious for your article and submit it to a top-class journal first. Sure, it is likely that your article will be rejected (along with 95% of the other hopeful submissions) but, if the journal undertakes a genuine double-blind peer review, your article is in with a chance.[1] Various measurements are used to determine the relative importance of a journal. If you look at the advertisements for different 'hard' social-science journals, for instance, you will often see that the journal's impact factor and field ranking is quoted. Because these evaluations are based on an analysis of citations, many authors in these fields believe it crucial (and a mark of the seriousness of a journal) that it is included in the Social Sciences Citation Index. Even though there is also an Arts & Humanities Citation Index, there appears to be far less concern with such ranking in the humanities and 'softer' social sciences, perhaps because journal articles are still far less important than monographs.

Other things to consider are how many subscribers the journal has and how visible it is on the Internet. Remember, too, that while

---

1 Nonetheless, do not underestimate the power of the invisible network. It is notable how some highly reputed international journals seem to have an over-representation of authors connected with the journal's host university, whereas many lesser 'regional' journals seem to be more international, often having a far wider range of authors.

one or two journals may dominate the pinnacles of your discipline, down in the academic undergrowth the journal of choice among scholars in your specific field may be a high-quality niche publication. Ultimately, you are going to have to make a subjective judgement about importance. If you are new to the game, seek advice from more experienced peers who may be willing to provide word-of-mouth feedback that you will never see openly stated (like 'Journal A may be the top journal but it takes three years to get an article published').

Be aware also that there is a growing chance that you will be required to hand over money to get your article published. There is already a long tradition for this in STM (scientific, technical and medical) journals. In these fields, where speed and volume of publication and number of citations are crucial, publishing a monograph is rare. As such, journals can get away with charging authors for the privilege of getting published. Being almost the only avenue for publication, they have the upper hand. This author-pays model is now spreading to social-science journals, but for a new reason: the increasing demand by funding authorities that the published articles of scholars receiving public funding should be freely available online (i.e. that there is 'open access' to the results of funded research).[2] Here, many journals publishers have adopted a hybrid 'double whammy' business model: journals are still subscription-based, but authors can obtain full and immediate open access to their articles against a payment of several hundred US dollars.

An unintended side effect of the success of the Open Access movement is the threat it may pose to many smaller journals which lack the resources to invest in going online, dare not risk losing subscriptions by giving away their content for free, and have contributors unwilling or unable to move to an author-pays model. Only you can decide what the right choice of journal, academically and ethically is, for you. Do you support the small, embattled, specialist journal,

---

2 To date, only journals have been affected by demands for open access but in time we expect that book publishing will be affected too.

do you gladly pay (out of your grant) to give free and open access to your work, is Internet accessibility an absolute must for you, or does the citation index trump all other concerns?

Getting your article published

Provided that your article is not immediately rejected at submission, it is likely to go through the following steps towards publication.

Evaluation. Not all journal articles are peer reviewed, as noted above. Nor is there a standard way in which evaluations are carried out; this varies between disciplines and from journal to journal. Experiments are also being made with open peer review and 'soft' evaluations based on social networking through the Internet. For the meantime, however, it is still most common that only one reviewer assesses an article (unlike books where the use of two reviewers is the norm). Almost certainly the reviewer is anonymous (albeit often identifiable in a small field) but so too are authors anonymous in double-blind reviews. Peer reviewers tend to be unpaid, doing a thankless job out of altruism and an interest in being on the leading edge of scholarship in their field. With luck they may receive a free subscription to the journal (and a Christmas present if they are especially favoured). Horror stories abound of reviews taking years to complete their reports but normally the turnaround is reasonably fast, so this is what you should expect – and demand, if need be.

Acceptance. If, based on the evaluation results and their own judgement, the journal's editors accept your article for publication (perhaps subject to specific revisions and adherence to a strict schedule), they will almost invariably require you to sign over to the journal your copyright in your article. This could be a problem if your article is a cosmetic makeover of a chapter in the book you are writing (see above).

Publication process. Normally, journal articles are published much faster than books. Indeed, today we are even seeing online versions of articles published as soon as the text is available, long before the print edition of the journal appears. The production process involves language editing, layout, proofing and printing/e-publication, often with little or no time for authors to provide input. Be aware that some journals expect their authors to deliver the final text in perfect, edited form; there is no checking for errors or omissions, with submitted text appearing uncorrected in the printed journal. (Seeing errors appear in print is horribly embarrassing, so make sure you proof your text well.) Likewise, journals can be unforgiving of late-stage textual changes and demand that you pay for these. Eventually, however, you will receive one or more copies of the journal (maybe with off-prints as well) with your article included. The journey is complete, and all that remains is the satisfying job of adding another entry to your list of published works.

Contributing a chapter to an edited volume

There are superficial resemblances between journal articles and contributions to an edited volume; both are short texts, for instance. But in many important ways, the latter is quite different:

- Often, it derives from a presentation made to a conference.
- Normally, you must be invited to contribute to an edited volume.
- Your chapter is not independent; it is one of several contributions addressing issues common to the volume. (Indeed, if the volume is at all good, its editor will create linkages between its chapters.)
- There is a tendency that the text emphasizes the 'meat' of an author's research, with discursive and methodological paraphernalia cut to the bare essentials.

Why would you write such a chapter instead of an article? Why indeed, given that an article in an international refereed journal counts for a lot, and a chapter in a book for almost nothing – always assuming any publisher takes the edited book, which is by no means a given. Again, this need not be an either-or choice. Given the differences between the two prose forms, you should be able to write chapters and articles so significantly different that they complement each other and build your publication list. Like an article, a chapter can be a quick way for you to assert your 'ownership' of new ideas and research material.[3] But what a chapter adds over and above a journal article is that it is published in a collection of such chapters on a common issue; the edited volume and its attendant marketing activities create a magnet for specialists working in your field (and related fields) to discover your work.

While there are many points of difference between articles and stand-alone chapters (and books for that matter), we see no point in describing the process of writing such chapters here. You can glean this in the following section and supplement this information with our other material elsewhere on the planning and writing process.

Editing a multi-author volume

There are several really good reasons for not getting involved in the work of a book editor. Editors are often given little academic credit for what can be a difficult and delicate task. Moreover, edited volumes are generally valued much less than monographs by book buyers. There is indeed a general feeling that too many edited volumes have not really been properly edited, but are simply disparate collections of whatever papers came to hand, with little attempt on the part of their editors to bring these bits and pieces together into an integrated whole. It is certainly true that such volumes have been published (*conference proceedings* are particularly notorious), although they are becoming rarer as they prove harder and harder for publishers to sell. But there are also examples of excellent collections where the collaboration of many minds, perhaps from different disciplines, on a single subject brings about real breakthroughs. Such outstanding works often suffer, though, from the general taint attached to edited books.

3 That said, while the writing may be as fast as for an article, getting the actual edited volume published could be a much slower process.

However, there are also a number of good reasons to offer yourself as editor. Editing a book could be a way for you to build your academic network and gain name recognition in a wider circle. You might feel that your field needs a collaborative volume on a particular subject, and that there is nobody else who can make it happen, or happen well. Perhaps you have to offer a route to publication in order to attract good contributions to a workshop or conference you are convening. Or maybe it is just simply your turn.

Whichever reason you have for accepting this potentially poisoned chalice, be aware that just as important as the academic challenge of forcing a coherent work out of a motley collection of contributions is the administrative challenge of forcing any extra work at all out of a large group of busy people. In fact, many good volumes have been edited by partnerships of editors where an established academic has used the clout of many years in the field to ensure a high academic standard, and a more junior academic has gained access to an impressive network of contacts by offering to take on many of the more administrative tasks.

Academic aspects

Getting the right contributors. Obviously the most important aspect is to attract contributors who have something interesting and important to say about your subject, but it can be very useful if you also think in terms of getting together a group with a variety of backgrounds. Try to attract at least one VIP in the field, if nothing else than just to write a brief foreword, and let the rest of the group consist of a mixture of established scholars and bright new people. If your book is interdisciplinary, get a good balance between the disciplines. If it purports to be in any way global in outlook, include contributors from different countries, continents and ethnicities.

Formulating the question. It is your responsibility to put into words the intended subject of the book (and perhaps of each chapter within it) in such a way that it is quite clear to contributors what you hope to receive from them, yet sufficiently broad to allow them to take ownership of their contributions. In doing this, you must also consider how you will later order and link the contributions within the volume.

Acting as peer reviewer. When contributions are submitted, you will have to comment on each one, possibly suggesting revisions to improve quality within the contribution or adjustments to improve coherence among contributions. This requires a delicate and diplomatic touch. There is good reason for peer reviewers generally to be anonymous, and because you are known to your contributors – perhaps personally as well as professionally – there is a clear risk of a reaction from bruised egos to carelessly worded criticisms. Remember to make positive remarks that can take the sting out of your more negative comments; it may sound obvious, but is often forgotten. But in addition to being a diplomat, you must also have the courage of your convictions and be prepared to live with the fall-out if you have to make the difficult decision to reject a contribution outright. On the other hand, remember that you are not alone; your publisher will also be commissioning peer reviews which often can be used in conjunction with your own assessments.

Writing an introduction and conclusion. Some edited books make do with just an introduction, but the best and most coherent ones also have a conclusion or epilogue by the editor. You could consider co-writing one or both with one of your contributors, although that might encourage a claim for co-editorship, too. Either way, it is hard to overstate the importance of the editor's responsibility to provide a narrative structure and a firm feeling of progression through the volume from introduction to conclusion.

Administrative aspects

Constructing a style sheet. You should expect that your publisher already has style guidelines to be used for the volume. All that you then need to do is simply tell your contributors to conform to these guidelines and check that they do so. If no guidelines are available, then you will have to create your own style sheet since both your readers and publisher will expect a uniform and coherent volume. Frankly, this is not a simple task. However, if you are forced into setting such standards, then you can get help from *The Chicago Manual of Style* or a similar work. In constructing the style sheet, you will have to balance desirability and expedience. It may be desirable that every aspect of every contribution conforms to exactly the same format, but the more detail you pile into your style sheet, the more likely it is that your contributors will disregard it as more trouble than it is worth. Does it matter, for instance, if you have both British and US terms and spellings? Is it more important that all bibliographic references conform precisely? Do you care whether east and West are capitalized or not? Be realistic when you set your requirements for contributors but also be aware that your publisher may return the manuscript to you and demand a more rigorous harmonization.

Enforcing deadlines. A great many edited works are repeatedly delayed because one or two contributors fail to meet their deadlines. If the contributions in question are important, you will have to accept the role of nag or supplicant. It is hardly fair to those contributors who deliver promptly that their work sits about gathering dust while a few mavericks play loose and fast with the deadline, and it is your responsibility to minimize this problem. It helps if you have laid out all deadlines before work begins, and if you remind everyone of upcoming deadlines in good time. As a last, desperate resort, do not hesitate to turn to your publisher, asking them to bear down on any recalcitrant, unreliable contributors.

Liaising with the publisher. Contributors usually have no direct contact with the publisher beyond taking receipt of one or more free copies when the book is published. You will have to produce the book proposal, negotiate a contract with your publisher, and see the book through the production stage. The publication contract is usually only between publisher and editor(s), and only the editor can hope for royalties. As we said above, edited volumes have low perceived value and are therefore not terribly attractive to publishers, so expect to work hard to land a publication contract.

Unifying chapter bibliographies. The easy and unattractive way out here is to leave a short bibliography at the end of each chapter rather than take on the laborious and, frankly, boring task of unifying the contributors' bibliographies into one. However, a unified bibliography sends potential publishers and readers alike a strong signal of intense editorial engagement with the volume and thus justifiably raises expectations that this volume should not be treated with the suspicion usually surrounding edited books. That said, nowadays edited volumes are being sold as individual e-chapters as often as they are sold as entire e-books; for that reason, then, the references may need to be organized by chapter. Your wisest course of action is to raise this issue with your publisher at an early stage.

Indexing and proofing. You will not get out of producing an index for the book, so set aside a few days for that. As for proof-reading, you could send chapters out to be checked by their contributors, but since proofing is generally done to a very tight deadline, expect to have to proof everything yourself, and view any input from contributors as a bonus. Do not tolerate any last-minute changes to their text from your contributors apart from necessary corrections; your publisher will certainly not be tolerant of such unpleasant (and expensive) surprises.

📖

Of necessity, this has been a short treatment of the issues involved in contributing an article to a journal or a chapter to an edited work, as well as in editing a multi-author volume. The actual process of writing these shorter works differs little from what is involved in writing a book, the subject we now turn to.

CHAPTER 5

Writing your book

A bad book is as much of a labour to write as a good one; it comes as sincerely from the author's soul.

– Aldous Huxley

WHEN IT COMES DOWN TO THE CONCRETE TASK of writing your book, it is absolutely imperative for you to seize and hold on to your reader's attention. The rule of thumb is that if your readers are not gripped by your book within the first 20 or 30 pages, the probability is that they will never finish it. The same rule applies to publishers and their peer reviewers, of course. Many book manuscripts are rejected by publishers not for lack of academic merit but because they are just badly written, and plain boring to read. Bear this in mind when shaping and writing your book.

Your readers must be coaxed along from start to finish with interesting text connected by a clear (yet subtle) narrative thread. This demands that your book has the unity, pace and direction we discussed in Chapter 2. At the same time, you must perform a delicate balancing act between grounding your study in the scholarly context of its readership on the one hand, and on the other hand letting it stand on its own merits as an independent and innovative piece of scholarship. And all the while there is the sometimes painful act of writing itself, with its issues of language, style and presentation.

You will of course have your own unique style and voice which will (and should) shine through in your academic writing. Likewise, the decisions you have made about the structure of your book reflect your personal preferences, attitude, understanding and experience as an academic reader and writer. However, there are issues relevant for all authors that can affect how easy or difficult it is to read your text.

In this chapter we will explain what these issues are, and why they are important. We will also lay out some general concerns about the technical aspects of writing (with much more detail available in Appendix 1), explain when and how to seek permission to use material originally produced by others, and lastly give a few ideas on how to achieve the least painful writing experience.

Language

What you have to say is obviously of paramount importance, but how you say it also matters greatly. Imagine being introduced at a drinks reception to someone with a huge, inflamed pimple on the tip of his nose. Everyone would stare in fascination at the great monstrosity

Which language?

This book is written in English, but your book might not be. While most tertiary education takes place in students' native languages, academic authors hoping to make an international impact must publish in the modern academic *lingua franca*: English. Indeed, even national assessments of research may be biased in favour of international publication, placing scholars for whom English is a second language at a distinct disadvantage in several ways:

- Their mother tongue may be quite different in nature to global English.[1]

1 The eminent historian-turned-publisher, Paul Kratoska, has met Japanese scholars who completely compartmentalize their English- and Japanese-language writing, so different are the thought processes and behaviour involved. For instance, one scholar said that 'it is necessary to become less Japanese, because English demands a directness that would be out of place

and nobody would be able to concentrate for one minute on what the poor man was saying. That is exactly the same effect that sloppy, unclear, error-filled language can have on a text. The reader will find it difficult, perhaps even impossible, to get past the poor execution to the potentially brilliant matter underneath, and will blame the author for thus obscuring good content behind poor form. Your aim

- Their English must be good enough to carry complex ideas and argumentation.
- Their English must be of such a high standard that it is readable, credible to (often foreign) evaluators, and does not threaten the publisher with higher editorial costs.
- Global scholarly discourses and interests may differ markedly from those dominant in their country.

If you are writing in a language not your mother tongue, then write your book in the foreign language from the beginning. You may struggle to express yourself in a second language, but it is even harder to finish a book in one language and mind-set, and then go back and translate it into another.

Beware also of the cultural differences in standards and approaches that can lurk underneath the more obvious language differences. For instance, strict neutrality (even invisibility) is expected of scholars working in the West, whereas in many developing countries social relevance and engagement (even activism) are the norm. Whereas dispassionate conclusions may be expected in Berlin, helpful recommendations as well are more likely to be appreciated in Hanoi. If you are aiming to be published in a different environment from where you normally work, then you will find it worthwhile to investigate what norms and approaches are expected (though hardly ever openly stated).

---

in Japanese-language material'. Paul Kratoska, 'English-language academic publishing in Asia' in ICAS 5 insert to *IIAS Newsletter*, no. 43, 2007, p. 6.

should be to write in such a way that the language flows seemingly effortlessly (no matter how much effort you have made to achieve this effect) and that the reading experience is equally effortless and enjoyable.

There are a number of practical steps you can take towards this goal and concrete points you should keep in mind, as we describe below. First, though, there are the three C's of all good writing: common usage, clarity and consistency (but the greatest of these is consistency).

- ***Common usage*** promotes quicker comprehension.
- ***Clarity*** cuts confusion and is vital for communication.
- ***Consistency*** gives your work uniformity and coherence.

Even if you get something wrong, or change your mind, or find you have to adjust to a new publisher's house style, then if your text is conscientiously consistent it will be possible to make the necessary changes with reasonable ease.

In all your writing, your purpose is to inform, not to obfuscate. Thus, avoid clichés, jargon, and unnecessarily difficult technical terms. Where possible, use words that are easy to understand, like 'blur' or 'cloud', instead of more complex and abstract words, such as 'obfuscate' above. Generally, the use of many words, and particularly the use of many long words, is a sign of insecurity in authors who do not feel confident that their normal language is good enough for the formal occasion of a manuscript. Also limit your use of the passive voice, which makes sentences more convoluted and generally increases the distance between the author and the subject matter. The passive voice is very common in academic writing (and indeed widely used in this book), but try to balance its use with active sentences that reconnect author, text and reader. Lastly, limit the length of your sentences – if one extends over more than two lines, it is a candidate for reformulation and division.

With an example from the Plain English movement, do not claim that

High-quality learning environments are a necessary precondition for the facilitation and enhancement of the ongoing learning process.

but rather tell your reader that

Children need good schools if they are to learn properly.

Style

Apart from issues of grammar and terminology, there are a number of stylistic concerns that you must keep in mind when you write.

Cutting the fog

A useful measure of readability is the *Gunning fog index*, which analyses wordiness, sentence length and complexity. The fog score indicates the number of years of formal education that a person requires in order to easily understand a text on the first reading. A good academic text should aim for a score between 12 and 15. To score a text, you need a block of about 100 words. This is how to calculate the fog score yourself:

(number of words divided by number of sentences)

plus

(number of long words[1] times 100 divided by total number of words)

multiplied by 0.4

Using this formula, the fog index score of the paragraph above (excluding the formula) is ((77/5) + (7 x 100/77)) x 0.4 = 9.8. The score is a useful tool with which to check your text at regular intervals as you write.

1 Words with three or more syllables, but excluding proper names, words with common suffixes like -es and -ing, compound words, and common words like *asparagus* or *influenza*.

Be confident that what you say is right. Diffidence and apologetic statements may undermine readers' confidence in your work just as badly as baseless exaggeration could, while arrogance can downright alienate them. Modest assertiveness should be the tone of your book, allowing your readers to trust that they are in safe hands.

Be subtle with your signposting. Something that is typical of theses and hence a common fault in new authors is excessive signposting. This is where an author starts each chapter with a mention of the previous chapter and an overview of what the new chapter will bring, and later ends each chapter with a summary of its contents and a foretaste of what is in store in the next chapter. When the signposting is especially bad, even the sections within a chapter will suffer a similar treatment. The effect is not pleasant; the reader feels rather firmly patronized. This does *not* mean you should do away with signposting altogether, but be subtle and courteous in how you use it.

Vary your text. Avoid repeating a word in the same sentence (or even paragraph, if possible). Vary sentence and paragraph length as well as the connecting words between them (within reason – a series of long, complex sentences followed by a burst of short, sharp ones can make the former appear dreary and the latter staccato). However, variation of language should not be used to disguise repetition of material. A classic error is to illuminate a text with quotations, tables or illustrations, and then proceed to spend almost as much space repeating or commenting on the information they contain. All this does is irritate the reader who understood you perfectly well the first time.

Keep speed bumps and diversions to a minimum. Remember at all times that your text should be a source of enjoyment and enlightenment, not a test of reader stamina. The smooth progression of your argument can be disrupted by speed bumps such as textual clutter (e.g. excessive footnotes, or author-date citations inserted in the main text) and words or phrases that are hard to understand or remember (such as foreign words that require definition or checking in a glossary). Technical terms can form another set of speed bumps. While some are certainly appropriate, remember that some of your readers may come from outside your immediate field and be unfamiliar with the more involved terminology. Avoid diversions such as cross-references that distract your readers and take them to other sections of the text, with the danger that they lose the thread of your argument or, worse, lose patience altogether because they perceive your text as badly structured. Endnotes are another type of diversion but, if you are using the author-date citation system, these may be unavoidable.

Use quotations judiciously. Too many quotations in a text can look like padding; it is as if you the author are letting others do your work. Keep to quotations that make or illustrate a necessary point or that express something particularly well or in an unusual manner. Instead of quoting a block of text, it may be more effective to paraphrase, quoting only a characteristic word or short phrase. And without fail, you must cite the author of any material you are quoting or paraphrasing. While we acknowledge that some scholarly cultures may see copying as a sign of respect, at the international level plagiarism remains one of scholarship's most unforgivable sins.

Avoid bias. A frequently heard complaint is that universities and their presses are plagued by political correctness. Be that as it may, you are likely to have a happier writing career if you are careful not to tread on any toes. Thus, gender bias is to be avoided (often achieved simply by using the plural form instead of the more clumsy 's/he' or 'he/she'), likewise any other form of discrimination through the use of particular terms. However, language is a living, evolving entity, and epithets that were once terms of abuse may later have been coopted as badges of identity, examples being 'Queer' and 'Creole'.

Be careful what you write. Libel laws vary from country to country but, in all jurisdictions, having to defend a libel case is likely to be a nasty and expensive business. For this reason, publishers' contracts invariably place the burden of legal responsibility for such matters on their authors. By all means be controversial in your study but, if you are in any doubt at all about something that you are writing, think very hard before you include it in your text.

Presentation

Presentation influences how your text is perceived (and evaluated) and in this respect, too, there are several general concerns that you would be wise to keep in mind when you write.

Visual readability. While good looks will not help make a badly written text more readable, a good text can soon be made harder to read with excessive use of bold or italic text, for instance. (In a similar way, an unfriendly font, miniscule type and too-tight line spacing can be off-putting to a publisher, even if these are cosmetic faults and easily fixed.) Also the over-use of headings, lists, tables and figures can produce visual 'clutter' that may detract from the reading experience as these (like the 'speed bumps' mentioned above) break the smooth flow of your text.

Uniformity and consistency. You have a great many choices to make about the appearance of your paragraphs, headings, etc., and you can save a lot of time and dull correction work if you apply a single set of standards right from the beginning. The only straightjacket you must impose on yourself is the Kevlar-reinforced straightjacket of complete and utter consistency. Then, if your publisher turns out to have different preferences, it will be a fairly simple matter to adjust your text by redefining styles (e.g. from single to double line spacing) and by searching and replacing text elements (from 'analyze' to 'analyse', for instance).

Conventions. There are many conventions regarding how things should be done in a book. Some are general to all academic fields (such as the order of the various book elements) while others vary from field to field (such as preferences regarding citation style). You will make life very much easier for yourself – and for your publisher – if you first discover and then observe the conventions in your particular field.

Compatibility and utility. Remember that your manuscript is not the final form in which your text will appear. It is a waste of time (even if it may be very tempting) to format your text to make the text fall nicely on the page. *Never* attempt to produce a 'designed' page by inserting hard formatting such as spaces, tabs, multiple returns, 'hard' hyphens, etc. as these will invariably have to be removed later. No one will thank you for wasting their time with counter-productive prettification.

All these points may seem rather prescriptive, but their essential purpose is to help you to excite and engross your readers, drawing them smoothly through your text from the point of initial uncertainty to that of ultimate satisfaction. Anything that stands in the way of this smooth progression – anything that distracts or irritates your reader – is a threat to the success of your book. Let your readers' thoughts be on *what* you are saying, not *how* you are saying it.[1]

You will find much more concrete advice in Appendix 1, where we set out what we believe to be the best practice for text preparation. If you are writing your text without already knowing which publisher you will approach when the manuscript is complete, we strongly urge you to use the Appendix guidelines. However, if you have already picked a publisher, you would do better to obtain their specific style sheet and work to the preferences listed there.

1 For some wonderful, occasionally laugh-out-loud funny examples of how *not* to write, you could do worse than dip into *Intellectual Impostures* by Alan Sokal and Jean Bricmont (Profile Books, 1998), part of their great crusade against the abuses of clarity and logic in (mainly) French radical postmodern and relativist scholarship.

Permissions and the use of copyright material

Academic endeavour is a form of intellectual bricklaying where scholars today build on the foundations laid by the scholars of yesterday, often re-using the same bricks in new and insightful combinations. The mortar that holds together the community-built edifice of scholarship is respect for the moral ownership of the originating scholar (or author, illustrator, photographer, etc.) to the original material. This respect is codified in copyright legislation. Quite rightly, violations can be a source of much trouble and expense, not to mention the loss of scholarly standing, so it is well worth 'doing the right thing'; indeed, your publisher will insist upon it.

Copyright covers a wide range of creative, intellectual and artistic works, giving the creator of an original work exclusive rights to it, usually for a limited period of time. (Part of the business of publishing involves the author assigning some or all of these rights to a publisher for their commercial exploitation.) It is always mandatory that you obtain permission to use copyright material, but the requirement is conventionally waived in the case of 'fair dealing' ('fair use' in the US) for prose text, which is taken to mean single text extracts up to 400 words or a series of extracts with a combined length up to 800 words (provided no single extract exceeds 300 words). Because your publisher may wish to avoid having to seek permissions, they may request that any quotations you make fall well within the general bounds of 'fair dealing'. There are, however, no such exceptions for copyright illustrations (diagrams, charts and photographs), poetry or music excerpts. Your safest bet is to do some research on the specific material that you want to reproduce, particularly to ascertain its age and see if it falls within the copyright term applicable in the country where the copyright is held. If in any doubt, seek permission.

If the copyright material you want to use has been published, you must get the permission of the publisher. If it is unpublished material, permission should come from the person who created the material. You do not need to make a formal request until your publisher has agreed that the material should be included in your book, but an informal approach could be useful (if, say, the material is owned by a library or archive that you are visiting and where you are friendly with the staff).

As a rule, publishers prefer that authors make the formal approach to copyright holders because academic authors have a good chance of being granted permission without fees or other restrictions. If a fee is nevertheless involved, academic publishers generally expect the author to pay, but this is something you might be able to negotiate. Often the fee depends on the purpose of your book, how many copies will be printed and where they are to be sold, and you will have to consult with your publisher to get this information before finalizing your permissions requests.

Your letter requesting permission to reproduce material could go something like this:

> Dear [publisher or copyright owner],
>
> I am seeking permission from you to reproduce [exact description] for which I believe you hold the copyright. The material is to be used in [an academic monograph/a reference work/a textbook/etc.] that I am writing entitled [your book title and subtitle], to be published by [your publisher]. My publisher tells me they expect to print [number] copies in hardback and [number] copies in paperback. The book will be available [globally/in all French-speaking countries/throughout Australasia/etc.]. I would be very grateful if you would grant me permission for this use of your material, and will of course ensure that your ownership is fully and clearly acknowledged in the resulting book.
>
> Yours sincerely,

Your publisher will demand that you forward to them all correspondence certifying that you have received permission to use the material. Furthermore, when giving permission, the copyright holder may require that you print an attribution statement with a particular wording, and they may also specify where this should appear (in the figure caption, preliminary acknowledgements, etc.). Do ensure that your publisher is sent all relevant information to comply with these requirements.

Sometimes, you will have to negotiate permission from your own publisher if you want to re-use material you have already published with them. Many publishers are sensitive about this because they fear that authors will publish a competing work to the detriment of the sales of the original work. Often, however, your publisher may be persuaded that this is a very minor danger and that an attribution could in fact work as additional publicity for the first publication. A common attribution in this case might be 'This chapter was first published in *Lost Cities of the Andes* by the author (Vancouver: ABC Press, 2001). My thanks to ABC Press for permission to reproduce this in an edited form.'

The writing experience

A few years ago, two Western scholars spent a weekend in a Japanese hotel. One hunched over a computer, furiously hammering out a text, the other sprawled on a Japanese-size bed, his legs jutting over the end, dictating. They talked to each other, and argued, and wrote. At the end of the weekend they had effectively written an entire book, one that went on to make an impact both in the world of anthropology and in political terms. It also sold out and made its publisher happy.

In contrast, this book has taken several years to write and has missed so many deadlines that there is no blood left to blush. A key reason for this delay is that it was a part-time project with other work having higher priority. (And it is hard to write in short, frenetic bursts, so even when there was time set aside for writing, it was regularly plagued by displacement activity and by the slow and painful progress that a colleague of ours diagnosed as 'authoritis'.) It remains to be seen whether our efforts will be worthwhile from our long-suffering publisher's perspective.

Hopefully, your writing experience will fall somewhere between these two extremes. *Hope*, of course, is not enough; you need attitude and action. Here are a few pointers on your way – good advice that all too often we ourselves failed to take.

Set your goals. This should be relatively easy if at the planning stage you have already defined what you want from your book. But there could also be time-sensitive issues, for instance a conference you wish to attend with book in hand, or a job to be found before the end of next year. Certainly, your writing task can be much easier if you have a clear target.

Map the work. The trouble with books is that they are big projects. A journal article or conference paper is often about 5,000 words long (and could possibly be completed in a weekend) but a typical book is 90–100,000 words. This is too big to conceptualize as a single entity, so you need to break the work down into discrete, manageable chunks. If you are really organized, you could sketch a flow chart or project plan. Not only does this map the tasks to be completed but it also shows the dependent linkages between them and flags up any fixed deadlines to be met.

Plan your time. If you are lucky and can devote all of your working day to writing, you should be able to draft an average of 1,000–1,500 words daily. But, as few of us can afford to write full time and most of us would be driven quietly insane by the attempt, in fact a 100,000-word book will take many months, if not years, to write (a page a day more or less equals a book a year). When are you free and willing to do this work? Your first priority is to estimate and allocate times to each of the tasks involved. You would be wise to:

- Be cautious with your time estimates (i.e. expect the unexpected disruption).
- Check your diary to allow gaps for planned absences (holidays, for instance).

- Block in all fixed commitments (e.g. allowing you to combine attendance at a conference with two weeks of research in a nearby archive).
- Consider any other work commitments unrelated to your book.

Make space for your writing. You will need courage, stamina and a little fanaticism to follow through on your plan. But, perhaps most of all, you will need discipline. It helps to establish a routine. Set yourself regular times when you write, but also plan and make sure you *take* your breaks. A brisk walk, bicycle ride or other physical activity can have an amazing effect. Not only does it clear the head and recharge batteries, but quite often you will find that a break from the computer monitor allows you unconsciously to draw threads of an argument together or generate new ideas and associations. A peaceful place to ponder and pace can also be immensely helpful.

Hone your skills. Arguably, writing is like sport: you need to get into shape and keep fit with constant practice; the practice also hones your skills. It is inevitable that you will occasionally struggle for hours over some trivial paragraph, finally getting it right only to discard it altogether the next week. This may be frustrating; it may feel like a waste of time and effort. But do not despair; what is really happening is that you are refining your ideas and, free of charge, sharpening your skills as a writer.

Maintain an overview. You will have to work to maintain your grasp on the full text so that you do not go off on some exciting tangent and lose sight of the original purpose. Your book is most likely far too big to keep in your head for extended periods of time; it is frighteningly easy to lose sight of its overall direction and thrust, its vital connective thread of argumentation and thought. Make sure that you frequently reacquaint yourself with long stretches of the text that lead to the section you are currently working on. A great, but more time-consuming, way to reconnect with the book as a whole is to skim read the entire thing from start to finish. It should not matter here that some chapters are finished text while others are only rough outlines, since your purpose should be to reconnect with the flow and direction of the work, and to spot any omissions or repetitions in the material. When you have finished a chapter, if not before, print it out and read it on paper – this makes for quite a different experience to viewing the text on screen, with errors and ideas previously invisible now suddenly obvious on the page.

Keep up to date. Finally, it should go without saying that time and tide wait for no one. Even as you write, another scholar will be publishing something that you need to consider. It is essential that you leave yourself enough time to keep up with news and developments in your field.

Survival tips for blocked writers

Writer's block can hit even the most successful writers, but the less experienced you are, and the more vital your writing is to your future career, the easier it is to get stuck. So, at the risk of descending to the level of the banal, here are a few tips that might help if you get really stuck.

Speed-writing and speed-planning

If your problem is being over-critical of your own work so that nothing you write is good enough to survive deletion for more than a moment, you may need to switch off your critical faculties for a little while. The aim is to 'disconnect' your logical, critical left brain and engage only your creative, risk-taking right brain. This allows you to produce a text that, while nowhere near perfect, can at least form a skeleton upon which you can flesh out a more substantial text, and which may contain nuggets of ideas that can be fruitfully expanded.

It is simple enough to do, although you may feel a bit silly at first. You pick a topic to write about, set an egg timer or similar to 5–10 minutes (no more, certainly not the first times you try this), and start to write. You must write as fast as you can, and you must write non-stop. If you cannot think what to write, just put down 'I don't know what to write, I don't know what ...', etc. You may *not* look at what you have already written and may *not* correct errors, i.e. you may not be critical of yourself until the time is up. You can write either on paper or, even better, on the computer with the monitor switched off. At the end of your 5–10 minutes, you will hopefully be surprised at the number of useful nuggets hidden among the typos and 'I don't know' exclamations.

A somewhat similar technique when dealing with issues of structure rather than text is to produce, as fast as you can, a mind map of all you want or need to include in your book (or chapter or article), allowing big and small points to mingle uncritically. This should produce a rats' nest of ideas that you can subsequently disentangle into a linear structure for your text. An example of a mind map is below.

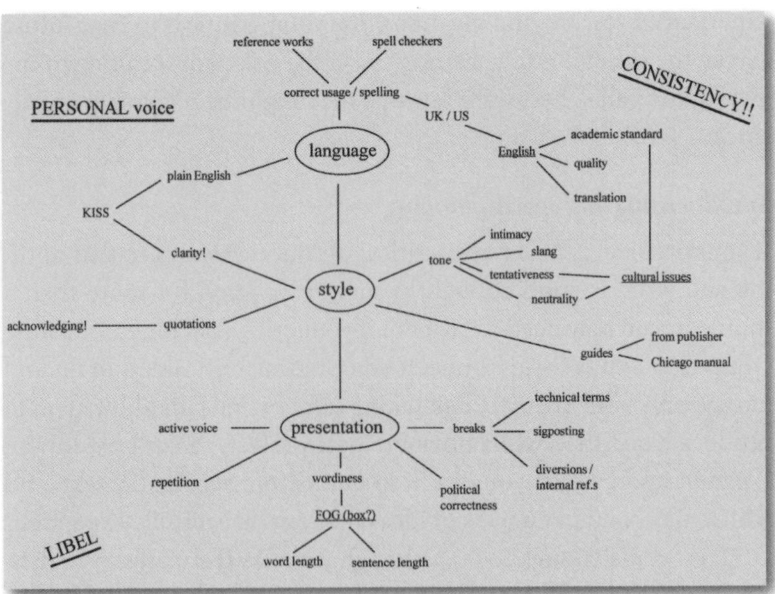

The mind map used to produce a draft of the first half of this chapter, some of which was moved to Appendix 1. This one uses size, capital letters, underlines and exclamation marks for emphasis, but one could equally well use highlighters and different-coloured pens to indicate connections and key points.

Writing groups

Getting together with other writers on a regular basis to review and comment on each other's work can be beneficial in several ways. In addition to the obvious benefit of getting helpful comments on your text, you will also have an opportunity to share ideas and complaints with like-minded colleagues, and if you have a problem with self-discipline you will probably find that the embarrassment of letting your writing group down is a good stick with which to beat yourself into action.

Writing groups should meet regularly, but not so often that they become a chore. A couple of hours once a fortnight is probably about right. The group should be large enough that occasional absences due to illness or holiday do not suspend activities, but small enough that everyone gets to present text regularly; 6–8 people could well be an ideal size. At the end of each meeting, select two or three participants who will distribute text for discussion about a week before the next meeting.

The intention should not be to have every word you write checked and commented on by subject experts, but to get advice on sections that you find problematic in terms of structure or voice – for instance, does your argument flow logically, are you talking down to your readers, do you get bogged down in detail, etc. Nobody in the group will know your subject better than you, so do not expect scholarly critique. In fact, the best groups can be those composed of members from related disciplines rather than direct colleagues, as this does away with any risk of professional competitiveness colouring the proceedings.

CHAPTER 6

Finding the right publisher

A good many young writers make the mistake of enclosing a stamped, self-addressed envelope, big enough for the manuscript to come back in. This is too much of a temptation to the editor.

– Ring Lardner

Is it wise to invest a lot of time and effort in completing your text without first soliciting a commitment from a publisher to turn it into a book when and if you submit the final version? Perhaps not. A well-written book proposal backed by a specimen chapter and an author CV/resumé is all that most publishers require for an initial review of the viability and desirability of a book project; indeed, it may be enough to allow publishers to make a decision. Quite a few presses are happy to offer a contract to publish an as-yet-unwritten or unfinished work, their position being safeguarded by a catch-all clause in the author contract that allows them to cancel publication if the work when submitted is not up to expectation and/or does not receive the backing of peer reviewers. For you as an author, such an agreement offers a measure of security and the best chance of getting material published while it is still fresh.

Identifying the candidates

There is no *one* right publisher for a particular text. As you will already be well aware, a number of publishers are active in your field. Accordingly, the search for that lucky press to which you will offer your work should aim first to narrow down the field to a group of good candidates, and then to prioritise the candidates so that if your first choice does not snap up your book, you already know who is next in line.

First, draw up a long-list.

- Check who is publishing in your field, simply by identifying the publishers with more than one recent book (a) on your own bookshelves, (b) in your subject category at your university library, (c) in the reference lists of books to which you would like to compare your own work, and (d) in the reference list of your own manuscript. You can broaden your results by finding a well-known book on Amazon or Google Books and then searching for other books with the same subject tags; Amazon book listings include the publisher name and publication date.

There is certainly no shortage of publishers (as can be seen from this bird's-eye view of the London Book Fair), but you would do well to consider the likely candidates carefully before deciding who should be given first refusal on your manuscript.

- Check who exhibits at your conferences, either by making the rounds at the next events (this also allows you to pick up contact details and perhaps chat to an editor) or by visiting the websites of the associations organising the most important events in your academic calendar.
- Check who is eager for new material, by reviewing book catalogues and by visiting publishers' websites to see how prominently they present their sections of material for authors. In other words, which publishers make it easy for a potential author to get in touch, and make it clear what format they would prefer author communications to take? (Later, you may want to ask yourself *why* a particular publisher appears so keen on new material.)

Next, you must whittle down your list to create a short-list of those presses that best suit your needs, your circumstances and perhaps your ethos. This involves asking yourself a range of questions about the general type of publisher you would prefer to work with, and checking your answers against the names on your long-list to see if there are any you can discount. Of course, not all the points discussed below may be of relevance in each individual situation, and you must also beware of being so picky that you leave yourself with no choices at all.

Academic acceptability. Is it absolutely essential for you that the press is recognised in the academic world as a guarantee of the scholarly quality of their books? Will you need to present your book as an academically validated element of a job application or research assessment? If so, you must eliminate from your long-list any publishers that do not operate a peer review process.

Commercial press or university press. Do you want a scholarly commercial publisher or a university press? While ultimately the former is motivated by profit for its shareholders, it must guard its reputation for academic quality even more assiduously than a university press since it does not have the reputation of a parent university to fall back on. On the other hand, although university presses are now expected to produce a reasonable level of income to cover their costs, they have a little more flexibility in their commercial expectations, but are still bound by restrictions associated with their not-for-profit status, and by the wishes of their editorial boards. University presses are not confined to publishing material produced by faculty at their own university; likewise, faculty are under no obligation to support their local press. If there is a press associated with your university, though, it could be a good place to go to for advice.

Size of list and of staff. Do you want a large publisher where you are likely to receive 'the standard treatment' or a smaller publisher where the service could well be more personal? Small publishers tend to be quick on their feet when the right project comes along, but may stumble with resource problems both in terms of staff and money. Large publishers, on the other hand, are far better resourced and able to offer a smooth (if perhaps bland) service. If you can find the information (which is generally easier for the smaller presses), then it could be interesting to see the average number of books published per editorial staff member, and to compare this to the general reputation of the press, to gain an indication of whether this is a slick and efficient operation, or an outfit in a perpetual mad rush.

Ivy-league, or hungry newcomer. Do you want a prestigious publisher? A precondition for getting tenure at many American universities is publication of a set number of books at certain, major university presses, even if they do not necessarily specialize in the author's field. On the other hand, a famous university press is probably the hardest place to get a book proposal accepted, simply because this type of press receives so many proposals that they need only accept the very best. A less famous press is perhaps more likely to focus on giving the author good service, and the younger the press, the more it must focus on building up a reputation for good author relations. In the case of journal articles, consider the circulation, citation ratings, and any national scoring systems operating in your country to determine which journals are at the pinnacle of your field.

Global publisher or international networker. Large publishing houses often have departments in several continents, sometimes just sales and marketing operations that leave all editorial work to the staff at headquarters, and sometimes full-scale sister operations geared towards the different markets and business styles of various regions. Many smaller houses aim to duplicate this global reach by joining forces and distributing or co-publishing each other's books. You will have to decide whether it is more important to you that the same business entity is responsible for all aspects, or whether you prefer a publisher who works through many local channels. Indeed, you may find that publishing through one of the minor partners in an international network may be the easiest way to get on the lists of their more important collaborators.

Innovative or mainstream list. Does it matter to you whether a press is mainstream in its publication programme or whether it strives to publish books at the forefront of research in your field? You can get a sense of this both by looking at the subjects of recently published books and by going through the names of recent authors. Among those whom you recognise, are there for instance many newcomers striving for recognition or a large contingent of older professors now able to write for their own pleasure before (or even after) retirement?

Value added. Judging both by the appearance of their books and by their reputation among previous authors, what benefits will the various publishers on your long-list bring to the table? How much effort do they put into the editorial work? Are all manuscripts copy-edited and all typeset pages proof-read by the press, or do they expect the author to either pay for or undertake this work? Are previous books attractively laid out and well presented, on quality paper and with good cover designs? Do the presses generally achieve good review coverage for their books, and do they appear to put in sufficient efforts to promote their books at academic events, in advertisements, and through direct mail to academics?

Subject specialist or ubiquitous presence. Would you prefer to publish with a press specialised in your area of study, or do you think a narrow focus can be a downside? While a specialist press may have a work similar to yours in production or already published that could discourage it from taking on a competing work, it is also worth considering that the narrower the subject focus of a press, the better it must know its subject, both academically and in terms of contacts with academics working in this field (which will come in useful for targeted sales efforts).

Book series. Many academic presses gather some of their books thematically into series run by outside series editors, usually established academics. It may be worth considering a series submission if there is one or more well-respected series that fit your subject. You are likely to get more thorough and comprehensive scholarly comments on your work from a series editor since he or she would be a specialist in your general field, but your study will be expected to have the same focus and concerns as the series (and to be a similar type of book). Moreover, it would have to conform to the series style in both text and appearance, and possibly to a pre-determined method of distribution or co-publication.

Speed of publication. How important is it to you that the book is published quickly? Be aware that speed must often be achieved at the expense of quality, and ask yourself whether you work in a field where the scholarship develops so fast that it is acceptable for you to risk a loss in quality in order to be among the first to publish on a new aspect – or, indeed, whether it is imperative that you have a finished book ready in time for a particular research assessment exercise or similar. You will have to accept that a proper peer review process takes time to complete, and that the speed with which this happens is in the hands of the reviewers rather than the press. But once a book has been positively evaluated and a polished manuscript delivered by you, you can reasonably expect the book to come out within 9–12 months (see Chapter 9 for a discussion of the many time-consuming processes the manuscript is subject to). If a press offers to do the job significantly quicker, you should review their commitment to quality. Likewise, if a press estimates that publication will take significantly longer, review their commitment to author care.

Price policy. Different price policies point to different commissioning strategies, and to different markets. A high-priced book is unlikely to sell many copies, so high prices are generally applied where books are aimed primarily at the library market, or where the perceived global readership for a book is so small that each copy sold must produce a good gross income. Some presses may look at first glance as if their prices are in the absurd range, but when you look closely at their subjects, the pricing may not be so unreasonable after all. On the other hand, if you aim to write a book with wide appeal or perhaps with potential for textbook adoption, then you must be sure to offer it to a publisher who is willing to produce reasonably priced paperback editions.

Distribution arrangements. The North American market is hugely important to sales of English-language books, so you must ensure that any non-US publisher you are considering either has a good presence in the area, or works through efficient local distributors. Likewise, if your book deals with a particular country or part of the world, make sure it will be readily available to customers there. Be aware that press size is no real guide to market reach. A small press can work very efficiently through a local distributor, while a large press can succumb to the complacency of thinking that a large home market means no further efforts are required (this can be a particular issue with American presses, both commercial and university-based).

Location. In most cases this will not be a concern, but do just check that the legal domiciles of your shortlisted presses are in countries whose business and copyright legislation you have no reason to mistrust. Also, if your press is likely to offer you a royalty, and if this is likely to be more than a negligible sum, you should check what the publisher's position is in regard to income tax for authors. Some publishers are required by their national tax authorities to deduct income tax at source. If that is the case with your publisher, you should check whether your country has a double taxation agreement with the publisher's country that will allow you to deduct any tax paid abroad from your domestic tax bill.

By the time you have considered all these points, and disqualified presses left, right and centre, you should be down to no more than a handful of publishers who fit your ideal profile. How do you prioritize where to send your book proposal first? This is probably the time to let personal preference play its part. Have you met editors or other press staff at academic conferences, and did you find them professional and easy to get on with? Have you had any other prior contact with one of the presses that can give you a leg up? Do you have colleagues who have published with anyone from your shortlist and who are willing to share their experiences to help you decide? Indeed, can you perhaps draw on a colleague who has published a successful book to introduce you and your idea to the editor with whom they worked?

Connections, connections

Do not be shy about using any connections you have with a more experienced colleague. Editors rely on and trust advice from such scholars, and hence will be more open to an approach from them than from an unknown scholar. They also know that later endorsements from such respected people in the field will help sales. Of course, there are risks in this approach. Your senior colleagues have their own reputations to protect, as well as their future prospects and credibility with that editor. Accordingly, they may wish to insure themselves against being offered a 'poisoned chalice' by wanting first to assess (and maybe require changes to) your manuscript. This additional layer of evaluation could be helpful, or it could be more than you wish to deal with.

Approaching the publisher

Maybe you have had an initial chat with an editor at a conference, or maybe you called the editorial department to discuss commissioning policy and requirements. But whether or not you have prefaced your approach with such a 'warm-up' enquiry, ultimately you will need to make a written approach to the publisher. Your contact should be direct as there are few literary agents working on specialized academic books.

Consider this to be similar to a job application. Although the candidates have been completely unaware of it, you have already acted as your own search committee to find the publisher best suited to publish your work. Now you must make them actually want to publish it, and much of the advice that applies in job searches is equally useful in this situation.

Whom do you approach? If you are hoping that your book will be accepted into one of the publisher's book series, find the name of the series editor (on the web or with a phone call) and make a direct approach. Otherwise, find out (by the same means) the name of the commissioning editor dealing with your subject area.

What should you send, and how? Although you may already have been in contact with the editor in person or by phone, e-mail, etc., the actual formal approach should be in writing (by first-class registered post if possible) in the form of a covering letter, a book proposal and other such enclosures as a CV and a sample chapter.

When is the best time to approach? No editor will thank you for receiving a new book proposal just before their summer holidays, especially if the proposal needs to be acted upon with some urgency. No proposal received then, or just before a major public holiday, is likely to receive the attention you would like it to receive. Of course, editors also travel, often for long periods in connection with a major conference or book fair, but this is not something that you can be aware of. (However, a preliminary e-mail to the editor can be useful in this respect.)

What if a publisher contacts you?

Of course, you may not need to approach a publisher. One may have already approached you. It does happen, especially if you are one of those lucky, important, established scholars who do not have to prepare proposals but who are contacted by a publisher keen to know if you have a manuscript on the go.

To differing extents, most publishers actively search for new manuscripts (e.g. by talking to scholars at conferences and keeping an eye out for what is being published in relevant journals). Normally, this search is restricted to a defined environment and will be undertaken by a commissioning editor or a freelance 'headhunter' (say, a scholar working part-time as a series editor for the publisher). You can be lucky and find yourself approached, but newcomers rarely find themselves within a publisher's magic circle at the time this is needed. Likewise, you could find that a publisher who approaches you is not the right one for your book.

Even if you are approached, this only gets you to first base; you still need to convince the editor that your study is publishable. Moreover, you must be realistic in your response. Take a good look at your work in progress, and consider the amount of time that is available for you to work on your manuscript. Publishers generally and editors especially live from season to season and need to have so-called lead titles (with broad appeal, good sales potential and prestigious authors) to offer in each and every season. If your book is selected as a lead title and you promise to have your material ready in time for the spring publication programme but then default on that promise at a late stage, you can put a bad dent in the appearance of the spring catalogue. This is at best a nuisance and at worst a real problem financially, and dangerous in terms of the publisher's reputation and the editor's job security. Authors who cause such problems may not be welcomed back the next time they have a book to propose.

Covering letter. Your letter should be short and to the point. If at all possible, address it to a real person rather than 'the commissioning editor'; a covering letter addressed by name always goes down well, and it proves that you have made an effort. If you have already met the editor or a colleague from the press, mention this too. You want to give the (quite truthful) impression that you have carefully chosen to approach this particular publisher because of their unique qualities, and that you are keen to enter into a close and friendly collaboration on your book project. Phrasing it right without seeming sycophantic, you must also be sure to mention why you have chosen this particular publisher/editor/book series for your first approach.

The book proposal. Different publishers have different precise requirements as to what information must be included in a book proposal. When you have decided which publisher you will pitch to first, check their website to see what details they ask for. If the website gives no indication, then it is worth calling up the publisher to ask for advice from the editorial department. Not every element is relevant in every book proposal, but this list gives you an idea of the information an editor needs to make a decision on whether to proceed with a book proposal.

Title and subtitle

- A preliminary title is sufficient for subsequent reference to the manuscript *but* note that this is the first element that the editor will see. First impressions matter. Have you properly thought through your title yet? For a discussion about what we believe characterizes a great title, see Chapter 2.

Author *(plus affiliation and contact details)*

- Necessary as the proposal will quite likely be detached from the covering letter.

Subject and contents *(be concise – see box opposite)*

- What is the main subject area?
- What is the main theoretical basis and discourse?

How to be concise

We suggest that you should describe the subject of your work 'very concisely'. What this means is that you should give yourself not more than half a page in which to describe the subject (i.e. 250–300 words). An ideal description might be broken into three paragraphs that (a) describe the work in broad, non-technical terms that an editor or librarian will understand; (b) elaborate on this in more technical detail for the specialist; and (c) by way of its findings, unique points, etc., spell out the value of your work to the scholarly community; and lastly state who outside the community of professors and lecturers should consider buying the book (under-graduate or graduate students, informed and inquisitive non-experts, practitioners in the field, such as NGOs, collectors, expatriates, etc.).

Begin your description at the broadest level and then narrow it down. For instance, 'This work is a history of X religious movement, specifically during Y period, focusing on the works of Z philosopher as it relates to ABC subjects'. (This is not a particularly gripping description, however. To make a more effective description, first raise an issue of wide interest then proceed to demonstrate the importance of your book in this context.) Thereafter, travel the reverse journey when identifying the importance of your work: 'This will be of central relevance to X specialized subject, while scholars of general Y-ology will find much of interest, and the whole faculty of Z may be affected by the conclusions.'

Keep the language clear and simple. There is always a temptation, especially early in a career, to prove one's right to a perch in the ivory tower through the use of complex, Latin-infested, abstract language. Practise the guidelines for effective communication discussed in Chapter 5.

- Why is this subject interesting? How does your work engage with current scholarly debates, in its own subject and generally?
- A draft table of contents is useful in this section – preferably briefly annotated

TIMELINESS AND NOVELTY

- Why publish on this subject right now – is there an anniversary or the like approaching, or has the subject been in the news recently?
- What is new and fresh about the approach?
- How does your work differ from earlier works by yourself or by others?
- How will this new project bring scholarship forward?

READERSHIP

- What level is the work aimed at?
- What academic fields will find the subject of (central and peripheral) interest?
- Does the work have a market outside its own subject area, or even outside the academic world?

- If the work has potential for teaching purposes, include information on courses where it might be used as a course text or be listed as recommended reading

AUTHOR CREDENTIALS *(do not just refer to your CV here)*

- Who are you? Include your academic and other professional association memberships.
- Why are you qualified to write this manuscript? Include degrees, specializations, and any points about fieldwork or similar.
- What have you written on similar subjects? On dissimilar projects? How well were your previous books received?

TECHNICAL POINTS

- What is the proposed length of the finished manuscript? (State word count including any notes.)

- How many tables are there?
- How many illustrations (line drawings, photographs, graphs, etc.) are there? Will any of this material be in colour?
- What is the current state of the manuscript?
- When do you estimate a full, final version can be ready?
- How freely will you be available during the production process?
- Are there immutable publication deadlines you must meet, e.g. for tenure assessment?

If you are at an early stage in your career, you could also consider getting endorsements of your work from more established scholars – particularly if what you are proposing is a reworked PhD thesis. But keep such endorsements brief. Their content is probably less relevant than the mere fact of their existence and the name of the writer.

Other enclosures. Your book proposal is not enough; its various claims must be substantiated by a full up-to-date CV to establish your credentials, a table of contents mapping the book (if not included in the actual proposal) and a sample chapter. Preferably, your sample chapter should be a key section in the study. The editor will use this to assess your command of both subject and language – essentially, to judge how much work will be required to make the study publishable. If you do not have a sample chapter yet, you will need to provide a more extensively annotated table of contents instead. Some authors submit the full text, but that is unnecessary at this stage and actively discouraged by many publishers. (Of course, if what you propose is a revision of your PhD thesis into a monograph, then a copy of this will be necessary at some stage, but wait for the editor to ask before sending it.) Whatever you do, do not block up the editor's in-tray by attempting to e-mail your full manuscript. Only if the initial assessment of your proposal is positive will the editor ask you to send a printout of the full text, if available, for peer review.

Proposal etiquette

With your prioritized shortlist of publishers, your book proposal, covering letter and other elements of the proposal package all done, you are now (almost) ready to mail out your material.

You now have to decide whether to send your material to one publisher only, or to several of your most-favoured publishers at once. Most academic publishers will be prepared to review book *proposals* that have been sent to several publishers at the same time, but simply refuse to consider *manuscripts* unless they can be sure there is no other publisher currently considering the same work. Academic books are not the subjects of bidding wars between multiple presses, and editors are understandably unwilling to spend time on material that could be withdrawn if a rival publisher indicates an interest. On the other hand, you will naturally be rather impatient to have a response to your proposal as soon as possible, which makes it tempting to send out multiple proposals at once.

What may well happen, though, is that you land yourself with a dilemma. What if publisher number four on your shortlist likes your proposal and quickly asks for a full manuscript to assess? Do you wait for responses from publishers one to three, risking that number four loses interest in meantime? Do you ring round to numbers one to three pressing for a quick response, at the risk of precipitating a 'no'? Or do you go ahead and send the full text to number four right away, thus cutting yourself off from the option of submitting it to publishers one to three in case they also turn out to be interested? It is perhaps better to send your proposals to only on publisher at a time and gently press for a fairly quick response before moving on to the next publisher, if necessary. You would certainly be wise not to risk instant rejection (and future blacklisting) if a publisher finds you guilty of multiple manuscript submissions.

While we have suggested above that you can contact editors and other press staff at academic conferences, do *not* go to book fairs in the hope of touting around your project. Book fairs are events de-

The editor, gatekeeper to the world of publishing. Your book proposal has to be good enough to get him all excited – clearly not an easy job.

signed for industry insiders – it is where marketing staff meet sales representatives and logistics suppliers, production managers see demonstrations of new software and meet with printers, and rights managers agree co-publications and translation deals. Quite often, editors do not even go to book fairs unless they are involved in rights trading.

The importance of the pitch

Before you send off your proposal to the publisher, review its contents one last time. As self-help books like to point out, you only get one chance to make a first impression, and considering the quantity of material tumbling across the desk of the average commissioning editor, you do not get long to make that impression. Your submission may well be given more time if you send it to a series editor instead as they have fewer proposals to review, but that in itself is not enough of a reason to aim for inclusion in a series. It is therefore crucial that you formulate an excellent covering letter to go with a convincing book proposal and appropriate enclosures that not only show your knowledge of your subject but also your appreciation of what is needed to make the book a success. Consider the hurdles that a book proposal must successfully clear:

1. An editor reads the covering letter and decides whether to invest more time in reading the book proposal and enclosures. If the decision is positive, then...
2. The editor reads the full proposal and decides whether the book project is likely to be commercially viable. If the decision is positive, then...
3. A full manuscript is requested and sent out for peer review. The reviewers report back with comments and a recommendation on whether to proceed with the project. If the decision is positive, then...
4. A review of the commercial viability and market positioning of the proposed book is undertaken, usually by the editor and the marketing department working together. If the decision is positive, then...
5. The editorial board and/or editorial director examine all positive peer reviews and the book's commercial prospects to make the final decision on whether or not to offer a publication contract, and whether this offer should be made contingent on satisfactory revisions as recommended by the peer reviewers.

The first assessment is done very quickly, based on editors' long experience of which type of books do well for their presses, and also on a certain element of gut feeling. Anything that falls outside the press's specialization is rejected without further ado, and this goes both for books on the 'wrong' subject and books of the 'wrong' type (such as edited volumes, which are rejected by many presses). Also likely to fall at the first hurdle is any manuscript accompanied by a covering letter that demonstrates the author's shaky command of English, a lack of appreciation of the realities of publishing, or an uncertain grasp of the subject itself.

The second stage represents a significant investment of editorial time in a project that is not yet certain to come to fruition – in other words, a potential waste of a scarce resource. You must strive to produce a proposal package that efficiently and effectively tells the editor exactly what he or she needs to know, without wordiness or obfuscation or wildly over-optimistic claims. The editor is an expert on publishing, not on your precise subject matter, so it is important that the pitch does not descend into incomprehensible professional jargon when describing the subject matter, and it is likewise important that the pitch includes enough information to allow the editor to assess the commercial potential.

These first two stages are about presenting your book project in the best possible (but realistic) light. Your target audience in stages 1 and 2 is small, often only one person: the commissioning editor (or series editor). In the subsequent stages it is the text itself that is judged, so your aim in preparing your book proposal is to get to stages 3, 4 and 5. Here, your audience expands; you need to convince not only the editor but also people elsewhere in the publisher's organization as well as outside experts. The needs and interests of each of these actors must be addressed by your proposal.

Waiting on tenterhooks

Now comes a time of waiting; it may not be long. Going back to the five hurdles mentioned above that each proposal must negotiate on the way to acceptance, it is clear that if a proposal falls at the first hurdle (the editor rejects it before even reading the full proposal and text sample), the author will have an answer very quickly. Likewise, if a proposal falls at the second hurdle (the editor reads the full proposal but decides not to pass it on for peer review), the author could have an answer within a couple of weeks of sending the proposal. Indeed, many presses reject up to 90% of the proposals and manuscripts they receive, mostly before going to the expense of peer review. If your proposal is rejected at this early stage, most likely you have written a poor proposal, or you have picked the wrong publisher to send it to. But if the proposal is passed on for peer review and later for assessment of its commercial potential and consideration by the editorial committee, these stages are likely to be much more time-consuming.

In other words, if the answer to your proposal is 'no', you will probably not have long to wait. A firm 'yes', however, can take months to achieve, and there is little the editor can do to speed things up – so try not to antagonize the editorial department by pressing for an answer that they are not yet able to give. The reasonable question an author can ask, and expect to have answered within a month of submission of the book proposal, is: 'Have you decided to pass my proposal and text on for peer review?' If the answer to that is 'yes', then the editor is behind you and is already spending money acquiring expert advice on your proposal. That is good news, and should help you overcome your understandable impatience at the sometimes glacial speed of the peer reviewers.[1]

Where now?

In pure statistical terms, the chances are that at this point the answer to your proposal *is* 'no'. Sometimes the rejection will not be outright; you may be invited to 'revise and resubmit'. In such a case, a period of dialogue may follow during which you revise your work to meet the publisher's requirements. Or you may choose to look elsewhere for a suitable home for it. However, if you have received a blunt 'no', then you need to move on; there is little point arguing with the publisher. Rather, be pleased if the publisher chooses to tell you in

1 By all means remember this impatient waiting when it is your turn to be asked for your expert opinion. If you cannot deliver a report within a reasonable time, decline the request. And if you accept the request, get the job done as quickly as possible.

any detail why your book has been rejected; such feedback is invaluable. On the basis of the knowledge of the industry, some publishers also helpfully suggest alternative presses which they think might be interested in your work.

Do *not* immediately rush off and submit your manuscript to the next publisher on your list. Pause a moment. Reflect on the likely reasons that your proposal was rejected. You might ask yourself the following:

- Was this publisher indeed the right one for your book?
- Was your approach to them handled correctly?
- Is there something wrong with your text itself?
- If so, exactly what is wrong, and what can you do about it?
- In what ways does the next publisher on your list differ from the first?
- What effect will this have on your revised proposal?
- How could your proposal be improved generally?
- Will you 'sell' this to the new publisher any differently?

However, you may have done your groundwork so well – approaching the 'right' publisher with a compelling and well-thought-out book proposal – that your work immediately sparks the interest of an editor who invites you to submit a full manuscript for peer review. This is excellent news, but it is not yet time to pop the champagne cork. Instead, you must now prepare for the peer review process.

CHAPTER 7

Getting accepted

A gem is not polished without rubbing, nor a man perfected without trials.

– Chinese proverb

CONGRATULATIONS! A COMMISSIONING EDITOR has reviewed your book proposal, liked it, and now wants you to submit the full text for peer review. This is not quite a cause for celebration yet (so far you have only got past the publisher's preliminary checks), but certainly cautious optimism is in order. Peer reviews are expensive, so an editor only invests in peer review if there is a good chance that positive reports and a publication contract will follow. But if a publisher is taking a gamble on you, then you must now focus your efforts on getting published with that one publisher. Any dealings with other publishers should cease at this point.

Preparing and sending the text

Now, before the peer review, is your last private moment with your work. Take the time, if you can, to quickly give it one last check (a preflight check, if you like; you are at the point of liftoff). Because first impressions are so important, ask yourself these things:

- Have I followed the publisher's instructions regarding presentation?
- Is the text complete, including notes and bibliography?
- Is it clean and presentable on first view?

- Have I spell-checked the entire text?

Although the publisher may give very specific instructions on the appearance of the manuscript (singled-sided, double-spaced, etc.), it is unlikely at this stage that you will be expected to conform to the publisher's specific house style in terms of language and formatting of the text; it would indeed be unreasonable to demand this before the work has been accepted. But be especially careful in following the publisher's delivery instructions. Even in these broadband days, there is no point getting your relationship with the commissioning editor off to a bad start by filling her e-mail inbox with a multi-megabyte file when you have been requested to submit the text *on paper only* for the peer review. A few other points to bear in mind are:

- If you *are* submitting the text on paper, be aware that publishers – and especially editorial assistants, who have more practical power than one might expect – hate dog-eared pages and sub-standard paper that can jam in the photocopier (apart from looking scruffy and unprofessional).
- Normally, unless they are an essential part of your argumentation or indeed the focus of your book, it will not be necessary to submit illustrations for the peer review. Where illustrations are necessary, it is usually enough that you include simple photocopies of these. Consult your editor.
- In contrast, you will be expected to submit any tables, charts or other figures (even if in only draft form) as these are an integral part of your text.
- If you have a choice of medium on which to submit an electronic copy, then doing so by e-mail attachment is quicker and certainly more environmentally friendly. Just bear in mind the above point about jamming inboxes; it may be wise to ask first, especially if the combined file size is larger than one megabyte.
- If submitting on disk, do so on CD or DVD (old-style diskettes and zip disks are no longer in general use) and remember to la-

bel the disk clearly with your name and the (short) title of your work.

Whatever the form in which you submit your text, always ask the editor to acknowledge its receipt.

External assessment

Each editor must usually cover a vast field of academic endeavour – all of cultural studies, say, or all reference works. It stands to reason that one person cannot know enough about every corner and hillock of every field. Editors, as generalists, must therefore draw on the expert and in-depth knowledge of peer reviewers to ensure that submitted manuscripts live up to rigorous standards of academic excellence.

Understanding peer review

Peer review (also known as *refereeing* in some academic fields) has a long and venerable history, even if today some scholars criticize it for being elitist, prone to bias, and overly slow. It is used in various areas outside publishing (e.g. by funding authorities to assess applications for research grants) but as far as academic publishing is concerned it performs a gatekeeper function – i.e. it is the process by which a publisher subjects a scholarly work intended for publication to the scrutiny of others who are experts in the same field.

In addition, peer review is supposed to encourage authors to meet the high standards of scholarship and conduct that are accepted in their disciplines. For these reasons, despite calls for new forms of 'soft' peer review, publications that are not peer reviewed are usually seen as being of inferior quality and even regarded with suspicion by scholars and professionals in their field. That said, on rare occasions, errors, plagiarism and outright fraud are found even in publications with the highest peer-review credentials.

Most publishers recruit two or more experts in the field to undertake this review. Among other things, these reviewers (often called 'readers' or 'referees') will be asked to make an evaluation of the text's theoretical, methodological and empirical merits and a judgement of its literary style and readability. In addition to a general assessment of the text, they may also be requested to answer specific questions (see box).

Typical peer review questions

Besides preparing a free-format, written report that analyses the manuscript, external readers may be asked to answer a number of specific questions. There are far more questions here than any one publisher would ask, so this is just to give you an idea of what is assessed in the peer review.

- Do you recommend publication? If yes, how much revision is required?
- Which main disciplinary field(s) does the work belong to? At what level?
- Which discourses, debates or topics does it address? Are there topics that should be added or omitted? How important is the topic to specialists working in these fields? In which other topics/fields would scholars find the work of interest?
- Would it be of interest to general readers? Why?
- What do you consider to be the contribution made by this work? Does it present new research? If not, does it treat familiar material in an original and stimulating manner?
- Is the scholarship sound and up to date?
- Does the author show familiarity with the literature of the field/topic? Are sources used appropriately?
- Has the author covered all necessary materials? Should anything be omitted?
- Is the work organized soundly? Would it benefit by being shortened?

- Are arguments stated clearly and logically, and supported by the material?
- How readable is the text? Can it be readily understood both by specialists and by non-specialists? Does its style conform to scholarly norms in its field?
- Does the work have any errors or omissions, inconsistencies or faulty logic?
- What are the competing books in the field/topic? In which ways is this work distinct from them? How is the work better and worse than its competing works?
- Where would you see the work attracting the greatest interest? Are there any special factors (e.g. local interest or an anniversary) that could influence sales?
- Is the work is likely to be useful for students? If yes, for what courses and at what level might it be useful? Would it be required reading or on a recommended reading list?
- Would *you* purchase the book if you saw it for sale in a bookstore? Why?

Normally, referees undertake the review on the basis of anonymity, but they may choose to sign their reports and even subsequently engage in a dialogue with the author. This can this lead to a far better book, and just as importantly can result in an endorsement from a well-known scholar that can be used to promote the book. Sometimes, a 'double-blind' review is made (that is, the author is also anonymous), though often the author's identity is quite apparent in the text. Indeed, such is the small extent of some scholarly fields that it can be virtually impossible for both reader and author to remain anonymous.

Why do reviewers bother with a largely thankless task, badly paid, diverting time and energies away from their own research and carrying the risk that one's identity will be guessed and future relationships affected? Altruism is a common reason, a desire to contribute or give something back to the field. (Such generosity and collegiality are often found in academia, making it a special place in which to work.) People also love to be told that their judgement is valued, even if the publisher's recognition and acknowledgement is given anonymously. Finally, a key incentive for many readers is that reviewing manuscripts allows them to keep up with developments in their field.

New forms of peer review

The anonymity of reviewers is blamed for many of the problems of peer review. It is criticized for being slow and plagued by elitism, bias and abuse. It does not reliably prevent plagiarism or fraud, and indeed often fails to detect errors. Moreover, it is condemned for smothering innovation. There are also issues of reviewers behaving badly or (by a process of 'criticism creep') ending up becoming co-authors of a work without the benefit of recognition.

Some scholars (and journals) see the answer in open peer review, where the reviewer's identity is made known to the author (and perhaps to eventual readers). Others argue for applying the 'wisdom of crowds' concept (pioneered by Wikipedia) to peer review, arguing that the system could be radically improved by the adoption of 'soft peer review', i.e. using the new 'Web 2.0' social networking tools – commenting, collaborative annotation and using tagging, bookmarking and hits – to measure popularity. Not everyone is convinced (some authors have a very understandable fear of losing ownership of their material, for instance), but new experiments are regularly launched in this area.

As the author of a book, you are unlikely to be affected by these developments in the near future, but it is a different matter if you are also writing journal articles. Journals publishing is very often far ahead of book publishing in testing and adopting new ideas, techniques and technologies.

From the author's point of view, an anonymous reviewer is in a position of great and unquestionable power. The author is utterly dependent on a good review but has no means to ensure fair treatment, and has not yet had a chance to build the sort of relationship with an editor that could protect the author from a reviewer in a rotten mood. However, although the peer review represents an awkward moment, it is also a vitally significant one. Perhaps the best way to look at the peer-review process is to liken it to the tempering of steel rather than as an ordeal by fire. Authors whose texts survive this process (and most do) usually find that working closely with a good editor to incorporate reviewers' advice and other editorial feedback into their text can be one of the most positive and productive aspects of creating a scholarly book.

What Churchill said about democracy applies equally to peer review: it is a lousy system, but to date all the alternatives have been even worse. We suggest that you grit your teeth and make the most of the situation.

Concluding the peer review

Although publishers normally ask peer reviewers to report within 2–3 months, in reality the peer review often takes much longer. The main problem is finding suitable readers who are available at short notice, and then getting them to deliver on time despite their other urgent and important work. Indeed, some never deliver a report at all, perhaps because they have taken a dislike to the manuscript and are reluctant to waste time reading the wretched thing just to say how terrible it is – or perhaps because the text is neither good enough to be a rewarding read, nor bad enough to be easily dismissed with a short report. Sometimes, the only resolution of this situation for the editor is to start the whole time-consuming process all over again.

Meanwhile, you could be getting increasingly frantic and stressed out at the lack of response. The only thing you can do is to nag, but *nicely*. Although the delay may get so bad that you have every reason to get upset, probably you will make greater headway with a combination of assertiveness, charm and humour. If you have heard nothing two months after you sent in your manuscript, politely query the editor or editorial assistant about what is happening. Extract from them a promise that you will hear back by a definite date; should you not hear, send another polite inquiry. Aim to ensure that the editor is more sympathetic to your need for resolution than to the peer reviewer's desire for (yet) more time.

Internal assessments and recommendations

Eventually, the peer review process will be completed. The normal practice is that the editor will send the reports to you and ask for a formal response. (Truly abysmal reports will most likely just result in summary rejection. The author ends up with a returned manuscript while the editor rues having gambled on netting a high-flyer but wasted money catching a turkey instead.) It is important that you make your formal response carefully and thoughtfully, keeping in mind that no final decision has yet been made to publish your book. That will come when the publisher's editorial board or editor-in-chief reviews all of the different elements of your book proposal together with various assessments and recommendations, namely:

- Your original proposal, including CV/resumé.
- The commissioning editor's own assessment of your manuscript.
- The peer reviews.
- Your formal response to the reviews.

plus

- An assessment of your book's commercial prospects.
- Financial projections.
- The commissioning editor's final analysis and recommendation.

Have no illusions: at this point you still need to 'sell' yourself and your book to a crucial audience. In any case, you will do your book no favours by ignoring or being irritated by the feedback received. Your editor has invested time and money in your proposal and is about to stake a degree of reputation, too. Enlist her in your cause, involve him in the formulation of your response, and make sure that the response you send is coherent and paints a rounded picture of an even better book project.

Commercial assessment

The peer review may be complete, but before a final decision can be made the publisher must assess the commercial prospects of your book. Important jobs here are to define the market (including positioning your book against its competition) and on that basis to measure the book's financial viability.

You did your bit in planning the book and considering the size and shape of its readership. The commissioning editor has already formed the opinion that the book has the *potential* to make a profit, or it would not have been put through the review process. Now the marketing department (with the editorial department) will review all available information in the light of their own specialist knowledge, resulting in a commercial assessment. This analysis will be part of the material submitted to the editorial board for their final decision on your book. Elements include the following.

The book. What is its likely lifespan and sales curve? If it is a time-critical book, how good are the chances of meeting the publication deadline? Are the book's length, format and level appropriate to the intended readership? Has it potential as a course book? If so, do its contents match the intended course contents? Is this a 'must-have' book or more likely to be a discretionary purchase? Has it special features such as regional interest or connection to an upcoming event?

Author. Are you an existing author who is cherished and must be retained at all cost? Are your views controversial? Are you well known with a wide network? Have you a track record as an author? Have you experience supporting promotional efforts?

Readership. A profile must be defined (discipline, level, location, book-buying budget, etc.). What does this readership need or demand? How and where does it buy these books? How well do current marketing activities reach the readership? Are there secondary readerships?

Market profile. Is it a new market for the publisher? If so, what will it take to reach this new market, and is that worthwhile? Who are the competitors? Are there opportunities for selling subsidiary rights to certain territories, languages or formats?

Market size and shape. How many similar titles already exist? (A high number suggests a large market – but also greater competition). How many copies have been sold of similar titles? Is there a journal or interest group whose subscribers/members roughly equate to your book's intended readership? Can a mailing list be purchased? What is its size? Given all of the foregoing, realistically how many copies of your book can be sold?

Financial projections

The next job is to estimate as precisely as possible the cost of producing and distributing your book and to compare that with the sales revenue that is likely to be earned. The outgoings include pre-printing costs for copy-editing, typesetting, cover design, and (depending on the type of project) expenses for language editing, proof-reading, illustration setting, permissions, etc. – elements that are hardly affected by the number of copies that can be sold. On the other hand, the cost of printing, sales representation and distribution is entirely determined by the price, the binding (hardback or paperback) and by the number of copies printed. The income includes the revenue from sales of the book itself, but also the earnings from the sale of subsidiary rights and from subventions; such additional revenue streams can make or break a project.

Each press has its own target for how much a book should ideally earn in net profits, expressed either as a sum of money or, more commonly, as a percentage of costs. These three elements – expenditure, income and profit – must balance if the manuscript is to be accepted for publication.

While attractiveness of design and creativeness of marketing can go some way to increasing market size, the two very largest and most crucial 'knobs' the publisher can turn in order to maximize the earning potential of a book are price, and – intimately related to price – format (hardback, paperback, e-book, etc.). A decision on which formats are viable is usually made at this stage, while price is often not fixed until later. The type of calculations involved in pricing a book are shown in the box opposite.

Pricing is a major area of contention between publisher and author. Publishers must make profits or they will cease to exist, and while no publisher is in profit on every single title, none can afford to knowingly and deliberately put themselves into a situation where profit is highly unlikely. As an author, however, you are more likely to argue for low prices and cheap editions that will deliver the highest possible number of copies sold, irrespective of profit (even though sales of a few hundred high-priced hardbacks would probably net you higher total royalties than sales of 1,000 cheap paperbacks).

This is a dilemma, but not an insoluble one. If you are in a situation where your publisher proposes publishing your book in hardback only, ask yourself – before you criticize their stubborn refusal to issue a paperback edition – whether a paperback would really be likely to deliver a five- or six-fold increase in the number of units sold, as required in our example. Perhaps a more viable route would be to ask for a commitment to produce a paperback if and when hardback sales exceed a certain revenue level that ensures the publisher's continued survival. Or you could endeavour to find outside funding to pay for (some of) the pre-printing costs, thus vastly improving the chances that a paperback edition would be profitable. You will get the best results from price and format negotiations with your publisher by being creative rather than confrontational.

Sources of income

The volume of sales required to cover costs is often unattainably high, especially for paperbacks. Today, an average academic monograph

Price and profitability

This is a simplified example of what project feasibility calculations might show, and the formula is full of 'knobs' that can be turned. Imagine the numbers in whichever currency you prefer.

Pre-printing costs (editing, typesetting, design, etc.)	12,000
Contribution to marketing budget (direct mail, ads, etc.)	1,000
Contribution to overheads (management, buildings, etc.)	2,000
Total pre-press costs	**15,000**

	Hardback	Paperback
Suggested retail price	**80.00**	**25.00**
Direct per copy costs		
Bookshop discount 33%	26.66	8.33
Sales commission 10%	8.00	2.50
Processing & packaging	4.00	3.00
Printing & transport	8.00	5.00
Total per copy costs	**46.66**	**18.83**
Revenue per copy	**33.34**	**6.17**
Sales needed to cover pre-press costs	450 copies	2,431 copies

If the figures for a particular project are unattractive, the publisher can attempt to adjust various elements. For instance, selling more books directly to readers rather than going through sales representatives and bookshops can greatly increase the income per copy sold, but will most likely require a good increase in the marketing budget. Likewise, bringing down production costs or increasing price can reduce the number of copies that must be sold to break even, but this will only work if it can be done without jeopardizing quality or alienating customers. Decreasing or completely abandoning author royalties would save a bit of money, but would it play havoc with the publisher's chance of commissioning good manuscripts in the future? Fortunes and reputations hang on the right decisions.

will sell around 300–400 hardbacks and 750–1,500 paperbacks, depending on the field. Many university presses must rely on the uncertain generosity of their parent institutions and survive on a variety of subsidies (free accommodation, partial payment of salaries, etc.) that help them stay afloat and keep them publishing 'narrow' books. Some have given up publishing narrow, specialist works altogether, to concentrate only on scholarly books with broader appeal. Commercial publishers, to a large extent, have had to increase their prices, streamline their organizations, and tighten up their commissioning policies. Fortunately, though, book sales do not represent the only source of income for publishers.

Rights sales

Two common ways of raising additional income are by selling foreign-language rights or by co-publishing books with presses in other parts of the world. Co-publications occur when one press (known as the originating publisher) takes on all the editorial and production work involved in publishing a work, but recoups many of the direct costs by offering to sell copies printed with the logo and ISBN of another press (the co-publisher) for sale in their part of the world – essentially a special form of territorial rights sale.[1]

Language-rights sales offer another handy revenue source, but not all books are suitable for foreign-language editions. While it is perfectly understandable that a novel could be published in 27 different languages (likewise, though to a lesser extent, certain popular non-fiction), at most one would expect a book on Aztec pottery to appear in Spanish and English editions (and quite probably only in one). An influence here is the fast growth of the English language as the medium of international scholarly communication. If nearly

---

1 Co-publications are now on the decline due to the rise of the Internet. It is far too easy today for customers to see that they can order a book from a co-publisher in Thailand at a fraction of the price that they would pay for the same book in Tokyo.

all Dutch scholars can read English without undue difficulty, what profit is there in a Dutch publisher buying Dutch rights to a book, translating it at great expense and attempting to sell it to a cosmopolitan scholarly readership that has already had access to a cheaper English-language edition for a year or more?

Subventions – in money and in kind

It is not unusual for a book project to confront editors with a bit of a dilemma: a good manuscript with a positive peer-review report and a clear market – but one that is too small to generate enough income from sales of books or rights. The only way forward is to appeal to the author for help either in increasing the income or reducing the costs so that the budget for the book can be made to balance.

Increasing income means providing a sum of money that the publisher can use towards paying some of the pre-printing costs. Some universities have special funds from which their staff can apply for grants to assist with the expenses of publication, and some outside grant-giving bodies are happy to include a sum for publication support in their general grants. If you have access to such money, grab it. Even if your publisher has not directly asked for publication subvention, the extra income could mean that your book is given VIP treatment – a specialist freelance copy-editor, colour illustrations inside, a professional indexer (instead of leaving indexing to the author), particularly attractive print quality, extra advertising, and the like.

Reducing costs could mean taking on one or more production jobs yourself, or paying directly for this. Can you call in a favour and get a job done at a particularly good rate? Do you know a freelancer just starting out who would be prepared to donate their services in order to build up a reputation? Is there support staff at your university who could be asked to help? Assistance could take the form of picture editing, arranging and funding copy-editing, basic layout work, or similar. Not every job is up for grabs, though. Many publishers utterly refuse to entertain the idea of passing specialist editorial or production work to authors or their friends. The extra time spent supervising authors attempting to typeset their books can be much more costly than passing the work to a professional typesetter. On the other hand, there are also publishers who insist that authors must deliver final typeset pages (so-called camera-ready copy) or suffer a reduction in royalties if they decline to take on this very technical task.

The key thing is to be creative. This could mean the difference between landing a publication contract and being very regretfully rejected.

Decision time

Finally, your editor has collected all the necessary material and performed all the relevant assessments and analyses with the help of colleagues and of outside experts. Now all that remains is for the editor to present concluding recommendations to the ultimate decision makers, and for them to make the final decision to accept your work for publication.

Is approval virtually certain? Well, life is full of surprises, some of them highly unwelcome. Even so, it would be strange if at this late stage (with peer reviews and a commercial assessment supporting publication) your book were turned down. After all, editors submit book projects for approval, not for rejection. Doubtful candidates should have been rejected long before – as we have said, a 'no' tends to come with unwelcome speed, while a 'yes' must be long and eagerly awaited.

Just who makes this final decision and how depends very much on the publisher. University presses often have rather ponderous formal approval processes involving large editorial boards meeting at fixed intervals. Some presses go to the slightly extreme extent of presenting book proposals to the full professorial board of the university. In such an environment, the pressures for 'equal treatment' over feasibility can play a role in the selection process. ('You haven't published a Classics text in three years; now it's our turn!') Commercial publishers may have less formal structures to make these decisions, but certainly there will be consultation between editorial, marketing and (perhaps) production departments with a final decision made by a senior editor. But while commercial presses may reach a decision faster than university presses, there will be nothing casual about the process; profitability and reputation demand stringent attention to all factors, with commercial and scholarly concerns being equally important.

If, against all expectations, your book proposal is rejected at this very last stage, then the commissioning editor should be able to explain to you what went wrong, and perhaps help you to adjust your project to tip the balance towards approval next time the board meets. Some publishers, though, practise a policy of 'no comebacks'; decisions are never reconsidered. If indeed the rejection is absolute and final, then you must start the whole process over again by finding another publisher – or you could consider taking the risky and labour-intensive decision to go it alone. In that case, skip ahead to Chapter 11.

But if you are accepted, then enjoy the moment, celebrate your achievement, *but do not rush to sign your publication contract.* Let it sit for a few days until the elation has subsided and you are able to review it with the eyes of a sleuth, the mind of a lawyer and the negotiating skills of a used-car salesman.

CHAPTER 8

Negotiating a contract

A verbal contract isn't worth the paper it's written on.
– Samuel Goldwyn

HURRAH, YOUR BOOK HAS BEEN ACCEPTED and you have received a publication contract already signed by your publisher, who now asks you to countersign. That is wonderful, but do not lose your grip on pedestrian detail. Your contract (sometimes called a 'memorandum of agreement') will be full of clauses and subclauses in language few of us can understand on the first read-through. Be thorough in your review of the contract you are being offered, and if you are in any doubt at all as to the terms and conditions in it, you should request clarification and seek advice before you even consider signing. If you are still in doubt, consult a solicitor for expert advice.

Before we say another word, let us be clear: we are not legal experts, and the chapter that follows is *not* legal advice; all we can offer is an explanation of the position of authors and publishers as we understand it.

Not all publishers issue publication contracts at the same stage of the process, but you can reasonably ask for a contract as soon as your work has been approved for publication. Note, however, that merely offering you a contract does not commit the publisher to your work. Almost all contracts contain a standard clause to the effect that the final text must be acceptable to the publisher in form, style and content. This get-out clause guards the publisher against sloppy work, grossly delayed delivery, ballooning size, borderline libellous material, etc. If you meet the terms of your contract regarding manuscript size and delivery date, and if what you deliver is a well-presented work that does not vary wildly from what you promised in your book proposal or from the version submitted for peer review, then you will leave the publisher with no cause or desire to invoke this clause.

Kinds of rights

The main purpose of a publication contract is to specify which rights you grant to your publisher over the material you have produced, and what the publisher will do for you in return for this grant of rights. Before we turn to the question of what is in it for you, we shall look at the different types of rights that come into play.

Copyright

At the outset, you own the full copyright to your text[1] – an intellectual property right (similar to a patent or a trade mark) that involves your right to copy the work, to publish it, to sell it, extract from it, translate it, or turn it into a musical with associated merchandising. But for most authors, these rights are fairly meaningless, because an individual author lacks the practical ability to exercise them. That is why authors attempt to find publishers to whom some of the rights can be assigned. Fiction authors want money in return for their rights, whereas all that many academic authors can expect is recognition and a few perks.

You can either transfer all your rights to your publisher in one great bundle, giving them full copyright over your work, or you can transfer rights to the publisher piecemeal, keeping all other rights for yourself or for sale to others. The minimum your publisher will expect is the right to produce, publish and distribute your work in book form for the entire term of the copyright (which is determined by national and international legislation and treaties, usually 50–100

1 Assuming, of course, that the text really is your unique and individual work.

Open Access and Creative Commons

The old model of copyright is suffering under the onslaught of new technical abilities to make material available rapidly, cheaply and collaboratively. New forms of author rights are emerging, the most promising of which so far is Creative Commons, which relies on the Open Access movement for much of its *raison d'être.*

Open Access

The goal of the Open Access (OA) movement is universal, free access to all publicly funded research so that universities become the stewards of their own research, making it available through organized repositories which are globally searchable. The aim is free availability on the Internet immediately on publication (or shortly thereafter), permitting all users to read, download, copy, distribute, print, search or link to the full texts.

OA raises three important issues. Firstly, it threatens the authors' ownership of their own research if universities or other grant-givers can require the work to be made public in specific ways. Secondly, it requires universities to build repositories which have the necessary hardware and software to store material, allow scholars to deposit new material, and enable anyone to search and access material (not cheap to do, and there is a risk of serious imbalances between rich and poor universities). And thirdly it begs the question: what space, if any, is left for publishers to inhabit – in other words, what value do publishers add to texts and how should they be compensated?

Publishers, who are almost invariably loath to let go of their legal rights, were initially hostile to OA because they felt that it did not sit well with traditional 'all rights reserved' copyright systems. Attitudes are changing, however. Some journals are experimenting with turning their business models upside down: instead of taking payment for their work from subscribers, they charge authors for publishing their work, or charge a set fee for the permission to make it available in OA repositories. No one is yet suggesting that whole books should be available at no cost to the reader (although Google Scholar comes close). However, several publishers are experimenting with providing free access to online extracts of their books, and the European Union is investing heavily in developing OA storage infrastructure. Many book publishers, though, still feel threatened by OA since it raises very fundamental questions about their place in the process of academic communication.

Creative Commons

Although many authors are disturbed by the potential of OA to restrain their freedom to publish, few oppose (or show much interest in) calls for a reform of copyright. To date the most successful challenge to traditional copyright has come from Creative Commons (CC), a new system of 'copyleft' licensing aimed at flexible handling of copyright protection for all kinds of creative work. CC licensing aims to develop new ways in which authors can define and limit exactly those rights that they reserve, while allowing other rights to be freely available. The aim, to quote the organization behind CC, is 'cooperative and community-minded, but our means are voluntary and libertarian. We work to offer creators a best-of-both-worlds way to protect their works while encouraging certain uses of them – to declare "some rights reserved"'. Publishers, on the other hand, are implacably opposed to such initiatives as – unlike OA – they actually undermine the whole business model upon which publishing is based. For this reason, usage of CC is spreading but generally only among self-publishers and those presses and journals offering free content (often because it is the author who pays).

years). The contract should state whether the grant of rights applies in all territories throughout the world, to all languages and to all formats (such as hardback, paperback, electronic, and any future formats). It should further be specified whether you are only granting the publisher rights in the entire, unabridged work, or whether the grant of rights also includes the right to extract, anthologize, serialize, etc.

We cannot overstate the importance of ensuring that the contract specifies very clearly *exactly* which rights you grant to your publisher. The parties to old contracts entered into when the Internet was still in short trousers now regularly find themselves at loggerheads over contractual text that does not clearly show who owns the electronic rights. Similarly, the ownership of rights to books that are out of print is a frequent source of disagreement now that e-books and print on demand are diluting the concept of out-of-print, and we would bet good money that future technological developments will give rise to new areas of conflict. For this reason, we would suggest that it is always best if the contract lists specifically those rights that are granted, thus clearly excluding all other and future rights, instead of simply granting 'all rights' and leaving it unclear whether this includes the right to do things that are not technically possible at the time the contract is signed.

You must also ensure that the contract clearly sets out the circumstances under which all rights granted will revert to you, which should be if the book is not produced by the publisher within a reasonable time, if the publisher allows the book to go out of print for a lengthy period, or if the publisher is willfully in breach of any of the terms of the contract in any way whatsoever.

Subsidiary and volume rights

Rights that your publisher does not exercise directly but may sell on to third parties are called volume rights (relating to the full work) or subsidiary rights (relating to alternative, abridged or derivative versions of the work). Some publishers take a very active approach to rights trading, as it is known, employing special rights managers and attending rights fairs. Translation (or language) rights are often traded, giving another publisher the right to produce, say, a French-language version of your book and sell that throughout the world. Likewise, territorial rights may be sold to other publishers who want to publish their own versions for their territories (say, a cheap edition for a price-conscious country) or who want to purchase copies of the original edition printed with the third-party's own name and logo as publisher (this is properly termed co-publication rights).

The various classes and types of rights that you are granting to your publisher will be listed in your contract, and for each one a level of royalty will be set. The most important is the royalty level set for sales of the unabridged book, which for academic works is often low or zero, reflecting the fact that the publisher has much practical work to do in order to realize modest sales revenues (more on book royalties below). However, royalties for the sale of subsidiary rights are often quite high, reflecting the fact that the publisher's main investment of effort has already been recouped through book sales. Thus, while an author may only be offered a 5-per-cent royalty on book sales, it is not unusual to be offered 50-per-cent royalties on sales of translation or serialization rights.

Set in stone or open to negotiation?

Apart from the grant of (limited) copyright, a publication contract sets out the rights and obligations of both the author and the publisher. This includes two groups of clauses: those that are more or less set in stone, and those where the publisher might be willing to negotiate special terms for special authors.

If you have been offered a contract for your very first academic work, it is easy to feel somewhat overwhelmed at the great honour that has befallen you and forget to be critical of the terms you are offered. Keep in mind, though, that the publisher has invested much time and effort in determining that they really want to publish your book, so your position is probably stronger than you think. Do not sign away your rights just for lack of the confidence to challenge the contract terms you are offered.

Standard clauses

Publication contracts are full of standard clauses that your publisher will be extremely unwilling to change, covering things like definitions and warranties and arbitration and termination and what happens if the author dies or the publisher goes out of business or the stock is destroyed in an earthquake. We will not go through every possible clause, but highlight the points where we think you should pay particular attention.

Delivery of final text. Your contract is likely to stipulate how you should deliver the text (on paper/on disk/in multiple copies), when you should deliver it, its approximate length (best defined in number of words), and how and when you should deliver any additional materials such as illustrations. You must take these things very seriously. If you make a promise here and fail to keep it, your publisher will have every right both morally and legally to cancel the contract.

Ownership of copyright and permissions. There will be a statement in your contract where you assure the publisher that the work is your own, i.e. that you own the copyright that you are about to assign to the publisher. Furthermore, the contract will most likely make you personally responsible for obtaining permissions to use any material under copyright to third parties, such as illustrations or extensive text quotations.

Inoffensiveness of the text. The contract will make you alone responsible for ensuring that the text does not contain material in breach of any laws regarding libel, *lèse-majesté*, invasion of privacy, national security or the like. Should you fail in this duty, you will most likely be required by contract to indemnify the publisher for any loss they might suffer as a result.

Author's production obligations. It should be stated if the publisher expects you to undertake, arrange and/or pay for copy-editing, proofing and/or indexing. In most cases, copy-editing is left to the publisher, with the author taking responsibility for proofing and indexing. The contract could stipulate the time frame within which each task should be completed.

Publisher's production and marketing obligations. The contract will contain the publisher's promise to produce, correct and publish the book. To safeguard the author's position, the contract should set out a maximum time frame within which the publisher must perform these tasks. The contract will also specify where and perhaps how the publisher promises to bring the book to the market.

Accounting and royalties. It should be clearly set out how the publisher will report on sales to the author. The minimum is an annual report showing number of copies sold, number of copies given away free (to reviewers etc.), number of copies lost or discarded due to damage, and total net sales revenue. These figures will form the basis for royalty calculations, and here the contract should state how often royalties will be reported and paid. On royalty levels, see below.

Remaindering and destruction. Remaindering means selling off excess quantities of stock at very high discounts (90% or more is common), sometimes in connection with letting a book go out of print. Your contract should specify the earliest time at which the publisher may remainder or destroy copies of your book. Also, there should be a promise in the contract to offer copies intended for remaindering or destruction to you first at the remainder price.

Going out of print. Your contract may specify the earliest time that your publisher can let your book go out of print, and it may specify certain conditions such as sales falling below a set annual level. It should be made clear what is meant by 'out of print' as opposed to temporarily out of stock while awaiting reprint. In fact, new print-on-demand technology means that some publishers no longer let any title go out of print. However, in case yours does, there should be a clause promising the reversion to you of all rights granted in the contract to the publisher, so that you are free to take your out-of-print book to another, keener publisher – or indeed to take on a self-publishing project to keep the book alive.

Protection against infringements. In addition, the publisher usually promises to protect, to the best of their ability, the rights granted to them against infringements. However, you should be aware that publishers may at times have to give up when it would be debilitatingly difficult and/or ruinously expensive to pursue a rights abuse. For instance, until China joined the World Trade Organization (WTO) in 2001, there was little that could be done against widespread copyright piracy within this potentially enormous market. Fortunately, with the Chinese market now part of the WTO, the remaining problematic areas generally only represent tiny market fractions, for instance a few countries where the legal system is in such an enfeebled state that prosecution is hopeless, or where the size of the black economy defies any attempt at meaningful legal action.

Clauses open to negotiation

Obviously, the keener the publisher is on acquiring your work for their list, the better your position is for negotiating an advantageous contract. Try to be realistic in your demands, though, and ask advice from colleagues with publishing experience to find out what that might mean in your particular case. If you come on too strong with demands for a sizeable advance and assurances of extra-speedy publication and harsh clauses on rights reversal for a project that promises to deliver nothing more than a standard monograph with global sales potential of 500–800 copies, you'll soon be looking around for another publisher. On the other hand, although some may believe that the meek shall inherit the earth, self-effacing authors should not expect to have juicy terms thrust upon them out of the goodness of publishers' hearts.

These are the points on which you have a good chance of opening negotiations:

Royalties and an advance. We have said before in this book that since profits are very narrow in academic publishing, many authors are offered no royalties at all on book sales, but can expect to receive other benefits instead (see below), and should also expect high royalties on subsidiary rights sales. Many more authors are offered royalties only after a sufficient number of copies have been sold to cover the publisher's direct investment in a book. Some publishers offer royalties on a rising scale, which has the advantage that the publisher can be reasonably sure of earning back the investment even if only a small number of copies is sold, while at the same time the author can expect to get a decent slice of the cake if the book becomes a success. Some publishers calculate royalties based on the catalogue price, but most pay royalties as a percentage of actual sales revenue after customer discounts. And there are often exclusions where no royalties are paid at all, such as copies sold to the author at discount and copies sold below production cost. As for an advance, forget it. This is something normally offered only to top authors, people so experienced and famous that they are highly unlikely to need our advice.

Free copies. Your publisher will always offer you a small number of free copies immediately on publication of your book, often with the proviso that these copies are not for resale. This is a good area to negotiate, because the value of twenty extra copies to the publisher (i.e. the production cost) is much lower than the value of twenty extra copies to you (i.e. retail price minus author discount). If your publisher offers you no royalty, you should be able to extract instead a promise of a goodly number of free copies – but note that the publisher's concern is that you may give away freebies to all your colleagues, thus completely flooding the potential market and making proper sales impossible.

Author discounts. You should be offered a high level of discount on your own book, and many publishers also offer a similar, or sometimes slightly lower, discount on all other books in their catalogue. Publishers routinely offer a 40- or 45-per-cent discount to wholesalers and major booksellers, and why should you not get the same?

Requirement for subventions. If you and your publisher have agreed that you must provide a subvention, this will almost certainly be mentioned in the contract. Do not sign a promise to pay over a subvention until you are quite sure that you have it in the bag. If there is any uncertainty, you could see if your publisher will accept wording to the effect that you will make all reasonable efforts to attract subvention funds up to a certain level and that you will pay over any funds that you do manage to attract.

Whether or not editions are specified. At the contract stage, the publisher normally already has a fairly firm opinion on whether your book should be published as a hardback only, paperback only, or both – or, indeed, whether a paperback should only be published if an initial hardback edition proves popular. Most contracts, however, do not mention editions. If you have strong views, ask the publisher to include a clause about editions and (keeping in mind our discus-

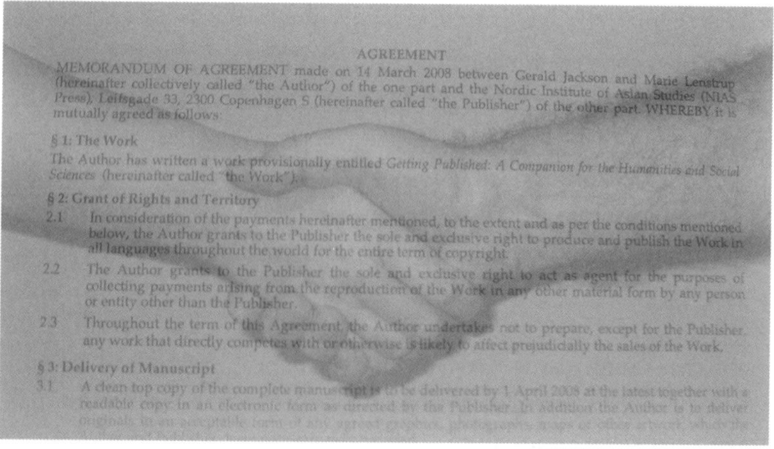

AGREEMENT

MEMORANDUM OF AGREEMENT made on 14 March 2008 between Gerald Jackson and Marie Lenstrup (hereinafter collectively called "the Author") of the one part and the Nordic Institute of Asian Studies (NIAS Press), Leifsgade 33, 2300 Copenhagen S (hereinafter called "the Publisher") of the other part. WHEREBY it is mutually agreed as follows:

§ 1: The Work

The Author has written a work provisionally entitled *Getting Published: A Companion for the Humanities and Social Sciences* (hereinafter called "the Work").

§ 2: Grant of Rights and Territory

2.1 In consideration of the payments hereinafter mentioned, to the extent and as per the conditions mentioned below, the Author grants to the Publisher the sole and exclusive right to produce and publish the Work in all languages throughout the world for the entire term of copyright.

2.2 The Author grants to the Publisher the sole and exclusive right to act as agent for the purposes of collecting payments arising from the reproduction of the Work in any other material form by any person or entity other than the Publisher.

2.3 Throughout the term of this Agreement, the Author undertakes not to prepare, except for the Publisher, any work that directly competes with or otherwise is likely to affect prejudicially the sales of the Work.

§ 3: Delivery of Manuscript

3.1 A clean top copy of the complete manuscript is to be delivered by 1 April 2008 at the latest together with a readable copy in an electronic form as directed by the Publisher. In addition the Author is to deliver

A gentlemanly agreement and a friendly handshake are all very well, but in our opinion a signed contract with all the details carefully scrutinized is a lot better.

sion in the last chapter of edition, price and profitability issues) negotiate a wording that satisfies both the publisher's need to take no unnecessary risks and your need to ensure the widest possible readership for your book.

Time of manuscript delivery. Most contracts mention when you should deliver the final version of your text. Be realistic about what you promise! And check what the publisher can do if you are late. Most accept some delay, but there are very great variations in how long publishers are prepared to wait.

Speed of publication. Some publication contracts contain a standard clause promising, in the absence of special problems, to publish your book within a set time after you have delivered your final manuscript. If the contract you are offered does not mention speed of publication, and if this is of concern to you – because the publisher has a reputation for delays, perhaps, or because you need the book out in time for an assessment or event – get a clause inserted into your contract. And beware also that publication is one thing, local availability is another. If your publisher uses a printer on another continent, finished copies right on time may still be thousands of kilometres away from where you need them.

First refusal on your next book. A promise on the author's part to offer the next work to the same publisher is included in some contracts. It is rarely enforced, but do not sign a promise you do not mean to keep. If you let the contract state that the publisher must evaluate this next project quickly, the promise costs you nothing since you are only committing to *offering* the publisher your work; you do not promise to sign any contract they might decide to offer to you.

Before you sign

Having reviewed the contract to ensure that there are no loose ends, consulted to make sure you understand all the implications, and negotiated the best terms that you possibly can, there is just one more thing you need to do before you sign on the dotted line.

Contract lawyers have a very useful concept that guards against signing contracts that may be the best you can get from your current negotiation partner but may not be the best option in a larger perspective. Meet BATNA, the Best Alternative To Negotiated Agreement. You must know the value of your work in order to know whether the contract you are being offered is advantageous to you. While you may have negotiated the very best deal that it is possible for you to get with your current publisher, the question is whether there is an alternative out there which would be even better, a personal BATNA – publishing with another press, for instance, or publishing articles instead of a book. If you take a little time to work out what your BATNA might be, you will have a clear basis on which to decide if the offer in hand is likely to be the best offer around.

But again, if you are in any doubt at all as to the terms and conditions in a publication contract offered to you, you should consult a solicitor for expert advice. Do not sign a contract that you do not fully understand. And if you do sign, always keep a copy in a safe place for future reference.

🕮

Now after acres of legalese come reams of proofs. Steel yourself for the production stage. It can actually be very rewarding to see your text slowly take on the shape of a proper book, and even if indexing does not really rock your boat, you should be so close to publication now that you can already sense the sweet smell of success.

CHAPTER 9

Working towards publication

In preparing for battle I have always found that plans are useless, but planning is indispensable.

– Dwight D. Eisenhower

YOU HAVE COME A VERY LONG WAY indeed, having completed all the creative and scholarly work on your manuscript and having found a partner who will help your ideas go forth and multiply. But it is not quite done yet. A thousand things small and large must be dealt with before bliss (and a book) is achieved. Although the publication process is in principle a reasonably straightforward one, the devil of course is in the details that we focus on in this chapter. You should also be aware that your book will be promoted from this time onwards in a process that is parallel to, and sometimes interacts with, the process of getting it into print (we examine these aspects in the next chapter.)

There is much to be done, but ultimately you will have a tangible reward for all of your work: a work of scholarship, a commercial product, a physical artefact to proudly hold in your hand – Your Book.

Enter the production manager

Although the publication process looks to be a reasonably straightforward one, it involves quite a range of people undertaking about a hundred distinct tasks. Making sure that everything is done (and done at the right time) requires superb organizational skills and/or a strong set of procedures in place. Some presses are renowned within the industry for their well-oiled production machines (and others for being utterly chaotic) but, even in the best-run operation, plans can be thrown into disarray.

Soon after the author contract is signed, your publisher assigns your project to a production manager (or production editor), whose first job is to work with you to plan the publication schedule for your book. It is vital that you are clear about when you are available to work on your book, and what your different contact details are. Make sure that you give yourself plenty of leeway in your timings so that things do not become impossibly tight and stressful at a later stage if unexpected delays occur. The end result of this planning is that a publication date for your book is set.

The handover to a production manager does not mean that you will cease to have any further dealings with your commissioning editor. In the next phase leading up to finalization and submission of the manuscript, the commissioning editor certainly has an important part to play. Thereafter, normally she is around and may act as your go-between in relation to all the other staff at the publishing house, even as confidante and advocate in some circumstances. And if there is a book launch on publication, the editor will certainly be there with a broad smile and glass of bubbly in hand.

Finalizing your manuscript

For many authors, the next stage is the very hardest mentally: to actually finish the manuscript. To place the last full stop, to recognize that this is as good as it is going to get and that any more fiddling about with the text will add only time without contributing quality, and then to let go and send your final words out into the world to stand or fall on their own merits – that can be very difficult indeed.

Revisions

First, after suffering the semi-public scrutiny of the peer review, you are expected to go back, make revisions to your text (perhaps significant ones) as occasioned by referees' reports, editors' opinions, and

From disk to bookshelf

The process of finalizing your book to the point of publication involves the following processes:

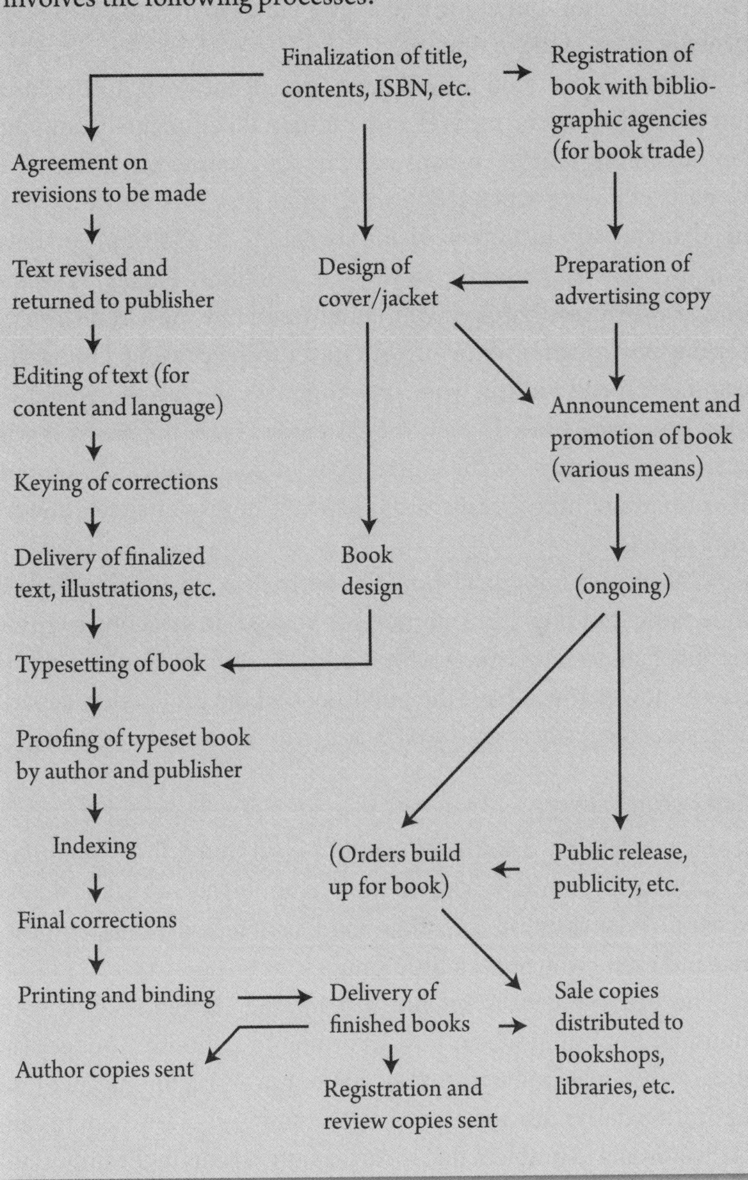

discussions between yourself and your editor to determine how these concerns must be addressed. And after all that, you are expected by your publisher to deliver a finished work that still looks fresh and unified, certainly not something that appears to be merely touched up to meet the worst of the critique.

At least you should have a good idea of the work to be done. You have the readers' reports and additional comments from your commissioning editor. Perhaps you saw the commercial assessment (or parts of it were explained to you); there may be something here, too, that you should address in your revisions. In addition, you have your own formal response to these evaluations. Finally, take the time to swiftly read through your manuscript one more time, briefly marking anything for follow-up but never really pausing. Doing this reading at speed reduces your unwillingness to read the wretched thing one more time. In fact, the faster you read, the easier it will be to keep a picture of the entire work in your head, and you will also notice anything that disturbs, distracts, bores or irritates you far more easily.

With all of this input, it should be fairly clear what revisions need to be done. Do them, but do not get bogged down with rewriting text that had nothing wrong with it in the first place. Speed is of the essence now that you have the publisher's whole production department standing ready to grab your manuscript as soon as you let it go.

Manuscript delivery

Keep your delivery date firmly in mind at all times. It is stressful to be running late, embarrassing to have to apologize or make endless excuses. To be early, on the other hand, is to feel virtuous, empowered and even (why not?) a little smug.

The delivery date is set not just for the convenience of your publisher. Bookshops often buy according to a monthly budget (in January, they may be buying titles due out in April, for instance), so publication delays disrupt their cash flow and may cause them to cancel their orders (a problem that is particularly serious in the important

US market). Many libraries lose any unspent money for book acquisitions at year-end, so a delayed book may mean less money to spend on other acquisitions in the coming year. As publishers know only too well, orders most likely to be cancelled are those for a delayed book. Think too about the poor eager reader – someone like you – who wants (indeed *needs*) to read your book before completing their own research project.

Similarly, it is important that your revisions do not cause the manuscript to vary wildly from the length agreed in your contract. Under-length books are regarded with suspicion, while over-length books increase the publisher's costs without increasing their income.

What exactly are you delivering at this point? That depends on your publisher's practice but certainly you will be delivering the full text of your book including all front matter, tables, figure captions, bibliography, etc. – that is, all text that is to be edited. In addition, you may be required to deliver your figures and other illustrations (especially if you have artwork that needs to be redrawn or created from scratch). Documentation of any permissions obtained should be delivered at the same time as the material to which they relate. Many publishers provide authors with a checklist to follow; if yours does not, you should request detailed instructions on what is expected of you.

The editing process

There are publishers and then there are publishers. Some do very little to an author's text beyond assigning an ISBN and slapping a cover on the manuscript. One place where this practice is found is in organizations where a close relationship exists between an in-house 'publisher' and the teaching faculty. Essentially, the 'books' published are course books or even lecture notes only intended for a specific purpose at that institution. This is not proper publishing as we understand it.

In a 'real' publishing house, editing a manuscript involves two processes: substantive editing of the initial text focusing on its structure and argumentation, and copy-editing of the finalized text focusing on its language and ensuring that it complies with the publisher's house style. In earlier times, much of this work was done by all-round editors who worked in-house, but today the two functions tend to be separate. Substantive editors are still likely to be found working in-house but copy-editors are often freelancers and may be located anywhere around the globe.

Substantive editing

Because of the pressures on publishers discussed elsewhere, in recent years there has been a decline in the amount of substantive editing (structural revisions) devoted to a manuscript. Instead, quite often the publisher may rely on any concerns regarding structure, argumentation and coherence being raised in the peer reviewers' reports, and perhaps in additional comments from the commissioning editor (which may have been made after only a hasty reading of your work). We would hope that you receive a coherent assessment of your text on such issues prior to final delivery; certainly, any book will be the better for undergoing a mindful edit.

Copy-editing

If substantive editing is the endangered aristocrat of academic publishing, then copy-editing is the ubiquitous cleaner, tidying up other people's messes. Copy-editing concerns itself with language, formatting and presentation issues. The copy-editor (either a specialist who may be a freelancer, or sometimes an in-house desk editor already familiar with your work) will read your manuscript very carefully from beginning to end, checking that grammar, spelling and punctuation are correct, correcting any deviations from the publisher's house style and normal scholarly conventions, and checking that your citations match your bibliography (missing references and redundant entries in the bibliography are common). In addition, unnecessary repetitions, unclear phrasing, faulty transitions and verbosity may be flagged for attention. It is unlikely that your copy-editor will attempt an extensive rewriting of your text or a general alteration of your basic style – copy-editors are not paid enough to spend time on such major surgery – but you may be consulted on anything that is unclear or needs fine-tuning.

The copy-editor also functions as a bridge between the author and editorial department who primarily are concerned with meaning, and the typesetter who is concerned with 'fit' and appearance. Thus, the copy-editor not only inserts corrections and queries but also marks up the text with typesetting instructions. If you get the copy-edited text back on paper, then you will see these notations marking a heading as 'H1' or 'A' (a first-level heading) or specifying indentation for a block quotation, for instance.

Depending on the size and complexity of the copy-editing job, you should receive your edited text back from the publisher within one or two months. The corrected text may be in electronic form or on paper. If in electronic form, then you are likely to see Word documents with tracked changes or documents showing the results of file comparisons. If you receive the copy-editor's changes on paper, you may see the pages annotated with correction marks in the margins and inserted in the text (see Appendix 2).

and discipline. Orienting yourself right from the beginning makes it far easier to write your article; there is then direction, coherence and relevance to its contents.

Think ~~audience~~ readership. Defining a target ~~audience~~ readership and understanding the needs and interests of your intended readers is a crucial part of that orientation. It will help you write a far more successful article.

Know your journals. Several journals may serve the subject and readership you are reaching out to. But each journal will have its own 'personality' and preferences. It is also likely that it will work to fairly strict rules on page length for each issue, balance

A copy-edited text. Note that in this instance the copy-editor made his changes in-line only (i.e. there are none of the marginal marks shown in Appendix 2). To leave room for in-line editing, many publishers demand that their authors deliver their manuscripts with the text double-spaced.

Your role in the editorial process

On receipt of the copy-edited manuscript, you will be given a deadline of only a few weeks to vet the changes and indicate any disagreements. Your main jobs are to:

- Check the copy-editing changes. Are they correct? Consistent? Appropriate to conventions/discourse in your field?
- Answer any queries.
- Vet the marking-up of text elements for typesetting.

Rage, offence, incredulity and humiliation: these are some of the emotions that can swamp an author when confronted with copy-editing changes for the first time. Try to avoid an emotional response. Take a deep breath. No one (not even you) is perfect, and someone coming from the outside with a fresh eye will always find details to query in a text. Go over each proposed change and accept all those that you do not have strong feelings against. Remember, too, that this is your last chance to make sure that the text is just as you want it. If you want to make substantial changes at this late point, you need to talk to your editor urgently, and certainly *before* making any wide-ranging changes). From this point onwards, any changes to your text will be met with the greatest reluctance by your editor. Slowly but irrevocably, the book – your baby – is slipping beyond your grasp.

There is another issue, however: if the editing has been done on paper, who is to key the changes? Some publishers expect their authors to carry out this task, thus saving on editorial costs; others are horrified at the risk of authors introducing new errors into the text. Your publisher should have made their position clear on this back when the contract was negotiated.

One last thing: before returning the corrected final pages to your production editor, make a copy so you can check the page proofs you will receive later against the original, copy-edited text.

After you have returned the edited text, your production editor will make a final check and gets any revisions incorporated into the digital file. Then, at last, design and typesetting of the book can begin.

Designing and typesetting your book

Publishers do not expect authors to design their own books, and in fact reserve the right to determine a book's final appearance. However, because of the time pressures book designers work under, the temptation to apply 'the standard treatment' to your book will be strong. It is up to you if you want to achieve a better result, something that brings to life your vision for the book. But how much say do you have in the final result? Each publisher is different, may be flexible in one area but will not budge a millimetre in another. Even so, chances are that your publisher will seize upon any good ideas that you have to make your book stand out in the crowd, shine among its competitors – and sell more copies. Once a copy has been sold, what you say becomes more important than appearances but – for a brief moment – the look and feel of your book is paramount. Content may be king, but design is the queen who by appearance attracts the most initial attention.

Inspiration need not come from the world of your research only. Other books can also inspire.[1] What works best for you as a reader? What attracts you aesthetically? Develop a sense of what works and what does not. If you can do this, then you will be able to communicate more knowledgeably and on more equal terms with your publisher on the book design.

The cover

The soul of a book should ideally be seen (or sensed) in its cover. That said, many publishers have house styles, and are likely to have a particularly strong visual unity between volumes in the same book series. As the author, you may not be asked your preference about the cover design but simply be presented with a fait accompli for proofing. At that point, the design budget will have been spent and any protestations from you are likely to fall on deaf ears. For this reason, it is important that you bring any design suggestions to your editor at an early stage.

1 Note that we use the word 'inspire'; we are not suggesting plagiarism.

Backroom or Bangalore?

Apart from the actual printing, binding and shipping of your book, the processes involved to create this physical artefact are largely intellectual and can be accomplished by various people sitting alone in front of computers. Indeed, often far more physical work and social interaction is involved in the original research, where people are interviewed or observed, archives searched, findings argued in conferences, etc., than goes into the publication of the resulting academic book. It is no surprise, then, that by its nature publishing (especially academic publishing) is one of the world's most globalized industries.

This book illustrates the phenomenon. It was written in Copenhagen (Denmark) and in a small Dutch town, reviewed in several parts of the world, edited in Britain's Orkney Islands, typeset back in Copenhagen (though this might just as well have been done in Mumbai, India) and proofed here too, printed on the outskirts of Kuala Lumpur (Malaysia) and the copy you are looking at now may be from one of several warehouses located round the world. Or maybe you have bought a reprint, printed digitally in Tulsa, Tokyo or Toulouse.

This globalization has its strengths and weaknesses. Traditionally, publishing houses trained their staff in-house in the different skills required to do their various jobs. It was of course expensive to train and maintain such a skilled workforce. Today, however, much of this work is outsourced to external freelancers or to specialist companies. The publishing functions typically outsourced are production control, copy-editing, translation, keying of text, design work and typesetting, often paid by the word or page and with a whiff of sweatshop in the air.

Although a professional designer will produce the cover, it is the publisher (ideally with your input) who will provide a design brief to sketch out ideas and elements to be included in the design. Some of the important decisions are as follows.

Colour or not? Technically, there is no reason today to restrict the use of colour on your book cover. A decade ago, it was far cheaper to print two-colour covers but that is not so today with modern printing presses. Of course, your publisher may have a branding reason to restrict the range of colours used; that is a different matter.

Illustration or not? A good illustration can transform a cover and dramatically increase the appeal of a book; a bad one can cause the book to look amateurish and unappealing. Your publisher should welcome suggestions from you for illustrations for your cover, particularly if you have copyright-free material. But your illustrations must be suitable. Keep in mind, for instance, that the image must leave enough room for the necessary cover text (title, subtitle, author name, publisher name and logo). A uniform background (like sea or sky) in a photo can be useful for that, or the cover could be designed with blocks of solid colour bordering an image.

Cover text. A printed book has more faces than its front cover; there is also the spine and back cover. In addition, hardcover jackets have inside flaps. All of these surfaces need to be designed; they also need text. Book spines invariably display the author's name, book title and publisher's logo. The back cover usually includes a longish blurb, with text based on material supplied by you in your author questionnaire or marketing form (see the next chapter). Ideally, the blurb should be augmented with one or more endorsements of your book from respected senior scholars in your field. If the book is jacketed, then the inside flaps should not be forgotten; normally, a shorter blurb and a brief author biography appear here. Too many books are published without text on the inside flaps, a wasted opportunity to give the customer a little extra help in deciding to buy the book.[2]

2 Sadly, though, the first thing an academic librarian will normally do on receipt of a boxful of new books is rip off any jackets and throw them out.

Typesetting

Once your text is finalized, typesetting can begin but first a design brief is drawn up. This specifies the trim size (physical dimensions) of the book; the layout of elements; the typefaces and sizes for body text, headings, captions and notes; the treatment of photographs; and so on. As with the cover, you could theoretically contribute to this brief, but in practice most authors show little interest.

Now your manuscript and the design brief are sent to a typesetter, who will take your text and illustrative material, setting it out on the page ready for printing. There is a lot more to typesetting (and its

Producing camera-ready copy

There is one case in which you do need to care rather deeply about how your book is laid out. This is if you are to take on the typesetting yourself, to deliver so-called 'camera-ready copy' (an archaic term for material fully ready for printing) to the publisher. Typically, such work is done using word processing software like Word, but increasingly scholars have access to (and are learning to use) the high-end desktop publishing software like Adobe InDesign that are also used by typesetting professionals. Frankly, neither struggling with Word's many failings (and its unsuitability for any sophisticated typesetting work) nor floundering with an unfamiliar, intricate program like InDesign will be much fun. If indeed you agree to take on this task, make sure that your production editor supports you with:

- A recommendation of the software best suited to your task.
- Detailed instructions on how to do the work, in language understandable to a non-professional. (This should include a specification of page size, margins, font size, etc.)
- Proper feedback on an initial sample, which you should prepare and submit before progressing too far.

sister, typography) than you would think. It is an art that only really succeeds when invisible. In many respects, the layout of your book is comparable to the background music added to a film. Its primary duty is to make your text clear and accessible, but ideally it should also enhance the meaning with mood and style. Though stylish, the layout must also be durable (indeed timeless), transcending fashion. Much creative energy goes into this art, which is the subject of passionate debate among its practitioners.

Little of this should be of concern to you, the author, except in two important respects. First, your material is converted to other

- Ongoing advice and support.
- Full review at delivery of the finished layout so that no errors slip through.

There are good reasons why an author might offer to take on such a specialist task and why a publisher might accept. The work may address such a small readership that it is uneconomic to produce in the traditional manner. Alternatively, it might include specialist features (musical notations, for instance) that are technically difficult and prohibitively expensive to typeset but which are vital to the study.

All the same, in most cases where authors prepare print-ready copy, the process is often strewn with misunderstandings, irritation and wasted time. Everyone usually agrees afterwards that it would have been quicker and easier to empty out an Olympic-sized swimming pool with a teaspoon. Do not do it if you can possibly avoid it. But if this really is the only way you can get published, at least approach the task with your eyes wide open. (Further advice on similar issues follows in Chapter 11, where we explore the intricacies of self-publishing.)

This is just a tiny selection of the fonts available to typesetters. It is easy to go overboard, so the art is in exercising self-control and demonstrating the beauty of simplicity.

formats at typesetting. Changes to your original Words files and JPEG images (for instance) are no longer possible; all subsequent changes must be made by the typesetter, who will likely be reluctant to make 'unnecessary' changes without extra payment. Second, errors can occur in such file conversions; for instance, your fancy Arabic script, keyed in Word from right to left, may turn into left–right nonsense (though to anyone other than an Arabic specialist it looks fine). The typesetter keeps an eye open for such conversion errors but ultimately it will be your responsibility at the proofing stage to pick up any such problems.

Proofing

Normally, initial typesetting of your book will not take too long, especially if no illustrations are to be added at this point.

First proofs

When your production editor has quickly checked the first proofs, a copy will be sent to you for proof-reading. At the same time, someone at the press or an outside professional proof-reader will vet this as well. What you normally receive is typeset text output on ordinary pages or a continuous (galley) sheet, in all probability not yet finally paginated (because too much may yet change). Whether or not your publisher employs an outside professional proof-reader, the ultimate responsibility for checking the proofs lies with you. Subsequent book reviewers may sniff at the failure of the publisher to properly edit your book, but you are blamed for making the original error.

At this point, the issue of extensive changes may raise its ugly head. Your publisher quite reasonably expects that text delivered for typesetting is final and that any last-minute content changes were made during copy-editing. Consequently, your job now is only to correct any typesetting errors but otherwise to make no changes.

However, something pertinent to your text may have happened that absolutely must be mentioned in your book, or there could be typos and factual errors that were not picked up in the editing process. Most publishers would accept such changes, but keep in mind that alterations to proofs are time-consuming, costly and can introduce further errors. Many typesetters charge publishers for *every single correction* apart from those that relate to fixing typesetting errors. (Not even typos are exempt; after all, these should have been picked up during copy-editing.) Charges can escalate rapidly, and eventually your own pocket could be at risk. The terms of your contract may well include a maximum amount of proof corrections you can make at the publisher's expense. Anything over and above that level will be charged back to you.

When marking changes to the proofs, follow your publisher's instructions carefully. Possibly you will be expected to mark the actual printed pages, using proof-reading marks like those listed in Appendix 2, but common alternatives are simple e-mailed lists ('p.

47, 3rd line from bottom, change "invariably" to "often"') or using the commenting features now available with Adobe Acrobat).

Second proofs

Once the text is completely stable, and any illustrations have been sized and inserted, the typesetter paginates the book and produces a second set of proofs for checking. In urgent circumstances, it is not unknown for authors to receive only a single set of paginated proof pages, but two proof stages are more common. However, second (paginated) proofs are *not* yet another opportunity to check your text. All you should do is check that:

- All corrections marked in the first proofs have been correctly implemented.
- Chapter titles in the table of contents match those in the text, not only in wording but also in upper or lower case. (The same applies for figure captions, etc.)
- Chapter titles in the running heads match (or are reasonable short forms of) the real chapter titles.
- Page numbers stated in the table of contents, list of figures, etc. are correct.
- Pagination of the book is consecutive (with numbering of the preliminary pages as a separate series using roman numbering).

Finally, as with the edited text, make sure that you retain a copy of the second proofs before returning them to your production editor. You will need this for producing the index.

Indexing

It is likely that the indexing of your book will happen at the same time as the vetting of the second (paginated) proofs, and that you will be expected do the work yourself on the basis of these paginated pages. An outside indexer has no hope of ever knowing your book as intimately as you do, but on the other hand, indexing is skilled work; you may not feel up to the task. If indeed you engage a professional indexer directly, then book a time slot early, and prepare a clear indexing brief.

An index may be unassuming, loitering at the end of your book with not a lot to say for itself. It is also one of the last things to be made, often under great time pressure. Nonetheless, the index is perhaps the most-used pathway to searching a book, accessed far more times than the table of contents. A poor index signals to the reader that this is an inferior book. Do not fail your book at this last hurdle, mere days before it goes to the printer.

There are many good guides available on indexing, hence all we shall do here is cover a few essential points. There are three main ways of preparing an index, none of them ideal. Two of them require that you have a single computer file generated from the typeset proofs, saved in Word and paginated to match the typeset proofs by playing with the font size or inserting hard page breaks.

- The ***traditional method*** is that, while you proof-read the text, at the same time you prepare a manual index, recording the entries with highlights or notes in the proofs, or keyed immediately into a text document.
- The ***mark-up method*** involves entering indexing tags in the book file itself. This can be as slow a task as the traditional method but, when completed, the resulting index is instantly generated and with luck should not need a lot of adjustment (e.g. to divide a large number of single-level entries into groups of two-level entries). Index generation can even be re-run repeatedly in conjunction with adjusting the tagged entries until the index is perfect.
- The ***quick and dirty method*** commonly used is to create a concordance file (a list of words to be indexed) then let Word automatically generate the index from your book file. Though quick to create, this is not recommended by us; the resulting 'index' will be full of junk entries that you must then weed out *and* it may lack entries you later realize are necessary. In the end, then, this method may save no time at all.

Indexing need not be a last-minute affair. You could prepare for this by producing a mind map of the book that identifies elements you wish to include. You could draw up a list of index entries (and sub-entries) minus the page numbers. If you feel confident that the text sent for typesetting will change very little during typesetting, you could even create a book file from this text in your word-processing program and begin entering index tags.

What to index. You must determine the final shape of your index before you start creating any entries. Will you have one comprehensive index (often best for readers), or does your book lend itself better to separate name and subject indexes? What text will you include? Obviously, your body text must be indexed, but what about notes that comment on the text? Citations and bibliography are usually not indexed; will you follow that practice? Some publishers think it unnecessary to index a glossary (indeed, sometimes an index becomes a kind of glossary), but consider it essential to index any illustrations and captions. Check for publisher preferences, then use your common sense.

Length. Indexes are like books: if too short, they may be treated with disdain; if too long, may be regarded as unwieldy and 'over the top'. Most important, ask your production manager how many book pages are available for the index before you start. Because indexes are generally set quite tight in at least two columns, your typesetter should be able to fit two word-processed pages from you on one typeset page in the book.

Structure. In our experience, adequate complexity and clarity of meaning are best achieved with two levels of entry. This allows you to split up major entries into several separate entries that remain bound together by the same first entry word or by the use of cross-references.

Organization. Publishers vary somewhat in their usage here but the generally accepted rules are as follows. Order your index alphabetically, numbers coming before 'A'. With sub-entries, ignore any initial pronouns, prepositions and the like (for instance, in an entry for 'slave trade', the sub-entry 'high tide of' comes *after* 'in African records' but *before* 'as understood in 18th century' – alphabetizing on 'African', 'high' and 'understood'). Your publisher may have a preference on whether sub-entries should be indented below their main entry or run as continuous text. Certainly, the former is easier to read, but space limitations may force adoption of the latter, more condensed arrangement.

Consistency. Remember that your index is part of your book and as such its page numbering should follow the same convention as the rest of your book. If page ranges are expressed as '123–126' in the body text, then they should not be expressed as '123–6' or '123–26' in the index.

Junk entries. Any entry or sub-entry that has more than about 15 associated page references is a junk entry, i.e. it spans such an extent of material that it is useless for searching purposes. Abandon it, or break it up.

Cross-references. Something that can really make an index useful is a judicious number of cross-references. In addition, if a term appears in two forms in your book (such as 'International Monetary Fund' and 'IMF'), let one index entry simply refer readers to the other entry. Use your common sense, however. Sometimes it is better to repeat an index element under several entry words rather than to refer the reader from entry to entry.

Printing, binding and delivery

Finally, after an express train of last-minute urgencies has thundered through your life, everything is quiet. No one calls with a voice edged with adrenalin. No urgent e-mails exclaim frantically in your in-box. Tentatively, the cheeps and chirps of life's other priorities begin to be heard again. At last you can say 'My book is with the printer' and attempt to move on to other things.

Meanwhile, somewhere else on our planet, your book is taking physical shape. Its electronic essence is drawn into the printer's pre-press department, a quiet, dust-free laboratory where visitors must take their shoes off before entering, a gamer's paradise of big-screened Macintosh computers and all manner of equipment that will produce giant printing plates where mirror images of your book pages are arrayed, normally in 16-page blocks.[3] Beyond the double doors, it is a different, almost primitive world with scenes straight out of the devil's kitchen and smells like a glue-sniffers' convention. But above all else, this is a world coloured by one thing: the noise of many huge lithographic printing presses tirelessly grabbing, inking and ejecting thousands of enormous sheets of paper. Beyond the presses, conveyor belts hustle the printed pages towards other contraptions that fold, collate, glue, trim and bind the still-warm paper into beautiful, finished books. Then these precious artefacts are packed in cartons, in shipping containers and trucks, and moved around the world to be shelved in cavernous warehouses where other conveyor belts, this time known as pick-pack lines, stand ready to process customer orders.

And now at last, the bell rings at the reception counter of your workplace. A courier stands there with a brightly coloured package. You sign, barely noticing as the courier leaves. Inside you can feel the copies. The Book, it has arrived. Now, truly, it is time to celebrate.

---

3 At this point, a set of printer's proofs will be sent to your publisher for checking that text pages are ordered correctly, cover colours match, etc. Only after their approval can the actual printing of your book proceed. This proofing process is one that you will not be involved in.

CHAPTER 10

Promoting your book

Doing business without marketing is like winking at a girl in the dark. You know what you are doing, but nobody else does.

– Stuart Henderson

THE JOY AND CURSE OF PUBLISHING is its variety. There are few other industries producing such a vast array of new products every year, each sold in relatively small numbers. A hamburger is fairly cheap to produce, is sold in the millions every day and the menu on offer is small; McDonald's business, then, is to get you to buy a burger and to come back for more, preferably tomorrow. A car is expensive to produce and its development costs horrendous, but millions of each model will be sold in its lifetime and again the selection on offer is small; Toyota's business is to get you to make a major purchase and return some years later to make another major purchase.

The book business, on the other hand, is all about keeping up a constant stream of unique new products (100,000 new titles each year just in the United Kingdom). Few people buy the same book twice, except by mistake or to give as a gift, and every new book has to compete against an overwhelming flood of other new books. With such a huge number of new titles published each year and the even more staggering number of titles in publishers' backlists, it is no surprise that even the most specialized bookshop can only carry a tiny proportion of what is available. The vast majority of academic books are too specialized to see the inside of mainstream bookshops, and would be lucky to make it through the doors of specialist or campus shops. Your publisher must rely on other channels to find customers for your book.

What is academic book marketing?

Marketing, at its core, means efforts to promote your book to a specific market, to make that target market aware that the book exists, and to encourage the market to buy it. Essentially, it means focusing on the customer. Serious marketing – that is, the marketing of serious books – is less about persuading customers with florid language and tempting discounts to buy something they may or may not really want, and more about keeping the academic world, the high-end libraries, the specialized bookshops and scholars in the field up-to-date about exactly what is on offer so that they can make informed choices.

A great deal of this work will be done by your publisher's marketing staff, but there is also much scope for you to get involved, both by feeding helpful information through to the marketing department to help them do their job as efficiently and effectively as possible, and by taking responsibility for your own success and engaging directly with marketing in ways impossible for your publisher to pursue. Here, we shall first look at the jobs you can rely on your publisher to undertake, and then at the many ways in which you can support these efforts to gain the greatest possible readership for your book.

The many tasks of the marketing department

Marketing involves balancing acts between the disparate requirements of different customer groups, and between tried-and-tested techniques and the need for flexibility and innovation, to ensure that finite resources of time and money are applied where they will have the greatest possible effect.

For instance, bookshops want their information early, briefly, and in a highly standardized format. Libraries also want information early so they can plan their budgets, but they want much greater de-

Everyday life in the marketing department

Staff communicate with

- bibliographic database services
- bookshops (real and web-based)
- individual customers
- libraries
- library suppliers
- regional distributors
- sales representatives
- warehouses
- wholesalers

by producing and distributing

- advance information sheets
- advertisements
- catalogues
- e-mail newsletters and alerts
- notices on e-newsgroups
- press releases
- review and examination copies
- single-book flyers
- subject leaflets
- website entries

and arranging and hosting

- author interviews
- book launches and signings
- conference displays
- lecture tours
- sales meetings
- trade fair stands

However, all these activities only continue for a certain length of time. Because of the focus on new products, publishers divide their books into two groups: (1) front list, which includes all the current and one previous season's books, and (2) backlist, which includes any title more than about a year old. It is the front list which is the focus of marketing efforts and of active promotion. Backlist titles, on the other hand, are generally deemed to have been given their measure of parental attention, and they must now continue to sell on their own merits with only the passive promotion entailed in being already listed in the publisher's catalogues.

This implies no lack of interest in backlist titles – indeed, they deliver a very welcome and important contribution to the turnover of academic presses – but it does indicate how important it can be that you continue to be actively engaged in promoting your book past the time when marketing staff are forced to turn their attention to newer arrivals on the scene.

tail. Sales representatives prefer their information in headlines and punch lines, while warehouses care only for accuracy. And readers differ from all of the above by wanting to know about books that are actually available here and now, and by being fickle creatures whose attention must be grabbed in creative ways.

The marketing department must gauge how to divide time and budgets between many competing activities to satisfy these groups. Some cost a great deal of money, such as printing and mailing catalogues, others cost a great deal of time, such as maintaining an up-to-date website. Some are aimed mainly at known customers, such as direct mail, others are aimed more at potential new customers, such as advertisements. But since very few orders read 'Hello, I'd like to order this book I read about on your website/in your catalogue/in your journal ad/in a review', it is often extremely difficult to pinpoint which of the many marketing activities resulted in an order. There are accepted and received wisdoms (such as 'advertising works') and tried-and-tested methods (thus, catalogue mailings usually prove their value by initiating a spate of new orders), but new methods like web-based marketing that may not yet have proved their value cannot safely be disregarded or the publisher risks being left behind if the new method proves magnificently powerful. In the end, most marketing departments end up doing as much as possible in as many areas as possible, but often with the sneaking suspicion that more could usefully be done if only the resources were greater.

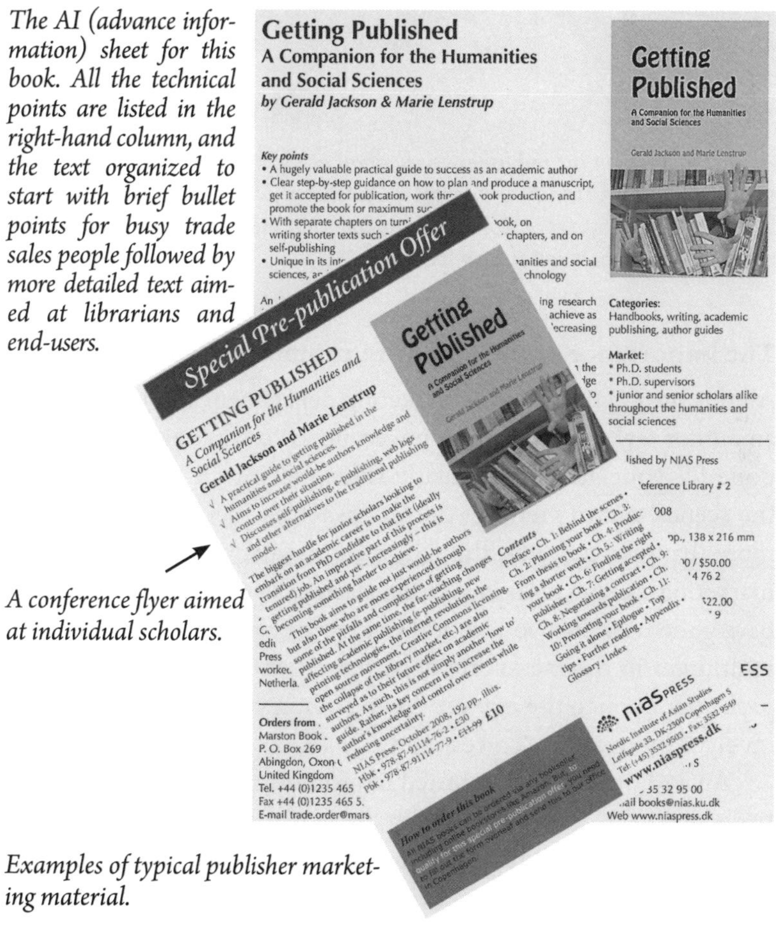

The AI (advance information) sheet for this book. All the technical points are listed in the right-hand column, and the text organized to start with brief bullet points for busy trade sales people followed by more detailed text aimed at librarians and end-users.

A conference flyer aimed at individual scholars.

Examples of typical publisher marketing material.

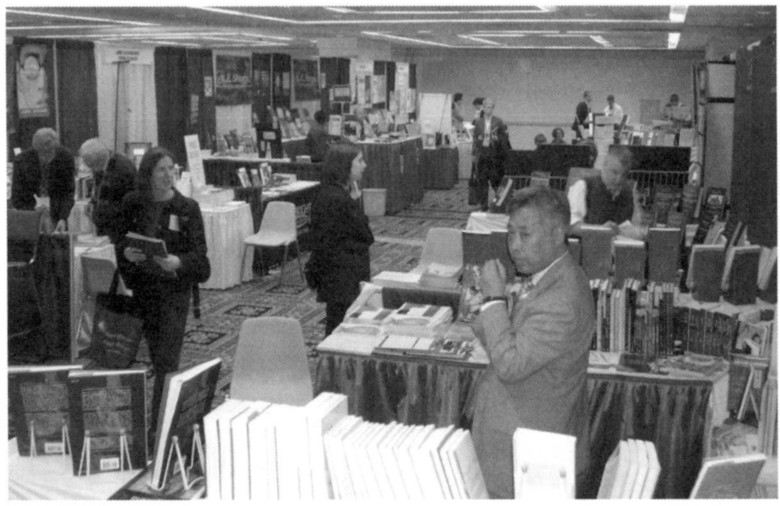

A quiet moment in the publishers' area at an academic conference. Apart from providing an opportunity to present books directly to their readers and meet with prospective authors, conferences offer publishers a welcome chance to network and to check out the competition.

The importance of the author in promoting books

All this busy activity in the marketing department can make you as an author feel rather left out, uncertain as to what exactly is being done for your book, particularly since much of it is done behind the scenes, out of view. If your publisher has been in business for more than five minutes, though, you can safely trust that essential marketing is being undertaken. If it wasn't, the publisher would soon have gone bust. But you should not leave everything to the unseen multitudes in the marketing department who are working hard to *push* your book to the market. As an author, you should get actively involved by creating a corresponding *pull*.

An author actively interested in promoting a new book, and actively seeking a conversation with the marketing department about how best author and staff can support each other's efforts, can make a great difference to the success of the book. Marketing professionals will know the potential trade customers (bookshops, wholesalers, library suppliers) fairly intimately, will be well aware of the annual conferences where the book should be shown, and will have a good general knowledge of the section of the academic community to which a particular title will appeal. But no one can have as much detailed knowledge as you do about the exact people who will make decisions on whether to use your book on courses and who should therefore be offered a reading copy, or about the one-off conferences and events which will gather academics working on the exact topics your book deals with and where it should therefore be displayed. And no one is likely to meet more potential readers than you simply in the course of a normal working day.

What you can do before publication

Book descriptions

It is vitally important for the marketing department to produce an excellent description of your book that will make it stand out from the crowd, and make clear exactly what it is about and who it is aimed at. In many cases, this will start with a description provided by the author which the marketing department can edit, add to, or rewrite. The basis for this can be text from your book proposal or from your preface/introduction, but often the marketing department will ask you for fresh material in a questionnaire sent to you after your book has been accepted and contracted. It is surprising how little interest many authors take in this process, even though it is the foundation upon which all sales and marketing work will be based – an excellent opportunity for you to affect the presentation of your book, and to adjust your book description to take account of any suggestions, criticism or revisions since you submitted the book proposal.

You may be asked for book descriptions at three different levels of detail:

- Long book description (200–300 words) for use in flyers, on the publisher's website, and other places where detail is desirable and space not costly. This could also form the basis for the blurb on the back cover of your book.

- Short book description (perhaps 30–50 words) for use in a seasonal catalogue, in subject leaflets, and other places where space is limited.
- Essential features in bullet form for use where time or space is at a premium, such as in advertisements and communications with booksellers.

Revisit the guidelines in Chapter 6 on how to produce a good book description, keeping in mind that it must be both comprehensive enough for libraries, concise enough for bookshops and appealing enough for end-users. And pay particular attention to clarity of language. The book descriptions will be read by many non-experts such as booksellers who must be able to see quickly and clearly what the book is about to judge whether it is right for their shop and under what subject category it should be displayed. Time is short, and an unclear text is unlikely to get re-read to extract the meaning. Complicated jargon will not win you admiration – it will just lose you sales.

Other marketing input

You are likely to be asked for a great deal of information, normally through an author or marketing questionnaire, which is intended to assist the marketing department in promoting your book. Some of this may cover details you have already provided to your editor or to other staff at the press. However, the marketing staff will not necessarily have easy access to this information, and may not have time to go and search through files and letters to find it. The questionnaire(s) will be an extremely handy and useful tool for the successful marketing of your book, so do not grudge the extra time it will take you to occasionally repeat yourself in one form or another. It is likely to be very well worth the trouble.

The details you are likely to be asked to provide can include the following.

- Your ***position and affiliation,*** which may be used as a shorthand way of validating you as an author.
- A short ***biographical note*** about yourself for use on flyers and possibly on the book cover.
- Your academic and other professional association ***memberships.***
- ***Other books*** you have written or contributed to and, importantly, any awards won for these books.
- Courses where the book might be used as a ***course text,*** if at all possible including the names of those teaching the relevant courses or making the decisions on textbook adoptions.
- Courses where the book might be listed as ***recommended reading.***
- Full names of journals that should receive ***review copies,*** with names of reviews editors if possible. Note that publishers will normally have decided on a target number of review copies to distribute, related to the estimated size of the market. Either prioritize your list, or find out what the target number is for your book so that your suggestions do not wildly exceed this.
- Contact information for your ***campus bookshop,*** and if possible the name of the book buyer. Shops will often be prepared to stock titles written by local faculty even if they are more specialized than normal stock.
- Any ***forthcoming events*** such as academic conferences, seminars, workshops or special courses where the book should be on offer either through flyers or directly for sale. Some authors are happy to handle sales themselves from a small stock provided by the publisher. If you are prepared to do this, say so. And do note that it is no use telling your publisher about an event taking place next week; you must give proper notice so there is time to agree a presence (and perhaps price) with the organisers, produce

material and get it to the venue. A month's advance notice is a minimum for most publishers, and more is better.

- ***Foreign publishers*** who might be interested in an edition of your book (and also indicate if any of your previous works have been published or translated, and by whom).
- ***Local or regional media*** who should receive press releases, including radio or TV programmes that might be interested in discussing your book with or without your participation.
- Professional or scholarly organizations whose members you think should receive a ***direct mail*** piece. Smaller and more specialized organizations are often the most useful because a larger proportion of their readers will be interested in your particular field of work. It could be helpful if you know whether the organization has a newsletter or journal, and whether they are likely to be willing to insert mail pieces from publishers.
- ***Electronic news groups*** or bulletin boards that should receive notice of your book. You should not leave electronic media only to the publisher; a notice posted by the author may well carry more weight with academic group members. In fact, many news groups only allow members to post such notices, feeling that publisher notices would commercialize the group in unwanted ways.
- Any ***awards*** in your field for which your book might be submitted. Although this may not result in higher sales, an award can boost the publisher's brand, it will look good on your CV/resumé, and may help you land a publisher for your next book.
- A ***photograph*** of yourself for possible use on the jacket and for publicity (remember to include credit information for the photographer if relevant).
- Suggestions for publications where your book could be ***advertised*** (but keep in mind that advertising budgets are usually very limited or non-existent, so be realistic and concentrate on specialized publications with highly targeted readerships and low advertising fees).

- Any ***other ideas***, such as prominent people who might provide endorsements, magazines which might excerpt your book, potential book signings, articles you have been asked to write which could spawn reader offers, etc.

If for some reason your publisher does not ask these questions, or only asks a few of them, then take the initiative and provide the rest of the details unasked. Probably not all your suggestions will be acted upon, but it is always worth a try. The marketing department is likely to be impressed and appreciative of your efforts, and you will keep your book to the forefront of their concerns.

Input on the title and book cover

We have already talked about the importance of finding a good title for your book in Chapter 5. The marketing people may have comments and suggestions for changes based both on how they think various parts of the market will react to your proposed title, and based on practical considerations such as length. Authors who are completely committed to titles that the marketing department strongly believes are wrong for their books may find themselves faced with an ultimatum.

Likewise, the marketing department will care very deeply about book covers, and any good publishing house ensures that the marketing staff are consulted on design briefs and cover drafts. We discussed your input on cover design in the previous chapter. Suffice it to say here that any suggestions you make must allow for the many and varied uses to which the marketing department will put your cover. It has to be possible to blow it up to poster size at conferences, reduce it to stamp size in advertisements, convert it to monochrome for photocopies, and still in all these different states have it sing out its attractiveness and distinctiveness, yet never lose its visual link to all the other covers from the same publisher. That is not a lot to ask, is it?

What you can do after publication

Your efforts after publication are particularly important because most of the publisher's efforts come before publication and immediately surrounding the publication day, with the main thrust falling in the year surrounding publication. Once a book moves from the front list to the backlist, the marketing department expects its earlier efforts to be rewarded with sustained, though slowly tapering, sales for several years. Titles adopted as textbooks are the exception, with sustained sales for many years and a good chance that a new edition will be produced in time to keep sales level or rising.

After publication, it is up to you as the author to support your publisher's slowly diminishing efforts to keep your book in the academic eye – especially in the (longish) period before reviews start to appear. There is a great deal you can do to help things along, by yourself or together with your publisher.

Get promotional material from your publisher. The marketing staff will be able to provide you with handfuls of catalogues and book flyers, and some may also have postcards or bookmarks or posters that you can use. This saves you having to produce hand-out material for yourself, and also has the advantage that, though you might perhaps be a little bit reluctant to blow your own trumpet loudly and confidently, the marketing people suffer from no such squeamishness.

Tell all your colleagues. Make sure that no one has any doubt whatsoever that you have published a new book, what it is about and how it can be obtained – in your department, in your faculty, in the professional associations and newsgroup where you are a member, at the conferences and workshops you attend. Independent or retired scholars could be at a disadvantage here and may need to work extra hard to access their network of contacts.

Arrange a book launch. This can be as simple and informal as a few bottles of wine and a handful of book flyers at the end of the working day or during a break at a conference. Or you can go all out with a tempting venue, a programme including presentations by your publisher and a lecture by yourself followed by catered nibbles and a book stand selling signed copies. Whichever way you go, aim to get a good diversity of guests – colleagues, VIPs in your field, press (local and/

Promotional DOs and DON'Ts

Do

- build a relationship with at least one person in the marketing department whom you can approach and who can be your conduit to colleagues.
- provide full information on whatever aspects you are asked about, even if you get asked the same question repeatedly by different people at the press.
- stay friendly throughout. It is only human nature to be willing to go to extra efforts for pleasant authors but not for prickly ones.
- be patient. There are finite resources of time and money, and a great many demands upon both. Be reasonable and selective in what you ask, but do ask.
- stay in regular touch after publication, but without becoming a time-waster.

Don't

- expect that your book will stay on the front list forever. While you may only have one or two new books to promote per decade, your publisher has dozens or even hundreds every year.
- be shy. Grab every opportunity to broadcast the merits of your book to the academic community and the world at large .
- expect a specialized academic treatise to be available from mainstream bookshops and chains, and do not harass your publisher about this.
- press for a paperback edition unless you feel confident of the appeal of your book. You will risk becoming an expensive mistake for your publisher.
- think your job is done when the book is published. There is so much more you can do which your publisher will greatly appreciate.

or academic), a tiny smattering of your smartest and most interesting friends, and (if geographically possible) a representative from your publisher. Your guests should be those most likely to talk afterwards about the event and, especially, about the book. Your publisher may well be happy to cover some or all of the cost of a well-arranged launch, and to supply promotional material for use on the day – particularly if you let the publisher in on your plans at an early stage.

Set up a website. Ensure that your book is mentioned on your own website if you have one and on your departmental or university website. Link these to one or more good Internet bookshops (you can even earn money doing so) as well as to your publisher's website. More and more authors set up separate websites for their books where they can augment the published text with additional material: detailed data that perhaps could not be included, updated information, colour photos, essays on related themes, etc. If you plan to do this, it may be worth mentioning in the book itself. Also be alert to opportunities for reciprocal links with other sites.

Use 'Web 2.0' to its full potential. The Internet is undergoing a shift from using web pages to announce something (one-way communication) to using a wide range of web-based tools to enhance social interaction. These new interactive uses are known collectively as 'Web 2.0' (and change happens fast here, so to take advantage of new developments, you will have to use the web to research the web). You should search regularly and widely for new material on topics related to your book – not simply to find new information but rather to be able to respond to new web material that allows you to plug your book.

If your book has a topic or associated material that lends itself to enthusiastic discussion, you could participate on social networking sites, mentioning the book in your profile. You could also write one or more Wikipedia entries relating to your subject, adding citations and external links back to your own website. You can do the same with contributions to article banks, which then syndicate your text all over the Web. Also, trawl Internet bookshops to take advantage of options for authors to add comments about their books (such as offered by Amazon) and encourage people who have appreciated your book to add their own reviews.

Lastly, you might consider starting a weblog (or blog) – a type of website where you can make a series of postings, often with a facility for your readers to post comments that you can reply to. Google and other search engines now listen in to this global conversation, so material from blogs is included in search results, adding hugely to the potential readership. Blogs are a superb way to publish your ideas and opinions, get feedback from others and build a community of like-minded people.

Use your contacts

It is not enough that you just let everyone you ever met know about your book. You should also call in favours (actual and promised) to promote your book. If there is a journal or two for which you regularly act as a peer reviewer, ask them to put your book at the top of their pile of material for review. If you have colleagues teaching courses where your book could be used either as text or as recommended reading, ask them to consider it. Don't rely solely on your publisher's sales representatives: if you do not see your book in the local campus bookshop, ask them to get it into stock. Let your publisher know well ahead of time about conferences you will attend so that they can arrange to have a stand or otherwise promote the book, and then drag all your contacts past this stand to show them the physical book. Promote your book in all your outgoing e-mails by adding a footer that mentions the book and contains a link to a website (yours or your publisher's) with more information. And lastly, carry with you at all times and wherever you go a small stock of book flyers, and be prepared to whip one out at the slightest provocation.

It is immensely important that you give all these efforts a personal touch. If you are asking a journal to review your book or a campus shop to stock it, then you should ask a real named person ('John Smith', not 'The Reviews Editor'), preferably in person (face-to-face or by phone). Your aim is to make it as difficult as possible for the other person to decline your request, and it is so much harder to say 'no' face-to-face with an eager author than by regretful e-mail.

If you follow the advice in this chapter, then you can be confident of having done a great deal more to promote your book than most academic authors, and can fully expect significantly better results for having taken the time and made the effort. Your publisher and the marketing staff are bound to appreciate your involvement – and to warmly welcome any new book proposal you later wish to submit to them.

CHAPTER 11

Going it alone

Hell is other people.
– Jean-Paul Sartre

MAYBE YOU HAVE HAD YOUR MANUSCRIPT REJECTED by every single publisher in your field because they all believe it is not commercially viable. Or maybe you have rejected all possible publishers for reasons financial, political or otherwise. Either way, you may be tempted – in view of the vastly improved facilities for private authors to lay out, typeset, print or post and market their own work – to dispense with the services of a publisher altogether. There is nothing technical to stop you doing so. There is a lot of work (or, if you prefer to buy assistance, a lot of expense) involved, but there is also great pleasure and satisfaction to be had from knowing that the final product is yours and yours alone.

However, academic publishers are not just leeches on the body academic, drawing off vital fluids to feed their shareholders and rejecting good honest scholarship in the process. Publishers actually add value to the academic books they publish over and above the value of the work. They act as gatekeepers to select the best texts, improve them through editorial efforts, dress them up in a form acceptable to readers (whether as printed books or electronic files), provide them with a voice and a route to market, and handle all the practicalities of matching supply to demand.

Arguably the most important service publishers offer to the academic community is through arranging peer reviews. It is the rigorous application of this globally accepted method that guarantees the quality of published scholarship and allows it to be used without further quality control for tenure decisions and research assessments. If you self-publish, you may be able to buy in many of the production and marketing skills that publishers provide to their authors, but you will not be able to buy the stamp of quality and approval that a scholarly press confers on its books. Your book may be viewed with suspicion by other academics, most damagingly by those on selection boards and tenure committees, and it may well be excluded from research assessments and disregarded on your CV/resumé. Only if that is of little importance to you should you consider self-publishing.

Making the decision

Before embarking on self-publishing, you should closely examine your text, your motives, and your resources to ascertain whether it is likely that the efforts you would need to pour into a self-publishing project would be worthwhile, judging by the criteria for success that you feel are most relevant.

Your text

If your text has been rejected by publisher after publisher, there is a reason, and you need to identify it. Scholarly publishing is quite unlike fiction publishing where (rare) gems can go unrecognized by dozens of publishers. Our kind of publishing is more mechanical in its application of two sets of well-defined selection criteria: the peer review process to determine scholarly value, and the publisher's experience to estimate commercial value.

Your text could have been rejected on the basis of either one, or of both, sets of criteria. It is very important that you are ruthlessly honest with yourself when you ask which situation is likely to apply in your case. If the work was rejected for both scholarly and commercial reasons, the best advice anyone can give you is to drop it and move on. If it was rejected for scholarly reasons but not for commercial ones, you have been looking in the wrong place for a publisher and should research which serious trade presses to approach instead. But if, as is increasingly common, the work is fine from a scholarly point of view but was rejected as being commercially unviable, it is a candidate for self-publishing.

Your motives

Self-publishing is not easy, so do not do it simply because you have already invested a great deal of time in writing the manuscript and are loath to admit that this effort has been a waste of time. You need to have a positive reason to self-publish, one that gives you a reasonable expectation of success.

A positive reason could be that you know there is a readership eager for your book, but one that is too small to attract a publisher to the project. Maybe you and a few colleagues are keen to use the book on a small course you are teaching. Or perhaps the work is a Festschrift for a revered professor and you are prepared to do whatever it takes to get it printed in time for her retirement reception. There are many good and valid reasons for pressing on where no traditional publisher is willing to go; we just urge you to make sure within yourself that yours is a good reason, too.

Your resources

You can publish your own work at any point on the scale of sophistication running from a photocopied and bound print-out from your normal word processing program deposited in a few free copies in your local university library all the way through to an elegantly designed and packaged, offset printed book fully equipped with dust jacket and ISBN – or, indeed, to a fully integrated multi-media experience freely available to all readers on the Web.

If the basic material is good, then there is likely to be a clear correlation between the effort you put in and the rewards you reap in the form of the size of circulation your work achieves. Only you can decide what is the right level of sophistication to aim for. Once you have decided what type of publication you want to produce, be realistic about estimating what investment of time and money it will cost to reach your target. Then double all your estimates, double them again and, if you still think it looks like a good and practicable idea, you are ready to go ahead.

Deciding on format

The first decision you have to make is whether you wish to publish your work in printed or electronic format. There is a popular idea that it is easy to publish research on the web, but that is far from true. To produce a text that is attractive enough to win readers, a great deal of time, effort and expertise must go into design, formatting and hyperlinking, and the amount of time that should be dedicated to promoting the work is the same as for a printed book. Web users will not be satisfied with a file that just reproduces your work; they will expect a text that takes advantage of the unique functionalities offered by the web, through links within the text, links to other web texts and to other media such as audio or film, and through the use of dynamic and interactive elements that would not be possible in a printed book. If your work was conceived as a printed book, it will be easiest to continue down that route.

Points to consider include:

- What format would your readers find most useful? How will your work gain the greatest circulation? In other words, which format will make the entire exercise most worthwhile?
- Would your work benefit more from the linking and multi-media capabilities of the web, or from the permanence and control over appearance offered by a printed book? (Web pages vary in appearance depending on the web browser and the configuration of the computer on which they are viewed.)
- How long do you want your work to last? If it is a relatively 'now' text, a web file could be a good option, but if the work is more timeless a physical book could be better as that would never need your input to migrate to new platforms or software versions.

- How important is it to you that your work is stored in libraries? Only a printed book equipped with an ISBN can be archived in perpetuity by your national library, and can be included (even if only by donation) in the holdings of research libraries.
- How technically competent are you with the software packages needed for either option? Would you need to invest a great deal of time in learning to use new software? Do you have that time to invest, and would you enjoy the learning process?
- How much money can you afford to invest? If you can do all the work yourself and have access to a university website, web publishing can be almost cost free. However, printing technology has developed which allows tiny print quantities at acceptable prices, so physical books are now within the reach of most purses.

Doing the work

Whichever format you settle on, there is editorial work to be done first of all. Writing a manuscript is a long and difficult task, and preparing it for printing is no mean feat either, so get help where you can. If you have received copies of peer review reports from those publishers who have rejected your book, read the reports as advice on editorial changes. Otherwise (or additionally), ask respected colleagues to read and comment on your work. Be aware, though, that most people will be reluctant to be critical to your face, so the comments you get are likely to be on the gentle side of truthful. If you are in a writing group, exploit it to the full. And get your life partner or best friend to read the text too – although they are probably subject outsiders, they can still do you great favours by spotting inconsistencies and typos.

Layout and typesetting

Start by buying yourself a good manual on desktop publishing (DTP). You will need much more detailed and technical advice than it is reasonable to include in this book.

To decide on the style you want for your book, look through the contents of your shelves with a view to form and appearance. Try to nail down the differences between styles you like and styles that have less appeal to you. Some fonts appear more up-to-date than others, some heading styles seem more professional than others, some types of page lay-out come across more stern and serious than others. You will need to apply an aesthetic, if not artistic, eye to determine (a) what the right general style for your manuscript is and (b) which specific style is most to your taste.

You must then define in precise detail exactly how you want your pages to appear, and where and how you want the various page elements to appear – main text, page number, running head left and right, footer left and right, footnotes, illustrations, etc. Next you must define exactly how each text element should appear, setting standards for font, font size, line height, style (plain, bold, italic, etc.), justification, indentation, space above and below, capitalization, etc. You will need to set these parameters individually for each text element in such a way that you arrive at a harmonious interplay between plain text, chapter and section headings at various levels, quotations, notes, tables and table legends, illustration captions, and so on. Your DTP manual should be of great assistance in this task.

Retail therapy

It is highly likely that you will have to buy dedicated page layout software. Standard word processors, while powerful tools for text production, are not geared towards page layout. They do not allow sufficiently detailed control over text elements in either appearance or position, and they are generally not good at handling very large quantities of text. The DTP manual should help you pick the software most suited to your needs.

If you plan to publish your work as a physical book, you must also have PDF generator software which will allow you to produce PDF files for your printer. On the other hand, if you are planning to publish your work in electronic form with no hardcopy option, you will need a web editor software package. The concerns as to de-

Self-publishing is not cheap. You can easily spend a considerable sum of money on computer hardware, software and manuals – here a large monitor for layout work, a scanner to deal with illustrations, a high-density storage device, a suite of DTP programs, and a handful of manuals and user guides.

signing the appearance of the work are similar to those for hardcopy typesetting, but instead of printing a PDF file for a printer, you must produce one or more hyperlinked webfiles for upload instead.

Lastly, you might consider investing in a large monitor for your computer. With this, you will be able to view two-page spreads at full size and hence easily be able to check text flow and consistency. In addition, the task of designing a wrap-around book cover or jacket is much easier if you can view the whole thing in one screen view without losing all detail.

Finding a partner

If you have decided on web publishing, you need to find a host site, either from your university or from an Internet service provider which can sell you a unique URL (website address) and space for your files. Ideally, the URL should be one that clearly relates to the title of your work.

If you have decided on a physical book, there is a range of options for how it can be produced, with more or less direct contributions from you in time and money. Note, though, that in order to be identifiable to libraries and other book professionals, and thus in order to be accepted by them as a valid book, your work must have an ISBN. You can obtain this for a small fee from your national ISBN agency (often, but not always, a branch of the national library). In return, you will usually be asked to provide on publication one or more free copies to be included in the permanent holdings of your national legal deposit library.

Working papers

Some departments and faculties publish working papers which range from rather informal, photocopied affairs mainly for internal consumption to more sophisticated, bound paperback books with some outside circulation. Indeed, several small university presses started life as working-paper programmes.

If you have the option to publish your text as a working paper, you will not have to come up with money for a printer's bill, and you may be offered a bit of secretarial assistance in laying out the manuscript. On the other hand, you may have little control over the production value of the book and there is likely to be no compensation for your efforts. In effect, working-paper series are a kind of 'academic-publishing-lite' rather than self-publishing.

Author-pays publishing[1]

There are several companies that offer assistance to self-publishers, usually employing print-on-demand (POD) technology to do so

1 Not to be confused with grant-assisted publishing. Academic publishers often have to ask for author contributions, e.g. to cover illustration costs or to part-fund publications that are deemed otherwise not commercially viable. This

(see below). Some work on the basis that the author pays the full cost of all editorial and typesetting work on the text (which can run into substantial sums of money) and gets a correspondingly healthy slice of any income from sales. At the other extreme, some expect the author to deliver a fully print-ready file but will then only charge a flat fee and/or a commission when a sale is made and a copy printed. Some focus on providing help with the editorial work, others offer typesetting and design, while yet others focus on helping you market and distribute your work. Some allow you to pick and choose services from an *à la carte* menu, others have more standardized offerings at potentially lower prices. This is a market in pretty rapid growth, so it is impossible for us to be specific here about the exact services that will be on offer. When the time comes, you will just have to search for the service that suits you best.

Bear in mind, though, that while there are some perfectly respectable businesses that exist to provide services to authors of manuscripts unsuited to traditional publishing outlets, any emerging market can attract cowboys. Be very thorough with background checks before you enter into any agreements, ask to see other books produced by the company you are negotiating with, and ask for contact details for a few satisfied customers.

Also keep in mind that the per-copy cost quoted by the company can affect you directly. You will most likely need to purchase a number of copies right away to use as thank-you presents for those who have helped you prepare the text, to provide to your legal deposit library, to give away as review copies, and to keep on your shelf for your own satisfaction.

Are author-pays publishing companies the same as vanity presses? The intended market of a vanity press is the author, and it makes little difference to the vanity press whether the book finds any other

---

does not generally harm academic value, as publishers have a vested interest in continuing to operate the peer-review process to safeguard their standing as reputable and trustworthy guarantors of good academic quality.

readers. In this sense, then, author-pays presses are vanity presses. On the other hand, the term indicates that anyone who engages with this type of press must be vain and only interested in seeing their name on the cover of a book, and that is not the case where you are engaged in a serious effort to produce and promote a book from a text that has been rejected by mainstream publishers on grounds unrelated to its academic qualities. It seems to us that the difference between vanity publishing and self-publishing is not defined by the type of press, but by the type of text being published. You are a self-publisher making use of a service that allows you to take control of (some aspects of) the production and distribution of your work, in the best tradition of the capable do-it-yourself project.

Ordering your own printing job

If you want full control over every aspect of your book and its presentation, you will have to engage directly with a printer. New print-on-demand technology makes it financially possible for a private author to order a small quantity of books directly from a POD printer. Essentially, POD marries the flat cost structure of digital printing (or, more bluntly, sophisticated laser printing) with the high-quality finish of book binding.

In traditional offset printing, the presses must be set up for each new print job, which is an expensive affair, but once that has been done, copies can be printed off at very little additional cost. That means there is a high initial cost to be distributed over the number of copies printed at low individual cost. The more books are printed, the lower the share of initial costs applied to each copy. Offset printing is thus good value for print quantities of hundreds or thousands of copies, but ruinously expensive if you only want dozens of copies, or even just a single one.

POD, though, has the same per-copy cost whether you print one copy or ten thousand. It is not cost-effective for printing large quantities, and the per-copy cost is such that it is very hard to make sufficient profit from selling POD books to cover a publisher's pre-

Self-publishers will come into contact with many industry insiders that authors normally never meet – here the printers at the coalface of publishing.

press production costs such as typesetting or cover design. But POD comes into its own when it enables projects to go ahead where profit is not an important motive. Thus, POD allows traditional publishers to keep their backlists available for ever as a service to their authors and customers, and it allows self-publishers to go ahead without risking large sums of money on printer's bills for quantities of stock that will clutter up the garage without any certainty of sufficient sales to turn it back into ready cash. You do, though, normally have to pay a title set-up fee and an annual file maintenance fee irrespective of the size of your turnover, and you should make sure that the prices you are quoted are competitive.

The quality of early POD books was rather questionable both in terms of the clarity of print and the quality of the binding. Now, though, these issues have been resolved, and it is hard for the untrained eye to distinguish between an offset paperback and one produced by POD technology. You will be able to order a small initial quantity to cover your immediate stock needs, and you can then ask your printer to keep your file on their computer so that they can print off additional copies for you as and when the need arises.

Promoting and distributing your book

It is extremely difficult to sell a self-published book through trade channels, not because any of the individual tasks involved are rocket science, but mainly because bookshop buyers are busy people who would rather spend half an hour talking to a trade representative who can sell them 50 titles than spend 5 minutes with a self-publisher who can only sell them one title (and that by non-standard means).

The situation is fortunately very different on the web, where individualism and fresh approaches are generally warmly welcomed. Your efforts should concentrate on promoting your book through web-based channels, and through other forms of direct communication with your potential readers. If you are lucky, your book will take on a life of its own and start selling by word-of-mouth.

You might consider disguising the fact that your book is a self-publication project by inventing a name and logo under which to publish it. The world wants to be deceived, and you may meet less resistance if you publish as A Great Big Publisher rather than as My Little Press. In fact, we have had people claiming to us that they remember meeting Mr So-and-so who we happen to know is the wholly fictional co-founder of a business that started out as a self-publisher.

Marketing and promotion

Revisit the section in Chapter 10 on what authors can do to promote their books. Everything we suggest in that chapter goes double for self-publishers.

In addition, you could consider taking on some of the jobs the same chapter explains as being the publisher's responsibility. For instance, if you believe you know exactly what publications your target readers subscribe to, you can use your newly-found design skills to produce an advertisement for their journal or newsletter, or at the very least write to offer a free review copy. If your book has an element of local flavour, you could approach local booksellers (but be aware that they will want a large discount on the retail price, and that they will want to be able to return any unsold stock to you for a full refund). And you should certainly make it your business to ensure that the book is on show at every academic conference you attend.

Since your book is unlikely to be available through bookshops, it is vitally important that every single piece of marketing and promotional material contains full details of how the book can be ordered.

Sales and distribution

It is increasingly easy for private individuals to access large markets through the web. Unlike previous generations of self-publishers, you will be able to sell your book directly to customers through Amazon Marketplace, eBay, Abe Books and whatever other private-to-private sales channels are available in your region. Some self-publisher services offer marketing and sales as an optional extra for a fee and/or a commission.

Web-based market places provide a mechanism for you to take payment from customers' credit cards or PayPal accounts. But it is not currently cost-effective for you personally to acquire the ability to process card payments, so for individual orders that you receive direct from a customer, you will have to ask for payment in cash, by cheque or by money transfer to your bank account. Buyers like using credit cards because they are fast, easy and safe. You will be asking your customers to use a less convenient method of payment, and on top of that there will be a time delay while you wait for their money to arrive or their cheque to clear before sending books.

The least you can do in return is be prompt and courteous in your order processing. Check daily for new orders, and respond immediately to enquiries. Confirm receipt of payment, and notify customers when books are dispatched. Be prepared to go to the post office to send off orders every single day – indeed, count yourself very lucky if you have to do so.

And give thought to the method of dispatch. It is cheapest to send books by second class mail, it is safest to send them as parcels with a progress-tracking system, and it is quickest to send them by courier. You may wish to consult with your customers on what method they prefer, or you may wish to specify that only certain options are available for certain destinations. It is your responsibility to ensure that the books your customers have paid for arrive without undue delay and in good condition. If your packing material is insufficient or your dispatch method inappropriate so that books arrive damaged or not at all, you will have to send replacements at no extra cost to the customer. It is well worth taking pains to get things right the first time.

Measures of success

As a self-publisher, you are the architect of your own success. Even better, you get to define for yourself what success means in your particular case. For an academic publisher, success is measured mainly in number of copies sold and amount of profit made, and only after that in the more intangible contribution that a book can make to the general prestige and standing of the publisher's brand. For you as a self-publisher the criteria for success could be just the opposite: good reviews and reader enjoyment may be more important to you than mere reader numbers, and an elegant appearance on the shelves of your office and your university library may well give you more pleasure than financial profit ever could.

EPILOGUE

Publishing revolutions

The future is here. It's just not widely distributed yet.
– William Gibson

THERE IS NO POINT TRYING TO PRETEND OTHERWISE: these are the pages that will seriously date our book. The ways in which academics, students, publishers, libraries, booksellers and the book industry as a whole have traditionally worked are being transformed by rapid technological developments and other change. Whole new fields of opportunity are opening up (sometimes resembling an abyss into which time and effort can be poured), and long-established practices must be revised or discarded as new realities take hold.

Little more than a decade ago, Web publishing was in its infancy, electronic books were little more than a glimmer in a nerdy eye, and few would have dreamt that a search engine could attempt to make every single book ever written freely available on the Internet. All that has changed now. No one knows what the publishing world of ten years from now will be like – the only certainty is that it will be different. So all that we can aspire to do, from our vantage point of late 2008, is to give some pointers to likely flashpoints for future developments that might affect you as an author (and a consumer) of books. The lack of clear signals to navigate by is nicely illustrated by *Print is Dead: Books in Our Digital Age* (published in 2007), where the author Jeff Gomez argues that books are a mere sentimental relic of a bygone age. He does so, however, in … (drum roll) … *a book*.

Electronic formats

As a general point, publishing has lagged behind academe in embracing new technology. Indeed, academics were among the first people to adopt the Internet as an integrated part of everyday life, and much new technology has offered immediate and obvious benefits for scholars and their research (and for university administration too). The advantages have been less obvious for publishers. Thus, although most publishers agree that it is desirable that their material should be available in an electronic format, few are able to make this a profitable exercise. Offering e-formats tends to be seen as a way of providing better service to customers and authors, and as insurance against being left behind if e-formats suddenly take off in a big way, but it is rarely viewed (except by specialist reference publishers and the like) as an important income-generating activity.

Some of this is quite likely just inertia and an unwillingness to invest large sums before one is quite sure of a good return. But in part, at least, it is because there are still a number of unresolved questions surrounding the best platforms to use for creating and safeguarding e-format, how to secure digital media against degeneration (a CD reliably lasts about 20 years, and a DVD much less than that – laughably short life-spans compared to books), and whether the publisher will have to keep investing in upgrading a work to one new software version after another – or, even worse, one new hardware standard after another. For journals publishers and for librarians, the issue of archiving is particularly urgent as they must ensure that decades-old journal issues remain accessible to readers today.

Once these various issues have been successfully resolved, and we expect that they soon will be, electronic formats could come to play a much bigger role than at present. There are evident advantages especially for the academic world where customers for specialist works are widely dispersed: how wonderful, for instance, to be able to send a book at no cost and with no risk from Oxford to Ulan Bator in less time than it takes to make a cup of tea. For the environment, too, e-formats hold great promise as they do away not only with the large physical object that is the book, but also with the significant amount of fossil fuels expended on sending heavy tomes from printer to warehouse to wholesaler to retailer to reader.

E-book readers

Handheld devices for reading electronic book formats were once trumpeted as real alternatives to printed books since, unlike files residing on desktop or even laptop computers, e-books are truly portable and versatile, just like printed books. However, these sturdy pocket-sized items have so far failed to engage a public otherwise hot for any new electronic gadget.

While one key barrier to adoption (in addition to cost and availability) has been the inferior reading experience compared to a book, the central problem has been the lack of uniform software and hardware platforms. Different e-books have employed different standards for the files they can display, so a work converted into the file format for one e-book would be unreadable on another e-book. That leads to a serious conflict of interest between device manufacturers on the one hand and publishers and readers on the other hand. While the latter would much prefer every title to be available for every e-book – just like every CD can play on every CD player – the manufacturers have wanted to license material exclusively for their own devices, barring manufacturers of competing devices from offering the same books. Recently, Amazon entered the fray with their own device which ties in with their on-going efforts to digitize as many books as possible and make them searchable on their website, but the device has not been particularly well received in press reviews. However, if a killer device were to come on the market it would probably revolutionize trade publishing as quickly as the iPod revolutionized the music industry.

Nevertheless, electronic formats in general and e-books in particular remain a promising option, partly because they offer publishers and their customers the opportunity to cut out a problematic middle man. Even the very best, most frugal and efficient shipper presents a largely undesirable link in the distribution chain. The further, and the more times, a printed book has to be physically transported, the greater the risk of damage in transit or outright loss. And despite shippers' best efforts, shipping is still costly in time (adding weeks or even months to a book's production schedule), costly in money (to the point where transport alone can cost as much as all the printing and binding work combined), and in fossil fuels (because books are heavy and fairly large objects to transport). Going 'e-' is clearly an attractive solution.

POD and the bookshop as content kiosk

Print-on-demand (POD) technology has developed to the point where proponents now talk of placing POD printing equipment in every bookshop so that, instead of carrying stock in the form of books, shops can become 'content kiosks' where customers browse through files before placing print orders for immediate execution.

Take our customer in Ulan Bator from earlier in this chapter. What if, instead of sitting at his office computer and ordering a book in electronic format from a British publisher, he were to go into his local bookshop and browse their infinitely large computerized inventory to order up books from seven different publishers around the globe. The bookshop manager would press a button to send a print order to the POD machine in the backroom, and our academic would be able to collect the finished books a little later – a system not quite as quick as making a cup of tea, but probably as quick as ordering a de-caff skinny latte with macadamia syrup from a well-known chain of coffee shops.

The initial investment in equipment is of course quite considerable and possibly out of reach of smaller shops. It is also quite likely that shops would continue to carry a certain amount of stock for impulse purchases, so we would be surprised if bookshop fronts became as small as passport photo booths. But it could happen, and POD systems are already being trialled in a few major bookshops and at least one large library. Whether the hugely increased convenience will make up for the atmospherically depleted browsing experience remains to be seen.

Free Internet repositories

As we mentioned in the discussion about Open Access in Chapter 8, many universities have set up Web-based repositories where they make available at no cost to the reader as much as possible of the research output produced by their academic staff. One could argue (probably against quite considerable opposition) that since the academics have already been paid by the university that employs them, it is perfectly reasonable for that university to treat any research output as their property – just like car manufacturers own the vehicles that their employees have produced during working hours.

How many people, though, would argue that all books ever written by any author in any situation should be made freely available by an organization that has had no input whatsoever into creating the books in the first place? Actually, there are those who would argue just exactly that. Way out ahead in the race to digitize everything ever written is Google Book Search, and other players include Amazon, Yahoo! and The Internet Archive. The aim is to make the entire 'dead tree' world searchable and inter-linkable with the electronic world, and progress can be counted in thousands of titles per day. Libraries are also active here as they seek to reinvent themselves in the Internet age by acting as Open Access repositories and 'publishing' their own e-content.

The benefits to users are evident. Apart from enabling a scholar to find with one Web search every single reference to the hair styles of Scandinavian bog mummies, there is a rich seam of links to be mined in every academic text. Footnotes, citations and bibliographies are obvious points for live links that facilitate scholarship by making primary sources much easier to access. No more jotting down the location of a book, trudging through the library, pulling it off the shelf, queuing for the photocopier – you will only be a mouse click away from the material you desire.

For authors and publishers, the worry is that copyright and book sales, and by extension royalty income, are being eroded. Perhaps the issue of royalty matters little for academic authors who rarely earn much, if anything at all, in royalties. It also seems, so far at least, that book sales are holding up and that, while Googling a book may be a handy substitute for looking it up in a reference library, it is not a substitute for buying and reading the entire thing. Some publishers have embraced comprehensive digitization as another element in their marketing tool box, while others have strongly resisted (on their own behalf and for their authors) what they see as efforts to appropriate their creations for selfish and sometimes commercial purposes. Small scholarly associations publishing their own journals have warned that if their subscription income (often the only money they have) disappears, they may have to close down altogether, and that free repositories thus risk being the cause of a decline in the number of channels for scholarly articles. Meanwhile, digitization continues apace, but with only limited access to view material still under copyright.

The content revolution

While global digitization for free consumption enjoys far from global support, the vast majority of publishers are very keen on digitization for good old paid-for consumption. How far advanced a publisher is in this arena is often less to do with preference and more to do with resources and the precise nature of their material.

There are two basic ideas underpinning publisher's efforts to digitize. The first is that digitized books (and journals) can not only be sold in their original entirety, but can be chopped up into smaller pieces such as individual chapters and articles, or even individual pages, to be sold as they are or to be re-combined with other chunks of material to create new products. This allows micro-sales of individual page views, bundle sales of subsets of the publisher's list to libraries as one-off sales or as subscriptions, and sales to content aggregators who collect material from many publishers and offer it (sometimes re-packaged) to many users. The second idea is that older material which publishers would previously have allowed to go out of print can continue to find new readers if only it is possible for them to search within the material to convince themselves of its usefulness.

Quite possibly the ultimate result will be a situation reminiscent of that which the music industry finds itself in, where downloads have made the album an archaic concept in a world where the relevant commercial (and, increasingly, artistic) entity is the individual song. Micro-sales and aggregation may have little effect on fiction titles. After all, who in their right mind would buy just two chapters from a prize-winning novel, or the last thirty pages of a crime thriller, or every page with a reference to custard in the novels of Charles Dickens? On the other hand, one can easily imagine that there would be a ready market for individual chapters from edited volumes of academic texts, perhaps even enough to revive the fortunes of the edited volume in general academic publishing.

Bite-sized scholarship

One aspect of making everything available electronically – some of it in small, handy chunks – is that cutting and pasting from search results to new text becomes very easy. In effect, 'new' text can be built using little other than blocks of material garnered from earlier works. One might worry that this will raise questions about what exactly constitutes fair use and what is plagiarism. Likewise, with the wealth of material available, it will become extremely difficult to uncover instances of plagiarism. And yet another concern could be that the facilities for bite-sized scholarship will threaten the tradition for long, sustained argument and reasoning that is a mainstay of scholarly publishing, particularly in the humanities and social sciences.

Perhaps an unintended effect of the digital revolution will be a radically different kind of scholarship based more on community effort than on individual achievement (making Creative Commons more common than old-fashioned copyright). In this environment, self-publishing and collaborative authorship could become more important. We are also likely to see a more rapid dissemination of research results via the Internet rather than via time-consuming print publishing, and with material in a constant state of flux to reflect the most recent reality and most up-to-date understanding – much like the difference, in fact, between the *Encyclopædia Britannica* and Wikipedia.

Creative marketing

You can expect to have books marketed to you in novel ways, and you should require your own publisher to be up-to-date with these new opportunities too. There is also scope for you to get directly involved in promoting your work through new avenues.

Already, good publishers and savvy authors make use of newsgroups and e-mail discussion lists to promote their books. Some publishers use weblogs to communicate with their authors and business partners, and we would expect it to become increasingly popular for authors to start their own blogs in support of specific books. Authors of trade books are beginning to use social networking sites such as MySpace and Facebook to talk about and promote their books, and we see no reason why that practice should not spread among academic authors. Another recent idea is to use podcasts (audio files downloadable by computer to an iPod or MP3 player) to broadcast material. As usual, the academic world got there before publishers: some universities have been offering podcasts of lectures for several years, while publishers are only now realizing the opportunities which could include podcasting author readings and discussions. The latest thing is footage from book launches and author interviews available on YouTube.

The book is dead, long live the book

Beset as it may be on many sides, we firmly believe that rumours of the death of the book have been greatly exaggerated. Sure, there are things that electronic media can do better than books: they are much faster and easier to search, they can integrate sound and moving images seamlessly, they take up hardly any space at all, and their storage capacity approaches infinity. But the book has its own unique advantages:

> I am very optimistic about print as a technology. Words on paper are a wonderful information storage, retrieval, distribution and consumer product. Imagine if we had been getting our information delivered digitally to our screens for the past 499 years. Then some modern Gutenberg had come up with a technology that was able to transfer these words and pictures on to pages that could be delivered to our doorstep, and we could take them to the backyard, the bath, or the bus. We would be thrilled with this technological leap forward, and we would predict that someday it might replace the Internet.
>
> – *Walter Isaacson, former CEO of CNN, on www.edge.org*

Top tips

Make a detailed structural plan of your book, but do not let it become a straightjacket. You need to have a clear idea of what you want to write before you start out. This will help you stay on track, and will be particularly useful if, like most authors, you write your book in bits and pieces, later to be brought together. But the plan should not be carved in stone – allow room for the material to influence the plan as you get into the flow of writing.

Think like a reader when you write. Ensure there is a narrative thread running through your manuscript and keeping the reader interested. Do not allow yourself to get bogged down in endless detail, especially these days when detail and background can so easily be provided on a book-related website. It is a real art to make the difficult appear effortless, and even the most serious treatise on an involved subject can wear its learning lightly. Remember that you are not writing to impress, but to communicate your knowledge and enthusiasm for your subject.

Consistency is King when you prepare your text. Different authors, editors and presses have different preferences as to the styling and formatting of text. Only if you have been scrupulously consistent throughout every aspect of your text preparation will you be able with relative ease to adjust the style and amend the formatting to suit the particular publishing channel you find for your work.

Do not be overwhelmed by the size of the writing task, by the efforts you must put into plugging your work to publishers, or by the practical work involved in turning your manuscript into a book. As they say, the longest journey starts with a single step. Likewise, do not be discouraged by critique and rejection. No one gets everything right on the first attempt, and you should not let the occasional negative reaction to your work dampen your spirits.

Choose your publisher with care. You are entering a fairly long-term relationship with an organisation that will have almost complete control over how all the effort that you have put into the text is treated, packaged and presented. If you have gone to the trouble of writing 100,000 words or more, it would be reckless not to check up on the likely publisher candidates.

Listen to the specialists at the press. When you get advice from your publisher, it comes on the basis of long experience and the best intentions for your book. It is depressing how many authors insist on disregarding the advice they receive, usually with negative consequences. So listen, and carefully consider the publisher's suggestions. They will not always be right, but you should have clear and strong reasons if you want to go against their advice.

Be shameless when promoting your book proposal to a publisher and your book to its readers. Do not forget a single positive thing you can say about yourself, the excellence of your manuscript or book and its likely rapturous reception among readers. Do not be afraid to push yourself forward, to cold call publishers, to send out polite reminders, and to draw on all your contacts to get your book accepted, reviewed and bought.

Be a team player, not a prima donna. Your book may be the most important thing in your life, but the publisher is handling dozens, perhaps even hundreds, of other books at the same time. Yours will not always be top of the pile. And publishing staff are only human: the more pleasant and helpful and professional and understanding you are, the greater the likelihood that others will respond by also rising to do their very best.

APPENDIX ONE

Practical style and presentation issues

Chapter 5 focused on the broad issues and general concerns relating to writing books. What this appendix offers is more in-depth advice on these and other technical matters. As with all such guides, we adhere to certain standards and conventions that not all publishers agree with. While it may seem to brim over with advice on how to format your text and your documents, it is in fact almost recklessly laid back when compared to the style guides of some publishers (which run to 50 pages or more) or to the North American gold standard, *The Chicago Manual of Style*, weighing in at over 900 pages. Our advice, then, is that you use this appendix but seek greater detail and explanation in the Chicago manual (though remembering that it has an American bias in some of its usage). Obviously, if you have a publisher for your book then you should consult their style guidelines for exact requirements.

Spelling and grammar

Not to be ignored. It may not be 'sexy' to warn about spelling and grammar but your publisher will care rather deeply about these things; a text that is clearly inadequate in this respect may lose credibility and be rejected. It does not help that English spelling and pronunciation parted company several centuries ago (most obviously in the case of British English), but while sociologists, for instance, may have something to say both about human rights and human rites, the two concepts really do need to be kept separate.

Reference tools. Spelling dictionaries are cheap and easy to find; use them, likewise a comprehensive grammar book with plenty of worked examples. Use the spell checker in your word-processing programs, but do not expect it to be able to catch all problems. For instance, incorrectly split or hyphenated compound words such as 'motor cycle' or 'motor-cycle' instead of 'motorcycle' would not be corrected. Some programs such as Word also check grammar, though rarely perfectly; this feature should only be used as a rough check before you carefully read through your text and find the myriad errors that need correcting in any draft.

Which English? If you are writing in English, you must decide which spelling variant to adopt – British, American, Australian, etc. – and set your spell checker preferences accordingly. If you are an American being published by a US press (or an Indian by an Indian press, etc.), the choice is obvious. However, for more globally oriented presses and authors, sometimes a 'mid-Atlantic' solution is best, for instance choosing the more international endings *-ize, -izing* and *-ization* over *-ise, -ising* and *-isation* only found in Britain and certain Commonwealth countries, but sticking to British terms and spellings of other words.

Use international spellings. While the local term or place name may be more correct to use, if you are writing for an international readership then in most cases you should use the internationally recognized and accepted form where there is one (e.g. 'sheikh' not *shaykh,* and 'Copenhagen' instead of 'København'). This aids recognition and hence cuts down on the 'speed bumps' described in Chapter 5.

Document formatting

Files. On balance, it is wise to operate with separate chapter files rather than a single book manuscript file. Computer processing will be faster, there is less to lose if something nasty happens to your file, and you can decide to add or subtract chapters without fuss (as we did with this book). And it is easy with modern word-processing software to search and update text across multiple files.

Chapter templates. Uniformity of style, while very simple if you operate with one book-length file, can also be achieved with multiple files provided you create them from the same document template. Because such templates often cannot be easily amended, it is important that you get this properly set up from the beginning with all the elements you need. This includes page layout, paragraph styles and the various other features described below. Of course, an alternative is to start writing your book with the basic design scheme provided as default by your word processor. You can simply leave things at that, or at a certain point you can use what you have written to create a more developed template, which you then apply to all of your documents. The latter is, however, by far the more time-consuming option.

Page layout. First you must define your paper size. Depending on where you work, your word processor's default paper size will be either US Letter or A4 paper, and this is the paper your printer will be set up to handle. Using a non-standard paper size is asking for trouble, likewise producing your manuscript in landscape orientation (or mixing portrait with landscape pages). You should give your document generous margins as your editor will need this space for writing notes. Imagine your completed manuscript being dropped and its pages tumbling across the floor. If for no other reason, you need the chapter name (or ID) and page number printed on every page in the header or footer. Some authors find that adding an automatic version date here also useful.

Hard page breaks. You will find less need for these if you use separate chapter documents. You should also know that most typesetting programs will ignore such breaks, so there is a danger that the typesetter will miss any hard breaks you have inserted unless you flag them up manually (e.g. with 'INSERT PAGE BREAK HERE').

Paragraph styles. Most authors use Microsoft Word and a great many key the whole text in the 'Normal' paragraph style, manually (but inconsistently) reformatting this to create headings and the like. Others create havoc for their typesetters by using a huge array of often-duplicate paragraph styles. You will save both yourself and your publisher a vast amount of time if you create just a few basic paragraph styles and use these consistently. Updating the look and feel of your entire text then becomes very easy for the typesetters. Be careful, however, if you create a new paragraph style based on another: if later you update the original style, the new style will also be updated unless you have reset the 'based on' link between them. Justifying your text may look more pleasing to the eye, but multiple spaces and many other errors in the text will be easier to find and correct if you left-align everything.

Line spacing. Some publishers demand manuscripts using double spacing but, for all purposes prior to submission to a publisher, it is wasteful to use such wide line spacing. The best idea is to use the line spacing that suits you best while producing the manuscript; afterwards, you can amend the style to double spaced when printing a hard copy for your publisher.

Font matters

While there have been major advances in typography in recent years, fonts are still a source of headaches for authors and publishers. Accordingly, you should bear the following points in mind.

Compatibility. There are thousands of different fonts out there. By all means choose fonts that you like but be aware that a document with uncommon fonts when opened by someone else may be unreadable or convert to a common font with strange results. The safe move is to choose standard fonts like Times, Arial and Helvetica or those that are Unicode compliant.

Readability. Some fonts are easier than others to read. Serif fonts (with 'feet') like Times are far easier to read in running text than sans-serif fonts (without 'feet') like Arial and Helvetica. Serif fonts are best for body text, while sans-serif are often used for headings because of the greater visual impact.

Font size. Choose font sizes that enhance readability and acceptability. The standard is 12-point Times, boring perhaps but eminently usable.

Flexibility. Make sure that you can easily switch fonts, if need be, by defining font usage in your paragraph style, *not* manually in the text.

Mixing fonts. It is common to assign one font for headings, another for body text. But within a paragraph, apart from inserting special characters or non-Latin script, avoid mixing fonts; it does not look good and it creates work for the publisher to correct it later.

Cost. Be aware that many fonts that may be free for you to use on your personal computer and printer are *not* free for commercial use (i.e. for high-resolution printing by your publisher); a licence must be paid (which the publisher may refuse or demand that you pay). Our understanding is that all of the specialist fonts that come 'free' with Word fall into this category.

Special characters and scripts. The text for this book was written in the Times font family, but the actual book that you are reading uses quite different typography. For us as authors, this did not matter; we wrote 'plain vanilla' text. Many authors, however, need to go beyond vanilla and insert symbols and other special characters into their text, examples being:

- Text with diacriticals or special accents (Vietnamese, for instance, uses multiple accents over a single Latin character).
- Non-Latin script (e.g. Cyrillic, Arabic and Chinese).
- Mathematical and scientific symbols (many based on Greek letters).
- Formulas (often a complex arrangement of super- and sub-

scripted Greek letters and other symbols and markers that must be precisely placed but still run into the main text).

In general, diacriticals and non-Latin script are less of a problem today than previously, owing to general acceptance of the Unicode standard for font mapping and the rise of Open Type fonts based on this standard. The common Unicode standard gives each character form its own unique identifier which allows easy swapping between fonts, so it is imperative that any font you use is Unicode compliant. That said, just because it is technically possible to splatter your text with (say) Arabic characters, this does not mean that you should do so. Consider the issues of readability and 'speed bumps' discussed in Chapter 5 and ask yourself what is necessary, not what is possible. (There are also wider issues with non-Latin script such as the input method and the direction of input, as discussed below.) In addition, Unicode standards have yet to be defined for all non-Latin scripts (at the time of writing, for instance, no standard exists for Lao script).

Many publishers refuse to accept works with diacriticals and non-Latin script due to the added production cost and general hassle, while others refuse to have non-Latin script in the main text but allow it to appear in a separate glossary that can be typeset separately from the bulk of the book. If it is necessary to include such special characters in your book, then the ability and willingness of a publisher to handle them must influence whom you approach with your script, and you may be asked to find significant sums of money to finance the extra typesetting costs that your choice causes.

Layout and punctuation

Extra spaces. The typewriter may be dead but its influence persists with underlines (see below) and spaces. A surprising number of authors still key two spaces after each sentence. This is unnecessary and your publisher will get you to remove the redundant spaces. Also, you should use tabs and never spaces to indent paragraphs and align text in lists. Never use multiple tabs (see Lists below).

Bold, italic and underlining. A significant but dwindling band of publishers still require that their authors deliver works in plain text, with any emphasis indicated by underlining only. You will need to check if your preferred publisher is one of these diehards. Otherwise, we suggest that you:

- Restrict the use of bold to headings. Bold (like CAPITAL LETTERS) is a 'shouting' style.
- Use italics for emphasis and for marking of foreign words. There has been a tradition not to italicize surrounding punctuation (parentheses and the like); some publishers still strictly enforce this. The same rule tends to apply with foreign plurals; if a foreign (italicized) word is pluralized with an 's' or 'es', this ending should be in plain text ('kamis') whereas foreign words pluralized in their native form are fully italicized (alim, ulema).
- Avoid <u>underlines</u> altogether (except for the traditionalists as above).

Super-script, small caps and other special formats. It is unlikely with modern typesetting software that these special formats will be lost in the text conversion process. However, as they can disrupt reading, be sparing in their use. If you can, turn off any automatic superscripting in your word-processor (e.g. for 'th' in words like '20th') as it is unlikely your publisher will want this format in the typeset text.

Hyphenation. Do not insert 'hard' hyphens (and it is best to avoid 'soft' hyphens, too) in your text except for compound words (e.g. 'nineteenth-century warfare'). Indeed, although sometimes the resulting line-end gaps may be ugly, turn off the automatic hyphenation feature on your word-processing software.

Punctuation. Refer to *The Chicago Manual of Style* or a similar guide for the detail of best punctuation practice. However, many common errors in author manuscripts concern the use of hyphens, dashes and quotation marks, so these are treated briefly here.

- Use ***hyphens*** to divide words and to create compound words (e.g. well-being, English-speaking, six-year-old).
- Use ***n-dashes*** (–, with no space on either side) to denote date and number ranges (e.g. 1995–97, pp. 234–298); 'from–to' (Moscow–Beijing railway); and 'between' (the Mongolian–Chinese border).
- To denote a 'thinking pause' in the middle of a sentence, use ***m-dashes*** (—, with no space on either side) if publishing in North America, otherwise use ***n-dashes*** (with a space on each side).
- Use double ***m-dashes*** (——) in bibliographies to mark 'ditto' author entries.
- Most but not all publishers use single ***quotation marks*** with double quotes within single ones. As these are fiddly to change, you would be smart to see what the practice of your preferred publisher is. Make sure that your word processor automatically produces smart quotes ('dog') rather than straight ones ('dog').

Lists. Numbered and bulleted points can be effective if used in moderation, but it is often easier on the reader if you weave your points into the text as sentences. If your glossary or a similar multi-column list looks unattractive, it is better to put the list into a table (which your publisher can later convert back to tabbed text) than to insert multiple tabs that will convert to a ragged mess in the typesetting program.

Headings. Unless you are writing instructional material, like this book, the use of numerous headings and subheadings has too much of a feel of a dissertation or report. Keep headings to a minimum; the reader can usually be moved along by the text itself. That said, the judicious use of headings can prime the reader for the content that follows and give structure and direction to a manuscript.

Publishers' preferences vary enormously on the capitalization of headings and on date style and other number-based formats. Consult a style guide and proceed with care (and consistency).

Quotations, notes, citations, etc.

Quotations. As discussed in Chapter 5, keep the use of direct quotations to a minimum and be careful how much you quote (otherwise you will need to get the copyright holder's permission to reproduce the text). Copy the exact spelling and punctuation of the quoted text (adding '[sic]' if necessary to acknowledge an error). If a quotation is longer than about four lines, break it out into a block quote.

Citations. Great care is required with your citations as these, being numerous and specific in their format, are probably the worst thing to have to change. Depending on your field of study and your publisher's preference, your citations will be either inline (the author-date system) or separate (the note reference system). Each system has its limitations. ***Author-date*** citations reduce the need for notes but they are a classic 'speed bump'; too many citations can make a text unreadable. At a glance the reading experience with ***note reference*** citations is much smoother, but a conscientious reader will be constantly distracted by the need to leave the body text, locate the relevant note and read its citation. Most readers choose not to do this and, as a consequence miss any comments made in a 'content' note.[1] Where possible, combine citations to reduce their distractive effect.

Notes. It is unlikely that you will have any great say in whether your book is typeset with footnotes or endnotes but as far as your manuscript is concerned you should be free to use either form. Create your notes by using the 'insert note' function in your word processor. This will mean that numbering and the link between note marker and note remain dynamic and can be updated easily. Do not write long notes; they are welcomed neither by publishers nor by readers.

1 The solution could be to use endnotes *and* footnotes, burying citations in the end notes but keeping the occasional comment close at hand in a footnote. Not many books have been published using this approach, though.

Cross-references. These are a potentially counter-productive diversion for your reader. Having frequently to flick backwards and forwards in the book is annoying, but a few well-placed cross-references can be useful. For the rest, make sure that you have an excellent index to help your reader locate again that interesting point you made. Cross-references may also be problematic for the author since there is a risk that the text that you are referring to has been moved – or even deleted. And because the pagination of your manuscript will never match that of the finished typeset book, you cannot insert actual page numbers in a cross-reference. Instead, you should refer to entities like 'Chapter 3' or 'Table 5.1'. Given their problems, cross-references should only be used where there is a significant benefit to the reader.

References/Bibliography. This should be restricted to a reference list that helps readers find out more about the subject. There is no need to include everything that has ever been written on the subject. Usually, a bibliography also lists every work cited in the book, but arguably this is not necessary if the full citation is found in a note. (Such a pruned list might better be given the title 'Further Reading' as it is in this book.) Order your list alphabetically by author, then chronologically if there is more than one work by an author (if you use the author-date reference, you must identify works from the same year of publication using a, b, c, etc.). For Internet references, put the date the web page was accessed in lieu of a publication date. Format your references (i.e. capitalization, order of elements, etc.) in a rigidly consistent manner so that if changes are required these are more easily made.

Non-text elements

Pictures may say more than a thousand words but they also interrupt the narrative, as do tables, charts and graphs. In each case, ask yourself whether this interruption to the flow of text is necessary, appropriate and desirable.

Keep separate. It is common for authors to embed tables and even illustrations in their chapter document, usually at the point they should be placed in the book, but handling is easier and picture quality better if each has its own file with just an insertion point marked in the body text (e.g., 'INSERT TABLE 3.1 ABOUT HERE').

Tables. A common mistake made by authors is to attempt to cram more data into their tables than is feasible. Worse, some tables barely fit a manuscript page but somehow are expected to fit on to a book page of half the size. In fact, a short table may be better summarized in the text while longer ones could perhaps be more profitably placed in an appendix. Consider, too, if a table is really the most effective way of presenting your information or if a chart or graph might be preferable. While it is aesthetically more pleasing to number tables consecutively for the whole book, in practical terms you may find consecutive numbering by chapter a far easier and more flexible arrangement. Never format your tables with the space bar. Right-align numbers and line up the decimal points. Notes relating to a table should be organized separately (best marked by symbols to distinguish them from your ordinary note markers in the body text).

Figures and illustrations. It will be your responsibility as the author to furnish your publisher with sharp-focus illustrations of the best possible quality. Their resolution will need to be at least 300 dpi at full size. Do not expect the publisher or printer to improve on quality that is lacking in the first place. Sub-standard line drawings, charts and graphs can be redrawn but it might be a point of contention whether author or publisher should take on this job (or pay for it to be done). You will probably be expected to deliver any illustrations electronically with a hard-copy backup. Many publishers' websites list their detailed and specific requirements as to format and delivery. Unless you have agreed with your publisher that some or all of your illustrations are to be printed in colour, any colour illustrations you submit will be converted to monochrome, so make sure they will still be meaningful in black and white. A 'quick and dirty' quality check can be made by photocopying any illustration you are in doubt about.

Graphic images and their formats

Essentially, there are two types of graphic images.

Bitmapped (or rasterized) images are made up of thousands or millions of pixels; the higher the printing resolution, the greater the density of pixels, hence 'dpi' (dots per inch). Key points are:

- High-resolution bitmapped images can be huge: many megabytes in size.
- Bitmapped images do not scale well as the original arrangement of their pixels needs to be resampled to the new size. Scale too far and the image becomes grainy. Similarly, the more an image is edited, the greater it degrades.
- Bitmapped formats are especially good to depict images with subtle gradations in colour, tone and density (photographs, for instance).
- Adobe Photoshop is the leading program for editing such files.
- The most common formats are TIFF, JPEG and BMP. Publishers use TIFF as this is a high-quality, open standard. JPEG is popular with authors (especially because this is the format of most photographs from digital cameras) but, being a file-compression format, it is not ideal. BMP is a format not readily usable outside a Windows PC. Publishers convert both JPEG and BMP files to TIFF.

Vector-based (or object-oriented) images use thousands of mathematical equations to define objects made up of points, lines, curves and polygons. Key points are:

- Because they are made up of lines of code, not actual pixels, these images can be quite compact in file size and yet be scaled up or down endlessly without distortion or degradation.

- Vector-based images are especially good for line drawings and other illustrations (like logos) with sharp, clear lines and solid colours.
- Adobe Illustrator and Corel Draw are the leading programs for creating and editing such files.
- The most common *open* format is EPS. You should avoid submitting artwork to your publisher with the proprietary AI or CDR formats created by Adobe Illustrator and Corel Draw, especially since these programs can save files in EPS format.

Other technical issues

Colour. With recent developments in printing technology, the cost of colour printing has dropped dramatically, but printing a book in colour still costs almost twice as much as printing in black and white only. Given the tight margins of academic publishing, colour printing throughout a book is rare. Instead, books are sometimes published with all of the colour illustrations grouped together in a colour section. If your book will include some colour illustrations, you must ensure that the colour quality is especially good; tonal imbalances in a grayscale image are far less obvious than all the many things (like over-exposure and colour imbalance) that can go wrong with a colour image. Be aware that images with an RGB (red–green–blue)

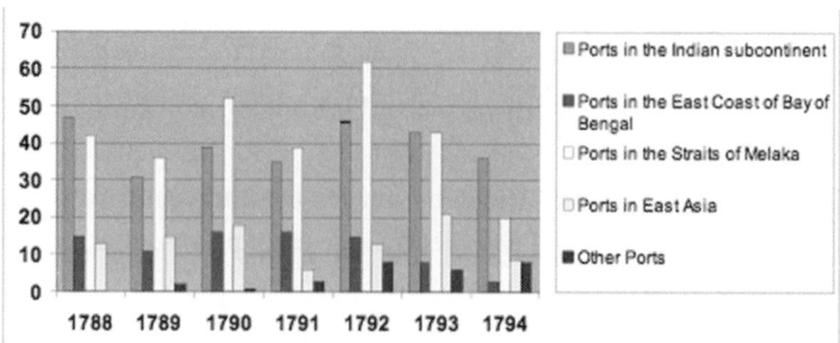

Beware of low-contrast illustrations which may look fine as a colour photograph but which risk losing all definition when converted to black/white. This chart was close to useless without colour and had to be redrawn using patterns.

colour profile, which is optimized for on-screen viewing, may appear less vibrant when converted to the CMYK (cyan–magenta–yellow–key [black]) colour profile required for printing. Do not expect your publisher to devote as much time, love and care as you or your technically savvy friend would in converting your RGB images to CMYK and optimizing them to the highest quality.

Computer operating system. Given the convergence of standards between Windows and the Mac OS in recent years, it should be irrelevant which type of computer you write your manuscript on.[2] Most typesetters and printers work on Mac machines which are fortunately very good at handling Windows files. That said, in a few instances there can still be compatibility problems between the two platforms. The most common are that standard fonts in older versions of Windows and documents produced in older versions of Word can be incompatible or very difficult to convert. These are 'old' problems, though, so if you have a recent computer and up-to-date software, you are unlikely to meet with problems.

Non-Western input issues. Not all text is written using the standard Latin fonts nor is it input in ways commonly used in the West. There are two issues here: operating system and input method. In many instances, a writer uses a Western-style operating system but keys in non-Latin script via a special input utility. Western scholars working with Chinese material will be familiar and comfortable with this approach (and provided fonts are Unicode compliant, there should be no serious problems). However, in some languages such as Arabic, text is entered from right to left and in many countries this is handled by using locally configured operating systems and keyboards. There is no problem if the typesetting and printing take place in the same operating environment, but there are *major* problems in importing

2 We should include Linux in this analysis but our experience here is quite limited. Our *understanding*, however, is that Linux (which like the modern Mac OS derives from UNIX) is also converging with the two other (major) operating systems.

right-to-left text into a left-to-right operating system. Publishers without experience of how to resolve these difficult issues often refuse to touch right-to-left works, which seriously reduces the pool of potential outlets for the author.

Word processor. Microsoft Word dominates the market for word-processors, but there are very good alternatives available (not least WordPerfect, Nisus Writer and – a fast-growing open-source rival – OpenOffice). For now, though, Word remains the 20-tonne gorilla in the playground. Whichever software you use, it must be compatible with Word because that is what your publisher's editorial staff are likely to be using. *Never* prepare your text using page layout software like Adobe InDesign or Quark Express. They are for laying out pages, not for processing words. You would not use hedge shears to trim your toenails either, would you?

Word processor settings. Most word processors have settings or preferences that tell the program to check your spelling and grammar, hyphenate your text, and auto-correct the entry of text. Word, for instance, has a huge array of auto-correction features selected by default, many of them annoying to specialist writers. Check out your word processor, identify those features you want and those that you do not, and fine-tune the options to help you in your writing.

Security. It goes without saying that you *must* back up your work very regularly to a secure storage device (preferably more than one). Make it a habit to run a back-up at least once a day. The rationally paranoid might want to ensure that back-up copies are kept in several locations in case of fire or other total destruction.

APPENDIX 2

Common editing and proof-reading marks

The following list of editing and proof-reading symbols is not exhaustive, nor does it cover every eventuality. However, we have listed the most common marks (both international and local variants) that you will encounter during the editing and proofing of your book.

Instruction	Mark in text / example		... in margin	Effect
Italicize	(text)	this was the idea	or ital	this *was* the idea
Make bold	(text)	Introduction	or bold or bf	**Introduction**
... bold-italic	(text)	Introduction	or bf+ italic	***Introduction***
... roman	(text)	this *was* the idea	or or rom	this was the idea
Capitalize	(text)	the red menace	≡ or caps	the Red menace
Small caps	(text)	in 55 B.C.	= or s.c.	in 55 B.C.
Lower case	(text)	of State power	or or l.c.	of state power
Wrong font	(text)	It is best that	⊗ or w.f.	It is best that
Spell out	(text)	the UN met in	spell out	the United Nations m
Leave as is	(text)	this is not right	✓ or stet	this is not right
Insert text	⋌ or ∧	gave to dog	(text)⋌	the⋌	gave to the dog
Delete text	/ or ⊢⊣	to his ~~his~~ dog	or	to his dog
Replace text	/ or ⊢⊣	to ~~his~~ dog	(new text)/	her/	to her dog

Instruction	Mark in text / example		... in margin	Effect
Insert space	⋌ or ∧	gave to⋌the dog	Y or #	gave to the dog
Close up	⁀‿	send ing home	⁀‿	sending home
Delete and close up	(text)	it is now on-line	⁀‿	it is now online
Insert/replace with period	⋌ or /	ended/In 1991	⊙	ended. In 1991
... comma	⋌ or /	Indeed/in the far	,	Indeed, in the far
... colon	⋌ or /	had one aim/to	⊙	had one aim: to
... semi-colon	⋌ or /	fast/It was also	; (here with ≢)	fast; it was also
... single	⋌ or /	a case of /moi/	‘ ’ or ‘ ’	a case of ‘moi’
... double	⋌ or /	said, ‘It is/in/ not	“ ” or “ ”	said, ‘It is “in” not
... hyphen	⋌ or /	the proof/reading	⊢⊣	the proof-reading
... apostrophe	⋌ or /	the printer/s proof	’ or ’	the printer’s proof
... parentheses	⋌ or /	or/we think/a pig	(/ /)	or (we think) a pig
Chg hyphen to n-dash	/ or N or N/	1789/1815	N or N (with /)	1789–1815
... m-dash	/ or M or M/	in Paris/-if not	M or M (with /)	in Paris—if not in
Transpose	⊔⊓	were not it for	⊔⊓ or tr or trs	were it not for
Indent paragraph	⊏	is unclear or needs fine-tuning. The copy-editor also functions as a	⊏ or □	is unclear or needs fine-tuning. The copy-editor also functions as a
Align text	‖	• Check the changes • Answer all queries • Advise your editor	‖	• Check the changes • Answer all queries • Advise your editor
New paragraph	⌐ or ¶ or //	fine-tuning. The copy-editor also functions as a	⌐ or n.p. or ¶	fine-tuning. The copy-editor also functions as a
Merge paragraphs	↩	fine-tuning. The copy-editor also functions as a	↩ or run on or runover	fine-tuning. The copy-editor also functions as a

APPENDIX 3

Compendium of publishing terms

This extended glossary covers not only words that you may have come across in this book but also a great number of technical terms that you could come across in dealing with your publisher. If a word appears in **bold** in an entry, this indicates a significant cross-reference to its own glossary entry.

Acid-free paper Paper with a pH value of 7.0 (neutral) or higher (alkaline). The key point however is that it is also free from wood-based impurities like lignin which react to heat and sunlight and cause the paper to turn yellow and become brittle. The best alkaline paper can last up to 1,000 years. To optimize the longevity of their collections, academic libraries prefer (and may only buy) books that are acid-free. In the US most university presses only print on **ISO**-certified alkaline paper. The label 'acid-free' is sometimes associated with **green publishing** but in fact most of the paper used in academic books today is acid-free and clear of any impurities; the difference is in the manufacturing process. Newspapers and trade fiction are printed on impure, often acidic paper that deteriorates rapidly.

Acknowledgements Text by the author thanking people for their help (or forbearance) in the preparation of the book. Thanking the publisher is unnecessary but it is fair and may be smart to express appreciation for outstanding support from individual press staff. (Believe it or not, one of the first things editors check in the final manuscript is if they are mentioned in the acknowledgements.) A very short acknowledgements section is too skimpy to stand alone and instead should be included in the **preface**.

Acquisitions editor *See* Commissioning editor.

Advance Money paid by a publisher to an author in advance of future **royalty** payments. Advances are normal in trade publishing but rare in academic publishing.

Advance copies Copies of a new publication received from the printer in advance of the main shipment and sent on to the author, to distributors and other key people (major book buyers and reviewers, for instance).

Advance information sheet Also known as AI or AIS. Single sheet of standard-size paper announcing a new publication to trade partners. The AI normally gives basic bibliographic details, key selling points, a blurb, cover image, brief author information and (not least) ordering/availability details. An example is shown in Chapter 10.

Advance orders Orders for a book received and recorded prior to publication. Publishers hope to build enough advance orders so that their release, when stock is first delivered to the warehouse, will cover the printing bill. Sometimes conflated with **back orders**.

Advisory board Group of scholars offering advice and support to the editors of a book series, journal, etc. *See also* Editorial board.

Agent (1) Person acting on behalf of the publisher (such as a **sales representative**). (2) Person acting on behalf of the author (usually a literary agent) who for a commission on all earnings finds a publisher for an author's work and acts as an intermediary, securing the best possible deal. Because earnings are so poor in academic publishing, such agents are almost unheard of. By contrast, in trade publishing they have taken on much of the gatekeeping role of commissioning editors, so getting accepted by an agent is often a crucial step towards getting published.

AI (or AIS) *See* Advance information sheet.

Alkaline paper *See* Acid-free paper

All rights reserved Note on the **copyright page** indicating that the publisher holds all **rights** in the book.

Appendix Supplementary material relating (but not essential) to the work and placed in the **back matter**. Increasingly, such material is being placed online rather than in an appendix.

Arabic numbering Numerals like 1, 2, 3, etc. used for pagination of a book's body text (as opposed to **roman numbering**).

Artwork (1) Illustrative materials like photographs, line drawings, charts, etc. prepared for reproduction. (2) Finished pages laid out with all text, illustrations and other elements incorporated.

Author Writer of a book or article. Note that this glossary often refers to the author in situations when it is equally applicable to volume **editors**.

Author alterations *See* Author corrections.

Author contract Contract between author and publisher defining rights and obligations between the parties, and formalizing **copyright** and transfer of the publishing rights from author to publisher.

Author copies Copies of a book that are given to an author by the publisher free of charge as per the terms of their author contract. These are among the **advance copies** sent out at (or even before) publication.

Author corrections Changes to the **proofs** made by the author. Traditionally, these corrections were made in blue with typesetter and printer errors marked in red. As per their contract, authors may be charged for 'excessive' changes to the final proofs.

Author-date system System of referencing based on a unique combination of author surname and year of publication (e.g. Patel, 2007), also known as the Harvard system. As opposed to the **note reference system**.

Author details Brief description of who the author is, including affiliation and previous publications. This is usually written by the publisher after referring to the **author questionnaire**. Used on publicity material like advance information sheets as well as on the back cover, its key purpose is to convince the reader that the author is a credible (and interesting) writer on the subject.

Author discount Discount rate at which authors can buy further copies of their own books (over and above their author copies), often around 40 per cent. Author sales can be a good source of extra income for publishers, who may also offer their authors a favourable discount on purchases of other books from their list.

Author questionnaire Detailed questionnaire that an author is asked to complete by the publisher, often delivered together with the author contract. Some publishers will refuse to begin work on the book until this questionnaire has been completed and returned. As well as asking for contact details, etc., it also seeks information that will help the publisher position the book (in terms of format and price) and develop a promotional strategy.

Author's proofs Output from typesetting in the form of page proofs sent to the author for checking (a matching copy will likely be sent to the publisher for simultaneous checking). It is common for authors to receive two sets of proofs: first proofs and second (or final) proofs. Today the author may not receive a hard copy but instead gets a PDF of these proofs, which are *not* the same as **printer's proofs**.

Availability An important status indicator for the book trade. While publishers may be happy to build up advance orders and back orders for a title, some online retailers refuse to take orders for a book (or even list it) unless copies are actually available (i.e. its status is 'available'). Two common notations for unavailable titles are **Not Yet Published** and **Out of Print**.

B/W (or B&W) Black and white (of illustrations), printed in black and tints of black only. Such images have a **grayscale** format (not a **bit-mapped** one). *See also* Colour.

Back (1) The **back cover**. (2) The book's **spine**, hence such styles of binding as 'rounded back' and 'square back'. (3) The **back margin**.

Back blurb *See* Blurb.

Back cover The **cover** on the back of the book, on which the **blurb**, the **ISBN** and **bar code**, and the publisher's **colophon** appear, often together with an endorsement and author details. (The back of this book is fairly typical of an academic book.) The back cover is far less likely to be illustrated than the **front cover**.

Back flap The flap of a dust **jacket** that folds around the back cover of a jacketed (hardback) book. A convention is to place the author details here. As opposed to the **front flap**.

Backlist Books published two or more seasons ago, sometimes called a back catalogue. This is where **long tail** sales come from.

Back margin The inside margin (or **gutter**), i.e. that part of the page closest to the spine. If this margin is too narrow then, after trimming and binding, the danger is that the two facing text areas will be too close together, making the book difficult to read.

Back matter *See* End matter

Back orders Orders received and recorded for a published (backlist) title that is (temporarily) unavailable. Sometimes conflated with **advance orders**.

Bar code Symbolic, machine-readable representation of a book's **ISBN**, sometimes (especially in the US) with the retail price built in. The bar code generally appears in the bottom-right corner of the back cover (see the back cover of this book for an example).

Bastard title *See* Half-title

Berne Convention The international agreement on **copyright**, instigated by Victor Hugo and originally signed in 1886. This built on earlier national copyright laws that only protected authors' economic interests by seeking to uphold and protect the creative rights of authors. A key feature was the protection of an author's copyright not only in their home country but also in every other country that is a signatory to the convention. At time of writing, more than 160 countries have acceded to the Berne Convention.

Bibliographic data All of the descriptive details about a book that are advised to the book trade and libraries for the purposes of identifying, cataloguing and promoting that title. Such bibliographic details can be more or less 'rich' and comprise title, subtitle, names of author/editor(s), illustrator(s) and translator(s), extent, number of images, maps, tables and figures, physical size and weight, binding and casing, edition number, series, imprint, ISBN, etc. Also included may be cover/jacket images and long/short blurbs.

Bibliography List of all books and other published materials used in the preparation of a written work. In more instructional books sometimes replaced, as in this book, by a section entitled 'Further Reading'.

BIC codes **ISO**-approved Book Industry Communication codes developed for the British book industry but now also used elsewhere to classify books by subject to a quite detailed level. These are used by bibliographic database services and are often the basis on which booksellers organize and order their stock.

Binding (1) Type/method of binding (perfect, burst, etc.). (2) Process in which a book is bound. (3) Cover material used in the binding (cloth, paper, etc.). (4) Hence also denotes the edition (hardback or paperback).

Bit-mapped (1) B/W format using black or white pixels only (no gray shadings). (2) *See* Rasterized.

Bleed Material (usually illustrations) extending up to and slightly beyond the trimmed edge of the page. As bleeds require a larger printed area, printers may charge more to print books with bleeds.

Blocking Stamping text, designs, etc. on a cloth cover, often using gold leaf (hence 'blocking text').

Blog From 'web log'. A type of website with a series of postings by one or more 'bloggers', often with a facility for readers to post comments. Postings are normally displayed in reverse chronological order (latest post first). Often, their content combines text with images (including embedded videos) and tools allowing the reader to index the material or submit it for attention/promotion on social networking sites. Dealing with any subject under the sun, blogs range from simple personal journals to sophisticated serial treatments of specific subjects. Blogs are the most explosive growth area on the Internet with over 110 million blogs indexed and about 60,000 new blogs launched each day. Unsurprisingly, blogs and their bloggers increasingly attract the attention of publishers' marketing departments who see the huge potential of their ability to 'speak' to large focused readerships.

Blues/blueprints *See* Printer's proofs.

Blurb Short text piece describing a book, used in marketing material and on the back cover (as the back blurb).

Body (1) The **body text**. (2) The **body pages**.

Body matter Another term for **body pages** (as opposed to **front matter** and **end matter**).

Body pages The main pages of a book (i.e. excluding the **prelims/ front matter** and often, but not always, the **end matter**).

Body text (1) The text block on a page, excluding running heads, etc. (2) The **running text** of a book.

Body type Font used for the main part of the text (excluding headings, captions, etc.).

Book (1) Set of printed sheets of paper bound together within covers. (2) **Title**.

Book block The printed pages of the book that have been folded, gathered and sewn in readiness for the actual binding.

Book buyer Person who decides which titles are to be stocked by a bookshop. Such people from the larger bookselling chains exercise considerable power, especially in trade publishing.

Book club Club whose members are often committed to buy a minimum number of books per year but who buy these at especially low prices. Book clubs are now in decline but were once a useful source of added income for publishers. Typically, book club editions are sold by the publisher at little more than cost so author royalties are not large. However, the increased **printrun** significantly decreases the unit cost of all copies printed.

Book design Specification by a book designer of how a book should look after typesetting, i.e. instructions and illustrations of the page layout, and of how the different elements of the book are to be arranged and relate to each other. Ideally, the cover design is an integral part of this process, but often in fact this is made separately.

Book designer Person, frequently the typesetter, producing the book design (and sometimes the cover design).

Book fair Large meetings of book trade professionals where publishers come to exhibit their latest titles and to buy/sell rights;

where printers, distributors, library suppliers, content aggregators and many others (like Google and Microsoft) aim to sell their services to publishers; and where librarians, booksellers, authors, agents and (often at restricted times) the general public come to browse. The world's leading book fair is held each October in Frankfurt but every month there will be several fairs held somewhere in the world, most regional but some specializing in a specific type of publishing (most notably Bologna for children's publishing).

Book proofs *See* Bound proofs.

Book trade The industry whose business is the making and selling of books.

Bookbinder Person (more usually a company) binding books.

Bookseller (1) Bookshop. (2) The owner, manager or leading person in a bookshop.

Border (1) The frame around, say, a figure. (2) The **margin**.

Bound proofs Page proofs that are bound and used to promote a book, e.g. to key booksellers and journalists. This practice is common in trade publishing but rare in academic publishing.

Boxed set Set of books packaged within a **slip case**.

Break The point at which a word is split at the end of a line, hence 'bad breaks' and 'line breaks'. Conversely, a break line is the last line of a paragraph.

Breakeven point The point, expressed in the number of copies required to be sold, at which costs are exactly covered by income.

Camel case Long words or word strings with multiple upper case 'humps' that help distinguish the individual elements (e.g. WordPerfect and PriceWaterhouseCooper). As opposed to upper and lower case.

Camera-ready copy (CRC) The finalized typeset book pages (or sometimes finished artwork) ready for delivery to the printer. Originally this was delivered as hard copy that was manually filmed, hence the name. Today, when authors produce their own CRC, this is usually delivered as a **PDF** file; direct filming is now rare.

Caption Title or descriptive text of an illustration or other figure, placed adjacent to it.

Case (1) The hard cover of a hardback book, often covered with **cloth** (with stamped spine text) and protected by a jacket. As an alternative to cloth, the book may have a **printed paper case**. (2) The form of lettering, i.e. upper and lower case (and the slightly tongue-in-cheek **camel case**).

Cased (1) Edition that is hardback, or cloth bound. (2) **Boxed set**.

Cast off Precise estimation of the extent of a book based on page size, word/character count, typefaces (and their size) to be used and number/type of illustrations and tables.

Catalogue (1) Detailed listing of a publisher's titles sent to booksellers, libraries, institutions, etc. with the purpose of promoting and facilitating sales. Typically, these only include recent and forthcoming titles. Smaller presses normally produce only one catalogue annually whereas it is common for larger presses (especially US university presses) to produce two seasonal catalogues. Large publishers may additionally or alternatively produce annual subject catalogues for key market segments. (2) Publisher's **list**, hence sometimes a backlist is referred to as a back catalogue.

Cataloguing in Publication (CIP) The system whereby, prior to publication, publishers pass details of new books to the British Library, US Library of Congress or other appropriate institution. They receive back a catalogue record, a **CIP data** block, for insertion on the copyright page. This speeds up cataloguing of the book by purchasing libraries and helps ensure that the job is done correctly. However, not all publishers have the time (or perhaps inclination) to offer this information, hence one often sees merely a note that 'A catalogue record for this book is available from the British Library'.

Character set All of the characters available in a font.

Characters per line The number of characters including spaces filling one line in a column of type. This is an important factor in **readability**, with 66 cpl regarded as an ideal column width.

Check digit *See* ISBN.

CIP data The catalogue record resulting from the **Cataloguing in Publication** process and normally inserted on the **copyright page**. An example can be found on page iv of this volume.

Cloth (-bound) Hardback, or cased. Today, the boards used for hardbacks are rarely covered with real cloth; more durable synthetic material is used instead.

CMYK Cyan, magenta, yellow and key (black), the four primary colours used in colour printing. *See also* Colour.

Coated paper Paper that has been given a coating on one or both sides, making it smooth and glossy. Such paper is used for book covers, jackets, colour sections and for the body pages if the book has many high-quality images.

Co-edition Edition of a book produced by (or for) a co-publisher. Often the only difference between the different co-editions are the cover/jacket and pages i–iv of the **prelims**, i.e. those parts identifying the publisher and stating the **ISBN** and **bar code**.

Co-publication The practice of two or more publishers publishing the same title at the same time, each in their own territory and under their own imprint. Thus, the book can look as if it has been locally produced when in fact the common practice is for a **co-edition** to be produced. The publisher who commissions and produces the book is known as the **originating publisher**, while partners who purchase copies of the co-edition or buy the right to print their own copies are known as co-publishers.

Co-publisher *See* Co-publication.

Collaborative publishing A once rare but increasingly fashionable **Web 2.0** form of group authorship often combined with self-publishing. Normally, authors use web-based tools like **Wikis** to produce collaborative content that often is then made freely available for others to use (through **open source publishing**) but with a **Creative Commons** licence. This shares similarities with but is not the same as traditional joint authorship, in which multiple authors write, exchange and critique each other's text (the method used to produce this volume).

Colophon (1) Publisher's or printer's identifying emblem, their logo. (2) Brief details about a book's or a journal's printer, where it was printed and sometimes the number of copies printed. In many countries these details are placed on a separate **colophon page** but increasingly this information is integrated into the **copyright page** as per British and American usage, while in journals it is often located on the inside cover page.

Colophon page (1) Normally the last page of a book on which the printer places their colophon (both meanings as above). (2) Common but incorrect name for the **copyright page**.

Colour Use of colour can be a major source of technical difficulty between authors and publishers caused by differences between **colour formats** and forms of **colour reproduction**. Not least, misunderstandings and errors arise because there is a marked difference between how a colour appears on screen versus on paper. Also, within each format, there are added variations (screen output is dependent on which computer operating system and version is used as well as settings on the computer monitor such as brightness and contrast; output from ink-jet, laser and lithographic printers are all different). The different base colours of **RGB** and **CMYK** formats are an added factor. The cost of **four-colour printing** has fallen but still remains high (printing costs can be doubled), so publishers are reluctant to use colour on the inside pages without good reason. If colour illustrations are unavoidable, costs can be reduced by grouping these illustrations into separate **colour sections**.

Colour format How an image is to be reproduced determines its format. Images that are to be printed in black and white will be **grayscale** while those printed in black and a **spot colour** will be formatted as **duotones**. Full-colour images for printing must have a **CMYK** profile (though the actual colours assigned may be spot colours and/or the four CMYK primary colours), while colour images to be displayed on screen must have an **RGB** profile.

Colour printing *See* Four-colour printing.

Colour proof Part of the **printer's proofs**, a copy of the jacket and/or cover with a close approximation of what the final printed copies will look like.

Colour reproduction Colour is reproduced on your computer screen by projection of **RGB** primary colour lights at varying intensities to create secondary colours. Colour is reproduced on paper quite differently, usually by overprinting of the four **CMYK** primary colours, but **duotones** and **spot colours** can be substituted.

Colour section Grouping of colour illustrations into a single **signature** that is printed in colour while the rest of the book is printed in black and white, thus saving on printing costs.

Colour separations Full-colour printing first requires separation of the four CMYK primary colours on to separate printing **plates**, one plate per colour.

Commission (1) The percentage-based fee payable to a **sales representative** or other **agent**, such as on the value of orders obtained or fulfilled. (2) To define a book project and find an author/editor to take it on.

Commissioned work Work conceived by the publisher, with its execution contracted to an author/editor.

Commissioning editor In the US often known as an acquisitions editor. A person who acquires the titles making up a publisher's list, by active commissioning of new projects and/or selecting from among the book projects submitted by authors. This key person in a publishing house may also take on the role as **publisher**.

Complimentary copies Free copies of the work sent by the publisher as a form of payment (e.g. author and reader copies) or in order to promote sales (e.g. review copies) or register the book with central libraries. Such 'frees' can comprise as much as ten per cent of the **printrun**.

Composition *See* Typesetting

Concordance file Document with a list of indexing terms used to generate an automatic index.

(On) Consignment (1) Books supplied by a publisher to a bookseller for normal sale but for an agreed period without payment unless and until sold. (2) Books held by a distributor on a publisher's behalf, i.e. the books remain the property of the publisher.

Content (1) Generally, the text and illustrative matter of a book. (2) Now also commonly used to refer to the **e-content** of an electronic publication.

Content aggregators Companies like NetLibrary which create vast digital libraries of journal articles, book chapters, etc. supplied by client publishers and sold as **e-content** to scholars and other readers, often on a **page-view payment** basis.

Contract *See* author contract

Copy (1) Text for publication, hence 'final copy', 'copy-editor', etc. *See also* Camera-ready copy. (2) Advertising text (or **blurb**).

Copy fitting Determining how (by adjusting font, font size, image scaling, etc.) the delivered amount of text, illustrations and other matter can be fitted into the allocated page size and extent.

Copy-editing Preparation of the manuscript for typesetting by correcting errors, applying the house style and indicating paragraph formats. Traditionally done on paper, increasingly this work is done on screen and often is outsourced.

Copy-editing marks *See* Correction marks.

Copy-editor Editor who carries out the copy-editing, often a freelancer.

Copyright This is literally the 'right to copy' an original work in a particular format. Normally, the author retains **moral rights** in the work but signs over to the publisher those publication **rights** whose formats or usage are covered by the **author contract** (usually full copyright in the work). On the expiry of its copyright protection, a work enters the **public domain**.

Copyright deposit *See* Deposit library.

Copyright notice Line on the **copyright page** stating who owns the **copyright** and the date of ownership. If a book appears after the end of September, publishers often put the next year's date here as it may be months before the book is actually available around the world; in so doing, they avoid having a book on its **release date** looking like last year's book.

Copyright page The back side of the **title page** (i.e. page iv of the **prelims**), also commonly called the imprint page or title verso (and sometimes misleadingly referred to as the colophon page).

Crucially, this page carries the copyright notice, ISBN, place of publication, date of first publication (and of the edition in hand), and publisher details plus (ideally) the **CIP data**. This page can become very crowded because it may also give fuller details like the publisher's address, **originating publisher** (if any), **typesetter** and main **typefaces** used, edition/printing history, printer and place printed, paper used (and statement if this is recycled or acid-free), and a credit line (for a cover illustration, subvention, etc.).

Correction marks Internationally recognized signs inserted in the text and margins to indicate required changes, used by editors and typesetters. The most commonly used of these are reproduced in Appendix 2.

Cost of sales All the costs incurred in getting a book to market, including for manufacturing, transport, marketing, etc. plus the author **royalty**.

Costing Calculation of all manufacturing, marketing and distribution costs plus likely author **royalty**, used to assess a book's commercial feasibility and determine its price.

Cover (1) Generally, the outside of the book. (2) More commonly, the outside of a paperback, though note that a hardback also has a cover (or **case**), often protected by a **jacket**.

Cover designer Person, often not the **book designer**, producing the cover and/or jacket design.

cpl *See* Characters per line.

Crop (1) To cut away part of an illustration. (2) To trim the printed pages after binding to their final size.

Crop marks *See* Printer's marks

CRC *See* Camera-ready copy

Creative Commons (1) New system of 'copyleft' licensing aimed at flexible handling of **copyright** protection for all kinds of creative work. As opposed to **digital rights management**. (2) The nonprofit organization managing and promoting this system.

Crossover titles Titles that have the potential to be of interest to more than one market, e.g. an academic book that also has local historical interest.

Cut marks *See* Printer's marks

Cutline *See* Caption.

CV Curriculum vitae, or resumé.

Dash *See* Em-dash; En-dash.

Dedication Brief note by the author dedicating the book to someone. This normally appears on the right-hand page opposite the **copyright page**, followed by a blank page. Publishers have been known to place the dedication elsewhere if space is tight.

Deposit library National library with which publishers are required by law to deposit copies of every book they publish in that country.

Design brief The material, specifications and design wishes passed on to the book/cover designer.

Desk copy Free copy of a book sent to someone who may want to (1) buy rights or (2) adopt the text for course use (also known as a reading copy).

Desk editor In-house editor who assists the **commissioning editor** and undertakes **copy-editing** and related work. In small presses this person might also carry out the work of the **production manager**.

Desktop publishing (DTP) Typesetting of a book or other work using a personal computer (and often its printing on a laser printer). DTP software has made it far easier for authors to **self-publish** their works to a professional standard.

Diacritical marks Accents and other modifiers to the standard roman alphabet, in earlier times (before modern **Open Type fonts**) often detested by publishers for the difficulty of typesetting these correctly.

Diazos *See* Printer's proofs.

Die casting (Now obsolete.) Casting of metal type using hot metal.

Digital printing As opposed to **lithographic printing**, direct printing of computer output often with technologies that avoid the need to create films, **plates**, etc. These use different output media, the most common of which is toner (as found in laser printers and photocopiers). Of the estimated 45 trillion pages printed around the world in 2005, only 9 per cent were printed digitally, but that proportion will almost certainly have increased since.

Digital rights management (DRM) (Often technological) measures taken by publishers or **copyright** owners to control access to or usage of digital data, e.g. by identification, trading, licensing, protection and monitoring. As opposed to the **Creative Commons** approach. *See also* Open Access; Open source.

Digitization Creation of **e-content** from previously printed (often **out-of-print**) titles.

Direct marketing Marketing communications sent direct to the end user, in the case of academic publishing either individual scholars or university libraries.

Discount *See* Trade discount.

Display (1) Specially printed promotional material, e.g. banners and posters. (2) Stand (booth, stall) at a book fair or academic conference. Also known as an exhibit.

Display type Large-size type used for display material.

Distributor Company (often another publisher) selling a publisher's list in a specific territory, frequently on an exclusive basis.

Domain *See* Public domain.

Dots per inch *See* dpi.

Double-page spread *See* Spread.

dpi Dots per inch, a measure of **resolution** for printing and scanning (hence of image resolution). Most academic works are printed at 300 dpi, so normally full-size illustrations need not be created at a higher resolution.

DRM *See* Digital rights management

DTP *See* Desktop publishing

Dues *See* Advance orders.

Duotone Typically, overprinting with black and one **spot colour** to create an economical colour cover. This practice is disappearing as the cost of four-colour printing is falling below that of manually setting up a printer with the inks for spot colour.

Dust cover *See* Jacket

E-book (1) Electronic book, i.e. a book-length work delivered in digital rather than printed form. (2) **E-reader**.

E-content Electronic content, i.e. a digital copy of all or part of the contents of a book, journal article or other work. Increasingly, such material is being sold for on-screen viewing or download to an e-reader.

E-publishing Publication of e-content, often in tandem with print publication.

E-reader Device used to store and display digital material. Some e-publishing advocates believe that in time e-readers will replace the printed book but to date adoption of these devices has been hindered by a high price, awkward construction, poor reading experience and lack of suitable e-content.

Edited volume Book to which several contributors have each provided chapters or the like for one or more editors to fashion into one volume.

Edition (1) Different bindings in which a title is available, e.g. 'hardback edition'. (2) Different versions of the same title, e.g. 'second revised edition'.

Editor Generic title for all sorts of people, most either found in the editorial/production departments or working as freelancers, e.g. **commissioning editor**, **desk editor**, **copy-editor** and production editor (**production manager**).

Editorial assistant Publisher's employee who assists (and often works as an understudy to) the **commissioning editor** as well as undertaking some of the work typically the responsibility of a **desk editor**.

Editorial board Group of scholars and/or publishing professionals who formally decide on which titles are to be published by a press. *See also* Advisory board.

Educational publishing (1) The publishing of educational material for students of all ages. (2) Sometimes understood to be publishing focused mainly on the schools market, hence excluding (tertiary) textbook publishing.

Electronic content *See* E-content.

Electronic publishing *See* E-publishing.

Electronic rights The right to reproduce the book in electronic form.

Em-dash Or em-rule (—), used as a separator in text, especially in US usage.

En-dash Or en-rule (–), used to indicate range and as a separator in text.

End matter All the elements of a book that follow the main text, such as **appendices**, **glossary**, **bibliography**, **index**, etc. As opposed to the front matter (or **prelims**).

End papers The sheets glued in to hide the join between a hardback case and the text pages within it. Sometimes these are coloured and/or decorative.

Endorsements Complimentary quotes about the book from prestigious or expert sources, printed on the **cover** or **jacket** of the book (and in trade publishing sometimes continued inside the book).

Errata slip Slip of paper inserted into a printed book listing important mistakes in the text noticed since publication. Insertion of such slips is annoying because it is expensive and indicates that the proofs were not properly checked before publication.

Escalator clause Clause in an **author contract** that allows for higher **royalty** rates as sales increase above set levels.

Exhibit *See* Display.

Export sales Sales outside the home market (as opposed to **home sales**), often itemized separately in royalty statements.

Extent The length of a book in pages, including the prelims. In printing terms, the extent equals the whole number of **signatures** to be printed (i.e. including any blank pages at the end of the last signature).

Face *See* Typeface.

Fair dealing/fair use (1) Convention not grounded in law allowing an author to use excerpts from **copyright** material without payment for the purposes of study, research, criticism or review. (2) Lawful photocopying of copyright texts for personal use and private study but not for sale or classroom use. *See also* Permissions.

Feasibility report Evaluation of the commercial profitability of and practical issues in publishing a book.

File copy Reference copy of a published book held in the publisher's archive.

Final proofs Finalized proofs of the book from the typesetter, usually delivered as **page proofs** with any illustrations included and pagination finalized. These are the proofs used for **indexing**. *See also* Author proofs; Proofs.

Firm sales Sales made on a non-return basis, often in the case of high-discount sales.

First option/first refusal The requirement, as found in some author contracts, that an author gives the publisher first right of refusal on their next work.

First proofs Initial proofs of the book from the typesetter, sometimes still delivered in **galley** format. *See also* Author proofs; Proofs.

Flap text Jacket text (including **blurb**, photo credit and biographical notes about the author) appearing on the front and back flaps.

Flaps *See* Back flap; Front flap.

Flyer (or flier) Small leaflet used in book advertising.

Font (1) In common usage (and how it is used in this book), a **typeface/type family**. (2) More properly, the full set of characters of a typeface in a specific style (indeed, in earlier times, with specific weights), e.g. Baskerville semibold italic. A key feature of the digital revolution in publishing has been the huge advances in typographical design, not least the development of **Open Type fonts**.

Footers Text (if any) at the bottom of each page, usually just containing the page number. *See also* Running heads.

Foreword Introductory remarks appearing before the **preface** and normally written by someone other than the author, usually with the intention to add authority to the overall text. (The author's own introductory remarks should be placed in a preface or, if longer, in an introduction.)

Format (1) The binding or **edition** of a book, e.g. hardback. (2) The **trim size.** (3) General layout of the book page, e.g. 'a two-column format'. (4) To convert text, apply paragraph styles, etc.

Forthcoming Title that has been announced but not yet published.

Four-colour printing Reproduction of colour by the overprinting of the four **CMYK** primary colours. *See also* Duotone.

Freelancing Work undertaken on the publisher's behalf by an independent contractor, especially common for copy-editing, design and typesetting. *See also* Outsourcing.

Frees *See* Complimentary copies.

Front cover The front face of a book on which title and author name must appear. Can be a powerful element in promoting a book.

Front flap The flap of a **jacket** that folds around the front cover of a jacketed (hardback) book. A convention is to place a **blurb** here that is different from that on the back of the jacket. As opposed to the **back flap**.

Front list Publisher's forthcoming and recently published titles, i.e. those expected to earn the most income in the near future. Normally the front list is understood to comprise the current season's books plus all books published in the season immediately previous.

Front matter *See* Prelims. *See also* End matter.

Frontispiece An illustration placed on the **half-title verso** or **tipped in** here.

Full-colour printing *See* Four-colour printing.

Galley proofs Traditionally, **first proofs** of the book that are output on galleys (long, continuous sheets of paper). If pagination is indicated, these are called 'page on galley' proofs.

Glossary Alphabetical list of terms (with explanations) that appear in the book and are related to the subject matter.

Gratis copies *See* Complimentary copies.

Grayscale A **B/W** format using black, white and gray shades produced as **tints** of black.

Green publishing Environmentally friendly/sustainable publishing. Conventional publishing is anything but 'green' – paper production is particularly toxic, and the ethical fig leaves represented by the use of recycled and/or acid-free paper and vegetable dyes do not address the issue of the fuel-inefficient global transport of printed books. Electronic publishing is touted as a green alternative, but the Internet is hardly carbon-neutral either: server farms consume enormous amounts of energy, for instance.

gsm Grams per square metre. *See* Paper weight.

Gutter (1) The two inside margins of a book. (2) The gap between two columns.

Half-title The first printed page of a book (page i), carrying only its title. This is not the **title page**.

Half-title verso The left-hand page opposite the **title page** (page ii), often used to carry details of other books by the author or books in the same series.

Halftone A **grayscale** image or other object whose (unprintable) continuous tones are broken via screening into a pattern of various-sized printable dots barely visible to the eye. This is why scanning an illustration from a printed source gives a far inferior result as opposed to scanning the original illustration.

Hard copy (1) Material that has been printed out, as opposed to being provided as a computer file. (2) Finished pages ready for filming (i.e. **camera-ready copy**).

Hardback Book more likely aimed at the library market than at individuals, produced with a **cloth** cover (and jacket) or **printed paper case** cover and usually with a sewn binding.

Harvard system *See* Author-date system.

Headbands and tailbands *See* Wibbling.

Headers and footers *See* Running heads

Home sales Sales in the home market (as opposed to **export sales**), often itemized separately in **royalty** statements.

House style Author style guidelines as set by a publisher or journal. *See also* Style sheet

Illustration Colour/halftone image or line drawing. Publishers tend to be more concerned about image quality than by how many illustrations there are (though obviously a book's extent will be greater and typesetting/printing costs higher if there are many illustrations).

Imposition Arranging print-ready pages on a **sheet** immediately prior to **plate**-making so that, when the sheet is printed and folded, the pages will be in the correct order and orientation.

Impression *See* Printrun.

Imprint (1) Properly, the name and address of the publisher. (2) In effect, the publisher's brand. A publishing company may have several imprints depending on the type of books or markets, e.g. separate imprints for adult versus children's fiction or scholarly versus popular non-fiction.

In print Published and available for sale. As opposed to **out of print** and **not yet published**.

Index Detailed alphabetical list mapping the contents of a book and designed to help the reader find information quickly and easily. This is the last section of the **back matter**.

Indexing Preparation of an index, sometimes by professionals but usually by the author. As many academic libraries put an index near the top of their checklist when making purchasing decisions, academic publishers generally insist on their books having an index.

Inspection copy *See* Desk copy.

Introduction The beginning of an author's argument, following any **preface**, list of abbreviations, etc. The convention is that short introductions are placed at the end of the **prelims** while longer introductions form the opening chapter of the book.

ISBN International Standard Book Number, the globally accepted unique identifier of book editions which must be used if the book is to be traded. Normally, ISBNs are assigned in blocks by national ISBN agencies to their local publishers but individuals can apply for a single ISBN for their **self-published** work. ISBNs recently changed from being 10 digits long to being 13 digits long. The code has 5 elements: a 3-digit product code ('book'); a 1–3-digit country/language code; the publisher ID; the book edition ID; and a check digit to pick up typos in the ISBN. Hence the ISBN of the paperback edition of this book is 978-87-91114-77-9, i.e. '978' (book), '87' (Denmark), '91114' (NIAS Press), '77' (paperback edition) and '9' (check digit).

ISO International Standards Organization. An international body setting world-wide standards, especially in industry and commerce.

ISSN International Standard Serial Number. The unique identifier for book series, journals and other periodicals with a function similar to that which the **ISBN** has for books.

Jacket The paper sleeve protecting hardback books.

Kerning The technical typesetting term for letter spacing.

Lamination Thin film, matt or gloss, coating and protecting printed paper or card. Book covers are often laminated.

Layout (1) The process of **typesetting** a book. (2) The page design, often made by a book designer, on which the typesetting is based.

Leading The technical typesetting term for line spacing. The normal leading for type is 1.2 times the **point size** (hence 12 points of leading for a 10-point font) and is often expressed as Baskerville 10/12 (for instance). Getting right the amount of 'air' between lines of type has an important effect on **readability**.

Leaf Single, double-sided page.

Legend *See* caption.

Library binding High-quality sewn binding.

Library supplier Specialist middle-man organization that liaises with libraries to determine their profiles, proposes concrete acquisition lists based on their knowledge of how new publications fit with a library's needs, and saves time for libraries by sourcing these books from their publishers.

Line spacing *See* Leading.

List All of the titles that a publisher has available, divided into the **front list** and **backlist**. In effect, the list is not just the corpus of works but also its current orientation, hence why a book may be rejected because it 'doesn't fit our list'. Sometimes also known as a catalogue (as in 'back catalogue', etc.).

Lithographic printing Conventional printing based on greasy inks and metal **plates**, as opposed to **digital printing**. Of the estimated 45 trillion pages printed around the world in 2005, 91 per cent were printed lithographically – although that proportion may well have dropped since.

Logo *See* Colophon.

Long tail The notion that sales of an item need never completely disappear provided stock is available and its existence is known; there is an infinitely 'long tail' to the sales curve. Hence, with the advent of the Internet and **print on demand**, small sales of backlist titles can be a significant income source for publishers.

Machine proofs Proofs of a book taken from the actual printing press. This is an extremely expensive procedure rarely undertaken. *See also* Printer's proofs.

Manuscript (ms, plural mss) (1) Strictly speaking, a handwritten text. (2) Body of text produced in any medium. **See also** Typescript.

Marketing questionnaire *See* Author questionnaire.

Marking up Inserting instructions for the typesetter on the copy-edited manuscript indicating heading level, indenting, etc., often made by the **copy-editor**.

Mock-up Draft of the layout planned for a text or cover, to give a quick indication of its visual properties.

Monochrome *See* Grayscale.

Monograph Strictly speaking, a (usually academic) book written by a single author. The term is also used to refer to co-authored books but should never be used of **edited volumes**.

Moral rights Among other things, the right of the creator(s) of copyrighted works to attribution and to protection of the work from alteration, distortion or mutilation. Moral rights are distinct from and independent of any economic rights tied to (assignment of) copyright. They are retained even if copyright has been assigned to the publisher or to a third party like a film studio.

ms/mss *See* Manuscript.

Net receipts Sales revenue after deduction of bookseller's discount, **commission** paid to distributors and sales representatives, warehousing charges, etc.

Not Yet Published (NYP) Standard industry **availability** notation, indicating that the book has been announced but is not yet available for sale.

Note reference system System of referencing whereby citations are placed in the notes. As opposed to the **author-date system**.

NYP *See* Not Yet Published.

Object-oriented *See* Vector-based

Offset printing *See* Lithographic printing.

OP *See* Out of Print.

Open Access Increasingly popular idea that the results of publicly funded research should be published as **e-content** and made freely available via the Internet for purposes of education and research (implicitly but not necessarily straight after publication). Open access does not mean that laws of **copyright** and the principles of **fair dealing** are suspended; nor is this the same thing as **open source publishing**.

Open source Software source code that is made available to the general public without licensing restrictions that limit its use, modification or redistribution. Often such software is collectively written by a committed developer community. The Linux operating system is a well-known example of open source software.

Open source publishing Dissemination of text that (normally) has been produced **collaboratively** and is made freely available for others to use and adapt, usually after attribution according to a **Creative Commons** licence.

Open Type fonts Scalable computer fonts conforming to the **ISO** open standard on typography and which can be used across computer platforms. Open Type fonts are now produced by virtually all type foundries and are available for a myriad of alphabets and scripts.

Orphan *See* Widows and orphans.

Originating publisher The leading publisher who commissions and produces a print-ready **co-edition**, usually also printing the final copies for the **co-publishers**.

Origination (1) The work and cost involved in producing a book up to the point of manufacture, including editing, design, typesetting, proofing and indexing (but excluding marketing, which is a **cost of sales**). (2) Sometimes conflated with **pre-press** work.

Out of Print (OP) Standard industry **availability** notation. With the growth of **print on demand**, far fewer titles are now going out of print. Indeed, we are currently witnessing the revival of large numbers of previously OP titles.

Outsourcing The practice of arranging for some regular tasks to be carried out by **freelancers, agents** or companies (e.g. indexers, **sales representatives** and warehouse operators respectively). In publishing, outsourcing has ebbed and flowed over the years. For instance, typesetting was such a specialized task that, up to 20 years ago, it was undertaken by external practitioners. With the **DTP** revolution much of this work moved in-house but now, to save on overheads, publishers are again outsourcing the work. Indeed, due to its widespread outsourcing practices, publishing is one of the world's most globalized industries.

Overrun (1) Text than runs over on to extra lines or pages due to additions made. (2) **Overs**.

Overs Extra copies produced by the printer above the number ordered by the publisher, to allow for copies that are spoiled during printing, binding or transport. Publishers are usually obliged to accept a limited number of overs but may only have to pay the **run-on** price.

Overstock Excess stock that the publisher has abandoned all hope of selling (often after an over-optimistic **printrun**). *See also* Remaindering.

Ozalids *See* printer's proofs.

Page numbering *See* arabic numbering; roman numbering.

Page proofs Print-out of the typeset book pages, usually on standard-sized paper with **printer's marks**, for use in proof-reading.

Page size The **trim size** of a book.

Page-view payments Charges levied by publishers or content libraries for access to their **e-content**, levied on the basis of the number of pages viewed or as a flat fee for access to the entire document.

Pantone (colour) An extensive library of **spot colours** where each colour is referred to by a unique code, allowing designers, printers and publishers to specify colours and tints to each other without sending samples.

Paper Nearly all modern paper is made from shredded, treated wood fibre (rarely now from rag) but comes in many different weights and colours, and may be **coated** or uncoated. The longevity of paper is an issue (*see* Acid-free paper). In high-volume **lithographic** printing, the cost of the paper is by far the greatest cost component.

Paper weight In effect paper density and thickness. Outside the United States (where printers and publishers still refer to pounds per 500 sheets), this is measured in grams per square metre. Paper quality is not intrinsically linked to weight though there is a perception that lightweight paper is inferior. In fact, the purpose is what counts. Typical weights are 80 gsm for text pages, 100 gsm for art paper, 130 gsm for jackets and 250 gsm for paperback covers.

Paperback rights The right to produce a paperback edition of a work originally published in hardback.

Papercase *See* Printed paper case.

PDF Portable Document Format, a fixed-layout format used to represent documents independently of the hardware, software and operating system used to create them. PDF reader software is free, while PDF creation software must be purchased (or is an integral part of certain DTP software). Generally, only users of the full Adobe Acrobat program can modify such documents but author proofs can be created in Acrobat that include tools allowing authors to annotate the PDF with requests for changes to the proof. PDF is one of the competing standards for **e-books**.

Perfect binding A form of binding where all of the pages are cut to size and then glued to the spine. This binding is typical for paperbacks and has a shorter lifespan than **sewn** binding.

Permissions Formal letters, often only obtained on payment of a fee to the **copyright** holder, permitting an author or publisher to reproduce material for which the copyright is owned by others.

Plate (1) In **lithographic printing**, the printing surface and means by which the ink is printed on to the paper. Usually made from metal, printing plates are created by the image for printing being 'painted' on to them with a hydrophobic emulsion that attracts the greasy inks. Traditionally, plates were created in conjunction with film, but a new technology using direct laser imaging is now gaining ground. (2) An illustration (or set of illustrations) usually printed separately on photographic or similar higher quality paper then **tipped** into the book. Such plates may appear as a separate **colour section**.

POD *See* Print on demand.

Podcast Recorded audio piece, such as a radio programme or lecture, that is downloadable to a computer or iPod.

Point (size) Unit of measurement for **type**. Point size measures the height (not width) of type, meaning that one 12-pt font can take up quite a bit more horizontal space than another one.

Point of Sale (POS) (1) The place in a bookshop or other retail outlet where goods are paid for. *See also* POS material. (2) Any retail outlet or other location where products are displayed for sale.

Portable Document Format *See* PDF.

POS material Promotional material intended for use by retailers to decorate their premises and attract customers to buy a specific product.

PPC *See* Printed paper case.

Pre-press (1) The work involved in converting the finalized (originated) book files or camera-ready copy from the publisher, filming, **imposition** and creating the **plates** to be used in the printing process. (2) Sometimes conflated with **origination**.

Preface Short introductory remarks by the author including background information about the book and, if too few to stand alone, any **acknowledgements**.

Prelims Preliminary material, i.e. all the elements of a book that come before the **body text**, such as **half-title page**, **frontispiece**, **title page**, **copyright page**, table of contents, list of illustrations, **acknowledgements**, etc. Also known as front matter, this section has roman page numbering.

Press (1) Printing press, a machine. (2) Printing company. (3) **Publishing house**.

Print on demand (POD) **Digital printing** system enabling the economical production of very small print quantities (as low as single-copy printing). As copies tend to be printed to meet actual orders rather than printed in large quantities for stock, inventory costs are much lower and the technology means that a (digitized) book need never go **out of print**, thus allowing for **long tail** sales. However, POD unit printing costs are significantly higher than for conventional (high-volume) **lithographic printing**.

Printed paper case (PPC) An alternative to **cloth** casing in which a paperback-like **cover** (but on much thinner paper) is glued on to the stiff boards and **laminated** in place. As a result, no protective jacket is necessary.

Printer's marks Marks placed on the printed **sheet** outside the book page that register (orient) the page and indicate where it is to be trimmed as well as any extra **trim** for **bleeds**.

Printer's proofs Unbound **proofs** of the book pages sent by the printer to the publisher for checking and approval prior to printing. These are output using many different technologies, hence the wide range of names for these proofs (common names being blues/blueprints, diazos, ozalids and Vandykes). Normally, they also include **colour proofs** of the jacket and/or cover. None of these proofs match exactly what the final printed copies will look like; to get this requires **machine proofs**.

Printrun The number of copies of a book printed at the same time, also called an **impression**, hence 'first edition, third impression' refers to the third printing of the first edition.

Process colours The three primary colours (cyan, magenta and yellow) used in combination with black in all colour printing. *See also* CMYK.

Process printing *See* Four-colour printing.

Production manager Also often called production **editor**. The person who coordinates the transformation of an unedited manuscript into a printed book ready for sale. While much or all of this work is done outside the press, generally the production manager is located in-house.

Production value Term referring to the quality of the physical elements of a book, such as the paper, binding and printing. The better the quality, the higher the production value.

Professional publishing Publishing in 'the professions', especially accountancy, law and medicine (but also in areas like architecture) where publishers tend to enjoy high prices and healthy profit margins.

Proof copies *See* bound proofs.

Proof-reader Person (often a **freelancer**) whose job is to check the printed proofs for errors and mark any corrections.

Proofing The process of checking (and marking corrections on) proofs. Also known as proof-reading.

Proofing marks *See* Correction marks.

Proofs Printouts of the book which at various stages are checked by the author, proof-reader, production manager, etc. These include **first proofs, final proofs** and **printer's proofs**. *See also* Page proofs. Proofs are sometimes used to promote a book (*see* Bound proofs).

Public domain Material that has no **copyright** (or whose copyright has expired) and may be freely copied by anyone.

Publication (1) Something that is published, a **title**. (2) The **publication date**.

Publication committee Probably less grand than an **editorial board** but carrying out much the same function, i.e. to decide if a manuscript is to be published by the press.

Publication date (1) The publication year, essentially the date on the **copyright notice**. (2) The planned, actual **release date**.

Publisher (1) **Publishing house**. (2) The person who defines/shapes a specific list. This can be the head of the editorial department or the owner of a small private press.

Publishing There are many types of book publishing (and publishers). Outside the humanities and social sciences, the dominant form of academic publishing is **STM publishing**. Nearby are **professional**, **textbook** and **educational publishing**, while serving the general public are several types of **trade publishing**.

Publishing agreement (1) **Author contract**. (2) **Co-publication** agreement between publishers.

Publishing house Company, institution or other entity that publishes books, journals, magazines, etc.

Publishing rights *See* Rights.

Rasterized (1) Graphics format based on dots (i.e. it is **bit-mapped**). Such images (e.g. **halftones**) differ from **vector-based** images in that they allow subtle variations of colour/tint but can only be scaled by resampling the dots. Repetitively resampled images quickly degrade in quality.

Readability Readability consists of two elements, language and the other literary factors being the ones most often focused on by authors. But almost equally important is the layout, especially the **font** used (**serif** fonts are much easier to read that **sans-serif**), **characters per line** and **leading**, because readers are discouraged by something that confuses the eye or otherwise is difficult to read. Scholarship that is worn lightly combined with a reader-friendly layout can be crucial elements in the success of a book.

Reading copy *See* Desk copy.

Receipts Publisher's earnings from sales, including sales of **rights** and **co-editions**. *See also* Net receipts.

Recto The right-hand page of a **spread**.

Registration marks *See* Printers' marks

Release date The date on which a new book is first supplied to retail customers. Some books, mainly at the trade end of the spectrum, have globally or regionally co-ordinated release dates, which means that outlets (wholesale and retail) that receive stock early are subject to an embargo on selling before the release date.

Remaindering The practice of disposing of books that are surplus to requirements (e.g. **overstock** and old **editions**) at a very cheap net price or a very high discount level to specialist remainder merchants, who then place these books with discount bookshops.

Reprint rights The right of one publisher to reprint, in substantially unchanged form, a work originally published by another publisher, e.g. a cheap edition, a book club edition or an edition to be sold in another country.

Repro Short for 'reproduction'. (1) The finished artwork or **camera-ready copy**. (2) Print/copy shop.

Residual rights Rights retained by the author (not passed to the publisher).

Resolution (1) The number of pixels in an area that can be displayed, expressed as dots per inch (**dpi**). (2) The clarity of an image.

Retouching Applying various image-altering techniques to improve quality or change certain characteristics of an image.

Returns Books that have not been sold by retailers or wholesalers and are returned to the publisher. Return rates are higher in the US than elsewhere and in trade publishing can get as high as 50 per cent. In academic publishing the rate is significantly lower.

Reverse out (1) To show text in white on a dark background. (2) To invert an image.

Reversion of rights Return of **copyright** to the author, one reason for which would be if the publisher fails to keep the book **in print**.

Review copies Copies of a book sent out to the media (both printed and electronic) in the hope that they will print, distribute or broadcast their own reviews of the book. Review copies are normally sent on the initiative of the publisher, but may also be based on a prior request from, say, an academic journal editor.

RGB Red, green and blue, the format used to reproduce **colour** on computer monitors. *See also* Colour.

Rights Publishing rights or **copyright**, which the author assigns to the publisher in the author contract. Generally, **moral rights** are not assigned. Specific rights can license use of the work in its original form (**volume rights**) or in a substantially altered form (**subsidiary rights**). Across these classifications, rights can also be assigned by market, territory or language.

Roman numbering Numerals like i, ii, iii, etc. used for pagination of the **prelims** (as opposed to **arabic numbering**).

Royalty Money paid to an author in return for the publishing rights, usually paid annually as a percentage of net sales **receipts**. In academic publishing, the royalty rate may be set at zero or no payment may be made until a minimum number of copies are sold to cover the publisher's excess expenses. Conversely, the authors of potentially successful titles may be offered an **escalator clause** in their contract.

Run *See* Printrun.

Running heads Headers, the line of text at the top of each page above the **body text**. Often, the **verso** running head is the book title, while the **recto** running head is the chapter title. *See also* Footers.

Running text The main text of a book, which runs over the pages (unlike notes, illustrations, etc., which are fixed).

Run-on Extra copies above the number of those originally requested. When publishers order a **printrun**, they are given a price for the number of copies ordered and usually offered a separate run-on price, which is much cheaper per copy since the printing set-up costs are part of the price of the printrun ordered. Low run-on costs may persuade a publisher to take a chance with a larger quantity than first planned. *See also* Overs.

Sales representative Publisher's **agent** or employee whose job is to solicit orders, especially for the publisher's **forthcoming** titles, especially from booksellers but also from **library suppliers**, wholesalers, etc. Especially because of electronic ordering but also owing to the rise of new Internet-based forms of promotion, the importance of sales representatives has declined in recent years.

Sans-serif *See* Serif.

Screening The process of creating a halftone.

Section *See* Signature.

Self-publishing The publishing of books and other works by their authors, rather than by established, third-party publishers. While self-publishers assume the financial risk of publication, bearing the cost of manufacturing and of selling their own book, they also retain all net sales income. Self-publishing is a feature of new, collaborative forms of authorship (e.g. **open source publishing**). To date, however, self-published academic works have a low status among scholars, institutions and funding authorities, mainly because they are not peer reviewed before publication.

Serial rights The rights to publish a work in instalments over several issues of a magazine or newspaper. First serial rights are for publication before the book is published, second serial rights for afterwards.

Series Group of books dealing with a similar broad subject and published in sequence under the same collective title.

Series editor Typically, a senior scholar whose academic specialization matches the profile of the series, and whose status and network function to attract new authors (and readers) to the series. It is not unusual for such scholars to actually initiate the establishment of the series.

Series page Where an academic title is published within a series, commonly the **half-title verso** page is used to advertise the series. Typically this states who the series editors are, describes the series and lists all existing and planned titles in the series.

Serif Often called 'feet', serifs are the small strokes at the ends of the main stokes of characters in serif fonts. As serifs help guide the eye, serif fonts like Times are preferred for running text, while sans-serif fonts (i.e. those like Arial without serifs) are often preferred for headlines because of their unfussy appearance.

Sewn pages/binding Form of binding where all of the large printing sheets are folded into **signatures** and stitched together before being attached to the spine. This binding is normal for hardbacks and has a much longer lifespan than **perfect binding**.

Sheet (1) Large piece of paper on each side of which 8 or 16 pages are printed then folded to make up a **signature**. (2) Commonly, a **leaf**.

Sheet sales Sale of the book in sheet form to a co-publisher (i.e. in unbound **signatures**), who will complete its binding using their own cover.

Short-run printing Printing of a limited number of copies of a book in a single **printrun**. Technological advances in **lithographic** presses mean that printruns as low as 300–400 copies are (just) economic. Totals lower than this make **digital printing** a better option in most cases, with single-copy printing now a realistic option with **POD** presses.

Signature (1) Printed **sheet** or 'section' folded into 16 or 32 pages. (2) The act of finalizing an author contract, hence (of an author **advance**), e.g. 'one third paid on signature'.

Slip case Open box inside which sits one or more volumes (usually hardbacks). The hard outer case is **cloth** covered or is a **printed paper case**. This protects the book(s) within and makes the whole product look classy and expensive.

Social networking Key characteristic of the **Web 2.0** revolution, this involves chatting, messaging, file sharing, **blogging** and other forms of interaction between communities of people who share interests and activities. Social networking websites are being used by millions of people everyday and increasingly are recognized by marketeers as a new channel for promotion.

Spine text Normally the author's (family) name and book title written along the spine and oriented so that it is readable (at eye level) when the book is lying face up. On cloth-covered volumes, this is produced by **blocking**.

Spot colour (1) Printed colours created with specially mixed inks rather than with the **CMYK** colours used in process printing. In fact, spot colours can be used very effectively in addition to process printing, e.g. over-printing an ordinary four-colour cover with a extra spot colour (say, with a luminous, transparent ink that simulates rain-drops). (2) The use of one additional colour on the page in addition to the normal black.

Spread Two facing (left-hand and right-hand) pages seen together. Viewing artwork as spreads rather than as individual pages is particularly important where there are many non-text elements such as tables and images, to ensure that the spread appears balanced and clear, rather than fussy and confused.

STM publishing Scientific, Technical and Medical publishing, usually of academic texts appearing in journals.

Stock (1) Something held together, in one or more places, e.g. books available for sale (hence 'in stock' versus 'out of stock'). (2) Paper available for later use (if regularly held by the printer, this is called 'stock paper').

Style sheet Document describing the **house style** adopted by a publisher or book series, normally covering both text appearance (e.g. how to show various levels of subtitles and how to set quotations) and text content (e.g. how to write numbers and what to include in references to other works).

Subsidiary rights Rights to present the work in a form different from the original or to adapt it to other uses, e.g. for serialization, foreign-language editions, film and mechanical reproduction (on photocopies and microfilm). As opposed to **volume rights**.

Subsidy *See* Subvention.

Subvention Money raised (usually by the author) to help cover the cost of publication.

Table of contents (TOC) List of chapters (and sometimes even sections) appearing in a book, followed by any lists of tables, illustrations, etc. Normally, the TOC starts on page v of the **prelims** but, if displaced by a **dedication**, appears from page vii.

Territory Area covered by a distribution, representation, co-publication or rights agreement.

Text block The main text on a page, excluding running heads, etc.

Textbook School book or academic text used for teaching students.

Textbook publishing *See* Educational publishing.

Tint Colour tone incorporating a solid colour and a certain percentage of white.

Tip in To insert an extra leaf between the pages of a book, often a colour **plate**, **frontispiece** or folding map. This practice is expensive and avoided by most modern publishers.

Title (1) Publication or **book** in all of its **editions**, which can consist of several volumes (as e.g. the *Encyclopedia Britannica*). (2) The name of a book, article or other work.

Title page This always appears on the right-hand page of the first full **spread** of a book (page iii), and carries the title, subtitle, author name and publisher details (comprising the **imprint**, publisher's name and/or **colophon**). Whereas the **cover** aims to attract the reader/buyer, the point of the title page (even if decorative) is to clearly identify the book, its author and publisher.

Title verso The **copyright page**.

TOC *See* Table of contents.

Trade discount Amount of discount off the published price given to booksellers and others selling the book. The standard discount for academic books is 25–33 per cent, depending on customer and market, but wholesalers and powerful retailers may force publishers to concede discounts as high as 60 per cent. Discount levels in trade publishing are even higher.

Trade publishing Publishing of titles with wide appeal, specifically aimed at the general public. Most of these are sold in bookshops but Internet sales are increasingly important.

Trim size The final trimmed dimensions of the book. Traditional names exist for all of the standard trim sizes but nowadays dimensions tend to be stated as a measure in height and width (e.g. the trim size of this book is 'demy octavo' or 216 mm x 138 mm).

Type area The area of the page available for printing, including the area used for **running heads** and page numbers.

Type family (1) In common usage and how it is used in this book, a **font**. (2) Correctly speaking, a group of fonts belonging to the same **typeface**.

Type style (1) **Typeface** variants like roman/regular, italic and bold. (2) The full character set of a typeface in a particular style, i.e. properly speaking a **font**.

Typeface (1) In common usage and how it is used in this book, a **font**. (2) Correctly speaking, a set or family of one or more fonts designed with stylistic unity and a consistent visual appearance (hence Arial is a typeface with several fonts including bold and italic).

Typescript (1) Strictly speaking, a typewritten text. (2) Word-processed text. *See also* Manuscript.

Typesetting The work involved in taking text and illustrative material and laying it out on the page ready for printing.

Unbound proofs Printer's proofs delivered in loose-leaf form or as individual signatures.

Uncoated paper *See* coated paper.

Unicode An ISO character-encoding standard for fonts and data storage that allows common mapping not just of the single-byte character sets found in Western alphabets but also of double-byte script systems such as Chinese, Japanese and Korean.

Unit cost The per-copy cost.

URL Universal resource locator, or web address.

Vandykes *See* printer's proofs.

Vector-based Graphical format based on objects (lines, squares, circles, etc.) whose properties are defined by the Postscript computer language. These are infinitely scaleable without distortion or degradation. All modern fonts are vector based. As opposed to **rasterized**.

Verso The left-hand page of a **spread**.

Vignette (1) Small illustration used as decoration (e.g. on the title page). (2) Halftone illustration that fades at one or more edges (e.g. used to decorate the opening of a chapter).

Volume (1) **Book**. (2) One of several physical books in a multi-volume set.

Volume rights Rights for use of the work in its first form, e.g. for co-editions, reprints and e-books. As opposed to **subsidiary rights**.

Volume sales Sales of the book itself plus income derived from the sale of volume rights.

Web 2.0 Perceived second generation of the Web with new functionalities (**social networking** sites, **wikis**, **blogs**, tagging/reviewing tools, etc.) that enhance and emphasize online collaboration and sharing among users.

Web log *See* Blog.

Wibbling On a hardback book, the two-coloured ribbon finishing the tops and bottoms of a set of **signatures**.

Widows and orphans First or last lines of a paragraph appearing either at the top (widow) or bottom of a page (orphan). Typesetters normally try to avoid these situations by type adjustments (e.g. by tightening or loosening the character fit) so that all or at least two lines of the paragraph fall on the page.

Wiki Website or similar online resource with word-processing functionalities that allows users to add, change and delete content collectively, Wikipedia being the best known example.

Work Usually a single book but in some cases the work may span multiple volumes.

Further reading

In writing this book, we have used a range of books and articles, and have also made extensive use of materials from the Web. There are useful ideas and advice to be found on many publishers' websites (also those to whom you would not consider offering your manuscript). There are also a number of useful community sites and a wealth of discussion lists and blogs to learn from. The trouble (and the beauty) is that the Web is a dynamic and constantly evolving entity, so that listing Web references in a book that we hope will last for more than a few weeks is a doomed enterprise. Before the ink is dry on this page, several sites will have closed down, opened up, or moved to another URL. Better, we thought, just to remind you that your network as an author encompasses far more than the few dozen colleagues in your department, or the few thousand delegates at the annual conference on your subject. There is a world of creative, opinionated and generous 'webbers' just waiting for you to click 'connect'.

That said, there is also a handful of printed materials that we think you may find useful, depending on your exact circumstances. These are our favourites, ordered thematically.

The Chicago Manual of Style, by The University of Chicago Press staff. The University of Chicago Press, Chicago, latest edition.

This *Manual* is the international gold standard for style, answering every last little question an author could possibly have about how to write. Seeing that it is published in the US, it will come as no surprise that the recommendations follow North American preferences with regard to spelling, punctuation, etc., but that does not stop the *Manual* from being an extremely worthwhile investment for scholarly authors in every corner of the globe.

The Oxford Colour Spelling Dictionary, edited by Maurice Waite. Clarendon Press, Oxford, 1995.

Unlike a normal dictionary, with its detailed definitions and examples, a spelling dictionary simply lists words and names in a single, clear A–Z sequence. This makes it a huge time-saver for anyone needing to check their spelling (especially for proper names, which most dictionaries leave out). A good spelling dictionary such as this includes all plurals, tenses, etc., as well as names of well-known people, places, companies, etc. Further, it glosses sound-alike words and names for clarity and gives full hyphenation for each word, making it indispensable for editors, typesetters and anyone involved in desktop publishing. In addition, both British and US spellings are given and cross-referred.

Getting It Published: A Guide for Scholars and Anyone Else Serious about Serious Books, by William Germano. The University of Chicago Press, Chicago, 2001.

The subject matter is rather similar to ours, but with more focus on the editorial process and relationship, and less focus on what happens after the final work has been delivered to the press. The style is much less prescriptive than ours. Where we may at times be a bit tiresome and school-marmy, Germano's style is more that of a benign and experienced editor dispensing advice and anecdotes over rather a pleasant lunch.

Thinking Like Your Editor: How to Write Great Nonfiction – and Get It Published, by Susan Rabiner. W. W. Norton & Co., New York, reprint edition 2005.

The advice in this book is based mainly on Rabiner's long experience as first an editor and then a literary agent in the field of serious trade non-fiction. Particularly valuable is a thorough and thought-provoking section on how to conceive and target a book project to a readership large enough to excite a publisher. The book is not aimed at academic authors, but at those hoping to write for the intelligent, general-interest reader – which often includes academics who have reached a comfortable stage in their careers where the pressures of building a list of academic publications can (temporarily) take a backseat to the desire to communicate an enthusiasm for the subject to a larger public.

Handbook for Academic Authors, by Beth Luey. Cambridge University Press, Cambridge, fourth edition 2002.

Although this book is perhaps beginning to show its age despite revisions for the fourth edition, it still contains much information of relevance. It is longer than our book and thus finds room for much greater detail on some subjects. It is particularly useful in explaining what influences pricing decisions, with many example calculations (invaluable for self-publishers), and on the intricacies of copyright and publication contracts.

From Dissertation to Book, by William Germano. University of Chicago Press, Chicago, 2005.

The title says it clearly: this book is aimed at new PhDs who want to publish their theses as books. Some of the advice on style and the writing process and what makes a book attractive to publishers is similar to that in Germano's other book *Getting It Published,* but there is also very useful advice on how to conceive, plan and carry out the tasks that are unique to authors who are reshaping a previous work rather than producing a completely new one.

Marketing Your Book: An Author's Guide, by Alison Baverstock and with a Foreword by Jacqueline Wilson. A & C Black, London, 2001.

Baverstock is well placed to give advice on all aspects of book marketing since she knows the game both as a marketing professional and as an author with several non-fiction books under her belt. Her advice is clear and concise, and although some of the points (e.g. giving interviews) may not be relevant for most academic authors, much of the book will be helpful if you want to take an active role in the promotion of your book.

Plug Your Book: Online Book Marketing for Authors, by Steve Weber. Weber Books, Virginia, 2007.

(Alert: Nominative determinism.) Weber shows how the Web can be used by savvy authors (and their publishers) to generate interest in new books, and hence increase sales. The book discusses how you can make the most of Internet bookshops, blogging, social networking sites, etc., with clear advice on exactly how to achieve maximum exposure. A self-publisher himself, Weber has much useful advice for those who must market their books efficiently at very low cost.

Publishing in Asian Studies, ICAS 4 insert to IIAS Newsletter # 37. International Institute for Asian Studies, Leiden, 2005.
and
Academic Publishing Today, ICAS 5 insert to IIAS Newsletter # 43. International Institute for Asian Studies, Leiden, 2007.

Both these newspaper-shaped publications contain a range of articles by book industry insiders on subjects such as the characteristics of small and regional publishers and publishing, the challenges of electronic publishing and the open access revolution, journals publishing, bookselling, and also (more) advice from the two of us on presenting and promoting a manuscript or book. At the time of writing, all articles are available at www.iias.nl. Another issue focusing on choice in academic publishing is expected in mid-2009.

Index

NIAS Press is the autonomous publishing arm of NIAS – Nordic Institute of Asian Studies, a research institute located at the University of Copenhagen. NIAS is partially funded by the governments of Denmark, Finland, Iceland, Norway and Sweden via the Nordic Council of Ministers, and works to encourage and support Asian studies in the Nordic countries. In so doing, NIAS has been publishing books since 1969, with more than two hundred titles produced in the past few years.

COPENHAGEN UNIVERSITY

Nordic Council of Ministers